Gifted IQ

Early Developmental Aspects

The Fullerton Longitudinal Study

Gifted IQ
Early Developmental Aspects
The Fullerton Longitudinal Study

Allen W. Gottfried
California State University, Fullerton
Fullerton, California

Adele Eskeles Gottfried
California State University, Northridge
Northridge, California

Kay Bathurst
California State University, Fullerton
Fullerton, California

and

Diana Wright Guerin
California State University, Fullerton
Fullerton, California

PLENUM PRESS • NEW YORK AND LONDON

Library of Congress Cataloging-in-Publication Data

Gifted IQ : early developmental aspects : the Fullerton Longitudinal Study / Allen W. Gottfried ... [etc.].
p. cm.
Includes bibliographical references and index.
ISBN 0-306-44683-9
1. Gifted children--United States--Longitudinal studies. 2. Children--United States--Intelligence levels--Longitudinal studies. 3. Gifted children--Psychology. 4. Children--Intelligence levels. I. Gottfried, Allen W. II. Title: Fullerton Longitudinal Study.
BF723.G5G54 1994
155.45'5--dc20 94-26562
CIP

10 9 8 7 6 5 4 3

ISBN 0306446839 (hb)
ISBN 0306484439 (pb)

A Division of Plenum Publishing Corporation
233 Spring Street, New York, N.Y. 10013

Printed in the United States of America

Dedicated to our gifts
Michael and Jeffrey,
Dick, Kim, John, Jim, and Darien,
Keith, Jonathan, and Alexandra,

and

to the children and families participating
in the Fullerton Longitudinal Study

Preface

We embarked on the research contained in this book because of the dearth of knowledge on the early developmental aspects of gifted IQ. This book represents an integration of our interests in the fields of intelligence, psychometrics, and developmental psychology. The research presented is based on the Fullerton Longitudinal Study, which entails the systematic investigation of a single cohort studied from infancy onward. It will become apparent in the reading of this volume that studies such as this one are rare in the field of psychology. This study comprises frequent repeated assessments of children's developmental status, information from a variety of sources, and objective data collected across an array of developmental domains. Extensive behavioral and home environmental information has been gathered across the course of investigation. The essence of the research contained herein is on the early developmental history of children who come to perform at the gifted IQ level during middle childhood. This is their early story.

Our special gratitude is extended to Mariclaire Cloutier, Editor, and to Eliot Werner, Executive Editor, at Plenum for their friendship, support, and providing the opportunity for us to share the scientific results of our scholarly endeavors. The Fullerton Longitudinal Study has been supported at various times by the following foundations: Thrasher Research Fund, Spencer Foundation, AMC Theatre Fund, and California State Universities at Fullerton and Northridge. We also extend our appreciation to the Child Development Department; Dr. Dan Kee, Chair of the Psychology Department; Dr. Stuart Ross and Bonni Kaahea at the Office of Faculty Research and Development; and Terry Jones, technician in the Psychology Department, all at California State University,

Fullerton. At California State University, Northridge, thanks are extended to the Department of Educational Psychology and Counseling and the Office of Graduate Studies, Research, and International Programs.

Over the years, many graduate and undergraduate students have devoted themselves to making the Fullerton Longitudinal Study possible. We thank them for their commitment, time, and effort. In particular, we would like to thank the following research assistants: Connie Meyer, Jacqueline K. Coffman, Pamella H. Oliver, Craig W. Thomas, Kandi Kipp, June Havlena, Leigh Hobson, Pam Paduano, Senia Pizzo, Rachel Goldstein, Arnel Sison, Adrian Schein-Sokolow, Zack Loukides, Kathleen Ellenberger, Veronica Zuniga, Shelli Wynants, Valerie Luoma, Catherine Lussier, Judit Au, Colleen Killian, and Charlotte Kies.

We especially wish to thank the children and families participating in the Fullerton Longitudinal Study. Without their dedication, this project would have never come to fruition.

Allen W. Gottfried
Adele Eskeles Gottfried
Kay Bathurst
Diana Wright Guerin

Contents

Gifted IQ

Early Developmental Aspects

The Fullerton Longitudinal Study

1

Introduction

The nature, characteristics, and consequences of giftedness and talent have intrigued behavioral scientists and educators for a century or more (C. M. Cox, 1926; Ellis, 1904; Galton, 1869; Terman, 1905; Yoder, 1894; see also Freehill, 1961; Witty, 1951). The study of giftedness and talent has captured ongoing intense international interest (e.g., Freeman, 1991; Gross, 1993; Parkyn, 1953; for volumes containing papers and research programs from scholars worldwide, see Heller & Feldhusen, 1985; Heller, Monks, & Passow, 1993). We recognize that there are many forms of giftedness (music, art, sports, business, scholarship, etc.); however, it is the intellectually gifted who have received the greatest amount of inquiry in the psychological and educational literature.

The focus of this volume is the scientific study of the early developmental history of children who come to perform at the gifted IQ level during middle childhood. The research contained herein presents a systematic, quantitative, and longitudinal approach to understanding the early ontogeny, behavior, and family and home environmental experiences of children who become intellectually gifted. This is their early story from a scientific developmental perspective. To this end, we sought to discover the differences between intellectually gifted and nongifted children when they were infants, preschoolers, and early elementary school children.

After a century of research on the phenomenon of giftedness, one can confidently conclude that there is no commonly accepted definition or conception of giftedness (Feldhusen & Heller, 1985; Hoge, 1988; Reis, 1989; Sternberg & Davidson, 1986). Moreover, although IQ tests have been by far the most extensively used instrument for assessing the intellectually gifted, there is no universally agreed upon procedure for measuring and identifying giftedness. Using IQ as our definition of giftedness does not negate our acknowledgment of specific domains of intellectual giftedness that are not measured by IQ. However, the continuing pervasiveness of the use of IQ as one of the indexes of intellectual giftedness by schools, and in the research literature, and the important achievements by those high in IQ, prompted us to use IQ as the criterion of giftedness in this research. We make no assumption that gifted IQ is a stable life-span trait, although there is evidence of stability in the early elementary school years (Cahan & Gejam, 1993). Proof of relatively long-term developmental stability should be founded on empirical determination that we intend to pursue in the course of our longitudinal investigation. IQ tests, which measure one's general cognitive repertoire, have proven to be a valid assessment for measuring one's relative intelligence (Humphreys, 1992). IQ scores furnish a demarcation or cutoff point, albeit statistically arbitrary, of who is and is not considered intellectually gifted at a given point in time (Humphreys, 1985). Again, we recognize and support the view of multiple forms of giftedness. However, in this research program, we are working within a specific frame of reference, that being the frequency distribution of IQ scores and its early developmental antecedents. In fact, we would have no objection to disregarding the term gifted IQ and title this book as simply "High IQ." However, the term gifted does tie this research to a literature, and that literature is referred to as the intellectually gifted. The fact is that IQ scores have provided the historical, ubiquitous, and objective basis for the determination of gifted intelligence.

Research, both past and present, on intellectually gifted children has focused almost exclusively on identifying such children, developmental outcomes once they are identified, and the educational needs and programs instituted for these children. A great deal of knowledge has been gathered concerning gifted children, but only after they have been identified or designated as gifted. The large body of developmental research in this area has dealt with the consequences of being intellectually gifted. The developmental course of gifted children prior to their identification is, heretofore, unknown. As Horowitz and O'Brien (1985) pointed out in their edited book commissioned by the American Psychological Association:

> Psychologists know very little about the developmental course of giftedness and talent, about the nature of environmental opportunities that nurture

> their realization, and about the nature of conditions that must change over time to ensure continued development of giftedness. (p. 450)

In their book as well as a subsequent article in the *American Psychologist* (Horowitz & O'Brien, 1986), they emphasized the importance and necessity of longitudinal research in answering such developmental questions. However, they caution researchers that without the commitment, time, and funds, such endeavors may prove unsuccessful. While longitudinal research has been conducted on the gifted, most notably the Terman (1925–1929) life-span study, research has been from the school-age years onward (see, e.g., Subotnik & Arnold, 1994). Even the multiple case follow-up studies or surveys, which have provided fascinating, insightful accounts of gifted children, have been conducted almost exclusively with school-age children (Feldman, 1986; Freeman, 1991; Gross, 1993; Radford, 1990). In his book on *The Origins of Exceptional Abilities*, Howe (1990) notes:

> Apart from some case studies of the home lives of particular individuals few of the investigations have been specifically involved with the early lives of those children who subsequently gain exceptional abilities. Other reasons apart, the impossibility of knowing in advance which children are the ones who will become extraordinarily successful creates practical barriers to any investigation of this kind. (pp. 110–111)

Our knowledge concerning the early development or antecedents of intellectual giftedness remains void. Well-respected scholars in this area have cogently argued for researchers to examine the early developmental aspects of intellectually gifted children. This is exemplified by both Horowitz (1987) and N. M. Robinson (1987) in their articles in the *Gifted Child Quarterly*. Horowitz stated that "the overall dearth of developmental research on giftedness is regrettable" (p. 165). Horowitz raised a number of significant and obvious developmental questions. For example, how early can we identify gifted children; how might these gifts be nurtured; what is the developmental course of gifted children, and is their course different from that of nongifted children; and if a child is gifted in one domain, does it affect other developmental domains? She also urged researchers to study environmental factors that might facilitate giftedness. Questions of this nature are addressed and have been central in our research. N. M. Robinson (1987) noted that:

> The sources and early history of markedly advanced intelligence have interested philosophers and biographers for centuries, and more empirical scientists for decades.... All these sources are, however, severely limited. The

> material is retrospective and no doubt highly selective, and leaves a great many questions unanswered. We now need systematic, contemporary investigation, not bias-prone biographizing. (p. 161)

She made a plea for researchers to search in a scientific manner for early cues and study the origins of developmental precocity. At the outset of her article, N. M. Robinson noted, "The time is ripe for extending our interest in gifted children downward to infancy and preschool" (p. 161). In our research program, we have taken on these challenges.

The present research is different from studies previously conducted. Figuratively speaking one could state that, after approximately three quarters of a century, our study ends where Terman's began. This volume presents an investigation focusing on development from infancy through the early school years of children who became intellectually gifted or nongifted. We assert that this is our contribution to the literature on giftedness.

In the Fullerton Longitudinal Study, children were not selected for sample inclusion because of intellectual or cognitive status. In other words, we did not select infants of high versus low intellectual performance. If we had, statistical regression would have certainly taken its toll as the children were prospectively studied. Instead, a relatively large sample of healthy 1-year-olds and their families were recruited. The sample was objectively, systematically, and intensively studied at that time and thereafter at specified intervals. As the children developed over the years, some eventually performed at the high or gifted IQ level and others did not. Hence, we were in a unique position to go back in time and examine the developmental-behavioral and home-family differences that existed between these groups. The data presented in this book are based on a scientific analysis of what these groups were like developmentally and behaviorally and what they were exposed to environmentally. Heretofore, investigations of the early life of gifted or talented children have relied on retrospective reports or unscientifically collected archival data. This is not the case in the Fullerton Longitudinal Study. From the outset of the investigation, data were collected contemporaneously, systematically, rigorously, and quantitatively by trained research staff. Most of the data were based on objective and standardized psychological instruments administered in the university laboratory and the subjects' homes. A battery of reliable and valid instruments has been employed. Additionally, we have included ratings and checklists from informants such as parents and teachers.

ISSUES INVESTIGATED

General Issues

In this section, we provide an introduction into the general issues and topics to be addressed in Chapters 3 through 6. It is not the intention here to furnish an exhaustive review or critique of the extensive literature on the various behavioral or family aspects of intellectually gifted children. Numerous books and articles have been published over the years as well as recently published compendiums containing conceptual and empirical reviews (see Heller et al., 1993; Subotnik & Arnold, 1994).

In Chapter 2, we discuss the subject sample, procedures, and methodology of the Fullerton Longitudinal Study as well as the statistical analytic strategy employed to tackle the specific issues advanced in each content chapter. Chapter 3 of this book presents the early intellectual and cognitive functioning of children who become gifted or nongifted. Chapter 4 focuses on early education, academic achievement, and motivational variables. In Chapter 5, the children's behavioral adjustment, social functioning, and temperament are analyzed. Chapter 6 addresses the home and family environment of these children from infancy through the early school grades. In Chapters 3 through 6, the specific questions, issues, and hypotheses addressed are enumerated at the outset, followed by the assessments employed and research findings, with the main conclusions summarized at the end. In Chapter 7, we put forth our developmental perspective or conceptualization on how young children become gifted as well as the psychological and educational implications of our findings.

Intellectual and Cognitive Functioning

There is a dearth of knowledge on the early intellectual or cognitive functioning of children who become gifted. This deficit in the psychological data base was first recognized by Hollingworth (1926) in her influential book entitled *Gifted Children*. She pointed out that "our knowledge of the infancy of the gifted rests at present upon the insecure and fragmentary data of parents' retrospections, and of the 'baby-books' which they have kept" (p. 150). The notorious problems of retrospective reports by parents were obvious, even during that era in the history of psychological research. Although Hollingworth considered baby-books to be of greater reliability than retrospective reports, she made reference to such issues as the selectivity of mothers who kept such records of their children's early development as well as the lack of universal criteria or definition of behaviors recorded (e.g., talking and walking). Acknowledging the limitations and state of the science at that time, she put forth her solution to discovering the early developmental aspects of gifted children. She proposed that:

> Direct study by psychologists would obviate these difficulties of interpretation, but the obstacles to the scientific study of infants are numerous. In the first place, infants are rarely collected for a considerable period of time, except in foundling asylums, where an unfavorable selection is obtained. In the second place, even if it were possible to collect any infants we might wish, we would not know with certainty how to choose in order to secure those who will be gifted children. In other words, we cannot now detect the gifted in early infancy. It is, nevertheless, becoming more and more possible to predict with reliability whether a given infant will later test in the highest percentile for intellect. If records were to be uniformly kept, for instance, of all infants born to parents both of whom are college graduates, we should find eventually that a large number of records had thus accumulated of the infancy of children testing above 130 IQ. (pp. 151–152)

Of course we have come a long way in the scientific study of infancy since Hollingworth's suggestion. Great strides have been made in our conceptualizations of infancy. Our knowledge of infant development has expanded manifold. Several longitudinal studies beginning in infancy have been conducted. Researchers have made arduous efforts attempting to examine the possible link or continuity between early behavior and later intelligence. Four areas relevant to the current topic are briefly reviewed.

First, psychometric and Piagetian scales of sensorimotor intelligence have been developed and extensively studied. There is an impressive body of data utilizing these measures. The findings demonstrate that they have not been successful with respect to long-term predictive validity (e.g., Bayley, 1970; N. Brody, 1992; A. W. Gottfried & N. Brody, 1975; McCall, Hogarty, & Hurlburt, 1972). Developmental researchers have continued to pursue other avenues in the search for continuity in individual differences from infancy onward. However, before presenting these other areas, there is an interesting and relevant study by Willerman and Fiedler (1974), who examined the relationship between sensorimotor intelligence and high IQ scores during the preschool years. About 50 years after Hollingworth's proposal, Willerman and Fiedler, in an article in *Child Development* using data from the Collaborative Perinatal Project, noted:

> While there are some anecdotal data on infant mental development of children later identified as intellectually precocious, there exists no prospec-

> tively gathered information based on objective tests. Data of this sort could be of some importance, since they might permit us to deal with the intrinsically fascinating issue of whether there are behavioral antecedents to intellectual superiority. (p. 483)

From that longitudinal project, Willerman and Fiedler selected children with a Stanford-Binet IQ of 140 or greater at age 4 years who were administered a research version of the Bayley Scales of Infant Development at 8 months. Results revealed that this superior group could not be distinguished from the total study population of infants at 8 months of age. Unfortunately, these were the only two assessment periods in the children's early years. In their research only one testing was conducted during infancy and no assessment was administered during the school-age years. Additionally, age 4 years has not been found to be a particularly significant age in terms of predictability, no less a reliable appraisal for determining intellectual giftedness.

Second, because of the failure of sensorimotor scales to predict subsequent intelligence, researchers have focused on specific abilities. One in particular has been early language abilities. Interestingly, the relation of early language development and later intellectual advancement has been examined bidirectionally. On the one hand, there are a number of studies in the gifted literature indicating that parents of gifted children report that their children were early talkers (e.g., Freeman, 1991; Hollingworth, 1942; Terman, 1925; Witty, 1940; among others see Gross, 1993). In fact, Gross (1993), who provided an impressive review of the gifted literature, noted, "It is generally recognized that intellectually gifted children tend to display a precocious development in speech" (p. 89). However, it is important to note that this conclusion is based on parents' retrospective reports.

On the other hand, there are longitudinal studies demonstrating a significant relationship between early language development and later intellectual performance. Fascinating data from two independent longitudinal studies were published in 1967, revealing highly similar findings. Cameron, Livson, and Bayley (1967) derived a language factor from the Bayley California First Year Mental Scale (this was the predecessor to the well-known Bayley Scales of Infant Development). Utilizing data from the Berkeley Growth Study, they then correlated this language factor during infancy with IQ between 13 and 26 years of age. This procedure was conducted separately for boys and girls. For the boys the correlations never reached statistical significance. However, for girls, the correlations were significant with magnitudes between .4 and .6. In London, England, Moore (1967) conducted a longitudinal study from 6 months through 8 years of age. He employed the Griffiths Scale of Infant Development, which comprises among other subscales a speech or language quotient. Most relevant are the correlations between infant language development and IQ. The correlations between the 18-month speech quotient and IQ at 3, 5, and 8 years were also analyzed separately for the sexes. For boys the correlations were .40, .22, and .20 (only the first was statistically significant). The comparable values for girls were .67, .66, and .50 (all *ps* < .01). Hence, these two longitudinal studies found a moderate to moderately high correlation between early language development and IQ several years later for girls but not boys. The differential sex relationship between early language development and later IQ has never been explained.

Other studies have also reported a relation between early language and later cognitive functioning. Roe and associates (Roe, 1978; Roe, McClure, & Roe, 1982) studied 3-month-old infants' differential vocal responses (DVR) to a mother-interactive versus a stranger-interactive session. The underlying assumption of this procedure is that DVRs to mother versus stranger interactions imply an early manifestation in perceptual association and discrimination, or of cognitive skills, with greater numbers of vocal responses to mother over stranger indicating more advanced cognitive development. DVRs were then correlated (partialling out socioeconomic status and mothers' education) to subsequent cognitive functioning up to 12 years of age across a variety of tests. The correlations with the Wechsler Intelligence Scale for Children-Revised Verbal IQ were .79 (.21 for Performance IQ), and .63 and .81 for the Wide Range Achievement Scale Reading and Arithmetic tests, respectively. Although the sample size was quite small in this research, the findings are intriguing and encouraging. A final study to be reported was conducted by N. M. Robinson and Dale (1992). These researchers followed a group of children between the ages of 20 and 30 months, who were precocious in their language development, until age 6.5 years. At various points in time they were administered language and intelligence tests. The results showed consistency in advanced language skills across the duration of the study and that early precocity in language skills was associated with higher intellectual performance. There are some methodological limits to this study; however, the findings are in accord with those above in showing that early language development is related to subsequent IQ.

Third, experimental research in infant perception has resulted in some contemporary assessments of cognitive functioning based on infants' proclivity to differentially respond to novel and familiar stimuli (e.g., visual recognition memory, tactile recognition memory, and cross-modal transfer techniques). This research will be discussed in greater detail in Chapter 3. The habituation and paired-comparison procedures have generated a considerable body of knowledge not only about basic perceptual and cognitive abilities of infants, but on the issue of cognitive continuity and predicting later intelligence as well (Bornstein & Sigman, 1986). Such measures have potential because assessments during the first year have been found to correlate significantly with later performance (see Fagan & Detterman, 1992). Although promising, a recent meta-analysis indicates that the correlations between 1 and 8 years (weighted average of normalized correlations = .36 or a raw median correlation = .45) have not yet reached magnitudes sufficiently high for discerning individuals (McCall & Carriger, 1993).

A fourth and final area of infant behavioral research to be discussed here pertains to early cross-time hand or manual preference and intellectual performance. A. W. Gottfried and Bathurst (1983) discovered that hand preference consistency measured across five assessments from 12 to 42 months of age was associated with a variety of intellectual abilities during this time frame. For boys there was no relation; however, for girls, those who were consistent compared to nonconsistent were performing significantly higher on the cognitive tasks. To determine if the preference groups displayed performance asymmetries indicative of left-hemispheric specialization for verbal processing, Kee, Gottfried, Bathurst, and Brown (1987) employed a dual-task procedure requiring finger tapping and rhyme recitation, administered at the 5- and 6-year assessments in our longitudinal study. Results for both male groups showed greater right-hand than left-hand finger-tapping interference; an asymmetry implicating left-hemispheric-specific processing for the concurrent verbal activity. In contrast, only consistent females showed this pattern. The nonconsistent females showed equal finger-tapping disruption in both hands. These findings suggest a link between the functional organization of the cerebral hemispheres and verbal-language precocity in females. Kee, Gottfried, and Bathurst (1991) followed these children from 5 through 9 years and intelligence and achievement tests were administered. The findings showed that: (1) early hand preference consistency across time for females predicted school-age intellectual precocity; (2) the locus of the difference between consistent versus nonconsistent females is in verbal abilities; and (3) precocity of the consistent females was also revealed on tests of school achievement (independent of intelligence), particularly tests of reading and mathematics. The parallel between our findings and those of Cameron et al.

(1967) and Moore (1967) is striking. However, even more interesting and relevant to the topic at hand in this book is a finding from our most recent study (Kee et al., 1991) that consistent females, compared to nonconsistent females, were more likely to perform at the gifted IQ level. The percentage of gifted performers in each group is 25% and 6%, respectively. Girls who exhibited cross-time consistency in hand preference were 4 times more likely to become intellectually gifted. For males the percentages were equivalent for the hand preference groups (17% vs. 13%). These data may imply some neurobehavioral basis, specifically verbal lateralization (and possibly differentially for the sexes) in the development of intellectual giftedness or in the potential to develop this quality. Data on cross-time hand preference will not be analyzed in this book because they have already been published. However, data on psychometric and Piagetian sensorimotor scales, language development, and infant recognition and cross-modal tasks will be presented along with major intelligence tests during preschool and early elementary school years.

Education and Achievement

As a group, intellectually gifted children are above average in their school achievement (Pendarvis, Howley, & Howley, 1990; Tannenbaum, 1983). The correlation between IQ and achievement typically ranges from .4 to .6 (Renzulli, 1986). The relation between gifted IQ and achievement is not a perfect one. For example, achievement test performance of the gifted can be affected by inadequate difficulty level, and report card grades may be influenced by extraneous factors such as student compliance (Pendarvis et al., 1990). Nevertheless, it is in the realm of education that the gifted excel both in terms of accelerated learning (learning at a level beyond their grade) and skill mastery.

Gifted children are often younger than their classmates. Terman (1925) reported that the gifted children as a group were younger than children of their grade, which could be accounted for by their entering school at a younger age. The implication of this younger age is that the children are accelerated in grade level (Terman, 1925). Indeed, Terman even calculated a Progress Quotient (standard age at a grade/child's actual age) and found the gifted to be accelerated in their grade according to this standard. Tannenbaum (1983) reports that high-IQ children often enter school early and show accelerated advancement. Further, the practice of accelerating children in school (i.e., advancing their grade level) creates the situation in which gifted children are frequently younger than others in their grade. The controversy between enriching the curriculum versus accelerating the gifted continues (George, Cohn, & Stanley, 1979; Pendarvis et al., 1990; Roedell, Jackson, & Robinson, 1980; Tomlinson-Keasey, 1990), with proponents on both sides. While educational acceleration is not a focus of the book, children's age at school entry will be examined to determine if gifted children, prior to their identification as gifted, tend to be younger in kindergarten than nongifted children.

What is the breadth of areas in which the gifted excel, and is there a pattern of early accelerated achievement that is maintained from kindergarten through the early school years? Terman (1925) found that when teachers rated 8- to 13-year-olds, the gifted evidenced a greater advantage in abstract and academic subjects, but little advantage on school subjects involving physical, athletic, or artistic skills. Roedell et al. (1980) report in their Seattle Longitudinal Study that there has been variability in the pattern of achievement on the Peabody Individual Achievement Test (PIAT) over a 4-year period beginning in preschool. For example, despite exceptionally high IQs for some of the children, not all were early readers, a characteristic typically attributed to young, gifted children. However, compared to an unselected sample of preschoolers not identified as gifted, the gifted group performed at a higher level on the PIAT. In the Terman study individual patterns of achievement were obtained (DeVoss, 1925). On the Stanford Achievement Test, individual children evidenced many instances of distinct patterns whereby some achievement areas were greatly accelerated, while others were more average. This was true for the gifted and nongifted groups. DeVoss (1925) interpreted this as indicating a specialization of ability. The individual differences in the pattern of abilities were unique to each child, not general to gifted or nongifted group status. Patterns of achievement for individual children will be examined in the present study as well.

The issue of continuity of academic achievement will be addressed. In the present study, we have measured children's achievement from ages 5 through 8 using standardized, individually administered achievement tests, and teacher and parental reports of achievement. Therefore, we have a unique opportunity to investigate the longitudinal, developmental trends regarding early childhood school performance and the degree of continuity of early achievement patterns prior to children's identification as gifted in the study. The availability of these different sources of achievement data permit us to examine the generalizability of achievement trends over time.

Motivation

An area that has received relatively less attention than gifted children's academic achievement concerns their intrinsic motivation. Academic intrinsic motivation is defined as enjoyment of school learning characterized by an orientation toward mastery, curiosity, persistence, task endogeny, and the learning of challenging, difficult, and novel tasks (A. E. Gottfried, 1985, 1986a, 1990). In the present study, academic intrinsic motivation was studied. Academic intrinsic motivation rests on the theoretical foundations of cognitive discrepancy, that is, provision of environmental stimuli that adequately challenge the child; mastery experiences for the development of competence; and the perception that the individual himself or herself is the "cause" of the outcome (A. E. Gottfried, 1986b). The theoretical foundations of academic intrinsic motivation are quite relevant to the issues that have been raised regarding the need to keep gifted children engaged in the school process (Tuttle, Becker, & Sousa, 1988).

Academic intrinsic motivation is positively related to intelligence (A. E. Gottfried, 1990). In this research, the higher the child's IQ scores, the higher the academic intrinsic motivation as measured by the Children's Academic Intrinsic Motivation Inventory (CAIMI) (A. E. Gottfried, 1986a). This relation was interpreted as indicating that children with greater intellectual performance find the process of learning more challenging and pleasurable than children with relatively lower intellectual performance and experience enhanced mastery of school tasks. The significance of this hypothesis to the present research is that there may be an intrinsic motivational foundation that supports the gifted child's academic achievement.

The literature, however, has provided little evidence regarding academic intrinsic motivation in the very young gifted child. Whereas A. E. Gottfried (1990) found that children with higher IQs had higher academic intrinsic motivation, gifted children were not identified as a separate group in that study. Henderson, Gold, and McCord (1982) reported that gifted children and adolescents had higher curiosity than their nongifted counterparts. Davis and Connell (1985) reported that gifted fourth and sixth graders had higher mastery motivation than nongifted children, as did Li (1988) for fourth and seventh graders, and Hom (1988) for third graders. Tomlinson-Keasey and Little (1990) found that childhood intellectual determinism of the Terman sample, a motivational construct bearing a resemblance to achievement and intrinsic motivation, predicted the maintenance of intellectual skills over the life course.

Motivation has often been assessed indirectly from other behaviors. For example, Hagen (1980) reported that motivation is evident in a student's achievement or by his or her active involvement in academic and extracurricular activities. These are indirect indices since factors other than motivation may influence both achievement and engagement in activities. Interest, although not synonymous with motivation (Krapp, Hidi, & Renninger, 1992), has been a widely used index of motivation (e.g., Terman, 1925). Terman found that more of the gifted children were reported to be interested in school, while more of the nongifted controls were reported to show a lack of interest in school. Gifted children also evidenced a wide range of extracurricular interests indicative of curiosity (Miles, 1946; Terman, 1925). In Janos and Robinson's (1985) review, a number of motivational characteristics were identified as being more prevalent in the gifted, such as independence, autonomy, and characteristics associated with achievement motivation.

Renzulli's (1986) conception of giftedness includes task commitment, defined as perseverance and a belief in one's ability to pursue significant work. This type of motivation bears a resemblance to intrinsic motivation, albeit it is not an identical construct, because the foundations of task commitment could be external sources of expectation rather than, or in addition to, intrinsic factors. However, observations of gifted individuals' task commitment, as reviewed by Renzulli (1986), provide additional support for the importance of further investigating the construct of academic intrinsic motivation in gifted children. Additionally, Feldman (1986) describes prodigies as evidencing an intense intrinsic motivation in their domain of giftedness.

The literature suggests that gifted children ought to be higher in academic intrinsic motivation. Gifted children's competence in academic school tasks may provide a foundation for the motive toward seeking cognitive challenge and mastery. To the extent that gifted children's needs for stimulation and mastery are met, then academic intrinsic motivation ought to be higher. Conversely, gifted children may become less intrinsically motivated in school if they are not adequately challenged (Tuttle et al., 1988; Whitmore, 1986). Monks, van Boxtel, Roelofs, and Sanders (1986) found that for Dutch seventh to ninth graders, gifted underachievers had lower school motivation than both gifted and nongifted students.

With an increasing emphasis on early identification of gifted children (Roedell, 1989) and a search for alternate methods of assessing early giftedness other than through standardized tests (Karnes & Johnson, 1986), increased attention needs to be given to early intrinsic motivation. Do gifted children differ motivationally from nongifted children? If they do, how early do such differences appear? The early development of academic intrinsic motivation in the gifted and the long-term course of such development from infancy are areas with no previous empirical data.

In the present study, children's academic intrinsic motivation was measured at ages 7 and 8. Further, direct observations of children's test-taking behaviors from infancy through age 6 were conducted. These test-taking behaviors, as measured by the Bayley Infant Behavior Record, have been identified as tapping cognitive motivation consistent with the early manifestation of mastery motivation (Matheny, 1980). Mastery motivation is one of the major theoretical aspects of intrinsic motivation (A. E. Gottfried, 1986b). Examples of behaviors observed include goal directedness, attention span, and orientation responses to the materials.

From infancy through age 8, data are presented concerning the early manifestation of cognitive-mastery motivation and academic intrinsic motivation. Heretofore, no other longitudinal research on the gifted has measures of early motivation, or of academic intrinsic motivation.

Academic Self-Concept and Anxiety

A. E. Gottfried (1982, 1985) studied the relations between academic intrinsic motivation, perception of competence regarding school tasks, and academic anxiety. This research showed that higher levels of academic intrinsic motivation are associated with more positive perceptions of academic competence and lower anxiety. Since children with higher levels of academic intrinsic motivation also tend to have higher achievement and higher IQs (A. E. Gottfried, 1985, 1990), gifted children may also be expected to evidence more positive perceptions of academic self-concept and lower academic anxiety. Certainly, their greater academic success and mastery of cognitive tasks alone would predict better perception of competence and lower anxiety. Indeed, there is also literature supportive of these expectations.

Schneider (1987) reviewed literature regarding self-concept of the gifted. He found that of studies comparing gifted and nongifted children, gifted children's advantage in self-concept was in the academic domain. When self-concept was examined in nonacademic areas, there tended to be no differences between gifted and nongifted children. More recent research continues to indicate that gifted school children have more positive self-concepts in the cognitive and academic domains (Chan, 1988; Eccles, Bauman, & Rotenberg, 1989; Hoge & Renzulli, 1993; Karnes & Whorton, 1988; Kelly & Jordan, 1990; Li, 1988). In the present study, we examine perception of academic competence with regard to reading, math, and school in general at ages 7 and 8. Inasmuch as studies of self-concept of the gifted are concentrated in the upper elementary and secondary school years, our data will provide an important look at younger children. Additionally, not only do we examine perception of competence in the academic domain, but we are also able to examine it with regard to children's perceptions of specific subject areas as well as school in general.

Regarding anxiety, there are reasons to expect either lower or higher academic anxiety in gifted compared to nongifted children. Relations between anxiety and school achievement, and anxiety and IQ, have typically been negative (Hansen, 1977), indicating that more capable students have lower anxiety levels. There are also studies indicating that gifted children evidence lower anxiety than nongifted children. For example, gifted children have been found to evidence lower general and school-related anxiety than their nongifted peers (Davis & Connell, 1985; Reynolds, 1985; Reynolds & Bradley, 1983; Scholwinski & Reynolds, 1985). Another point of view was presented by Yadusky-Holahan and Holahan (1983), who suggested that the gifted may experience higher anxiety than nongifted children attributable to self-imposed pressure and pressure to succeed imposed by parents and teachers.

In the present study, academic anxiety (worry related to school tasks and tests) is examined at ages 7 and 8. Based on the literature and previous work (A. E. Gottfried, 1982, 1985), the gifted children were expected to show lower academic anxiety than the nongifted children. A. E. Gottfried (1985) found that academic intrinsic motivation was inversely related to children's academic anxiety and positively related to academic perception of competence. Higher academic intrinsic motivation is associated with lower academic anxiety and more favorable perceptions of doing well in school.

Behavioral Adjustment, Social Functioning, and Temperament

The nature of gifted children's nonintellectual functioning has received somewhat less attention than their intellectual and academic accomplishment. By nonintellectual functioning, we are referring to aspects of development such as children's behavioral and emotional adjustment, personal and social competencies and activities, and temperamental characteristics. Do these aspects of functioning relate to children's advanced or higher development in the intellectual realm? Several researchers have noted the paucity of research on these nonintellectual aspects of development, which is particularly evident with respect to development during the infancy, preschool, and in the early elementary school years (Austin & Draper, 1981; Horowitz, 1987; Janos & Robinson, 1985; Lehman & Erdwins, 1981; N. M. Robinson, 1987; Roedell et al., 1980). In addition, the methodological problems inherent in investigating these areas of development have also been detailed, including the lack of widely used standardized measurement tools (Austin & Draper, 1981; Janos & Robinson, 1985; Roedell et al., 1980), lack of equivalent comparison or control groups (Austin & Draper, 1981; Janos & Robinson, 1985; Schneider, Clegg, Byrne, Ledingham, & Crombie, 1989), bias in identification or selection of research subjects (Ludwig & Cullinan, 1984; Roedell et al., 1980), and failure to consider potentially important moderating variables (Janos & Robinson, 1985; Schneider et al., 1989). Finally, even among the relatively few studies addressing these aspects of development in gifted compared to nongifted children, inconsistent findings have resulted. Some studies have reported that gifted children score more favorably than their nongifted peers on assessments of social, emotional, and/or behavioral functioning, while others report no differences (Austin & Draper, 1981; Gockenbach, 1989; Ludwig & Cullinan, 1984; Olszewski-Kubilius, Kulieke, & Krasney, 1988).

In the current literature on gifted children's development in these areas, the early writings of Lombroso (1891) during the late nineteenth century are often contrasted to those of Terman in 1925 (cf. L. E. Brody & Benbow, 1986; Ludwig & Cullinan, 1984; Pendarvis et al., 1990; Solano, 1987). Lombroso held that the intellectually gifted were at risk for maladjustment ranging to insanity, whereas Terman concluded that gifted children surpassed average children with respect to adjustment.

Although Terman and his colleagues did not have the psychometrically developed measures of social or behavioral adjustment that are now available to researchers, they collected a large body of data regarding the play interests, play knowledge, and play practices of gifted versus control children. Children rated their participation and preferences for play activities. Activities were conceptualized to fall into one of three categories: active-solitary (e.g., spinning tops, riding bikes), social-active (e.g., tag, hide-and-seek), or social-quiet (e.g., "playing school," dominoes, cards). The latter category was characterized as requiring less physical strength and skill than powers of imagination or logic. In addition, children were tested on their knowledge about various play activities, and parents and teachers provided information regarding the children's play behaviors.

Terman's results showed that the play interests of the gifted and control groups were only slightly different; age and sex of child were much more influential than intelligence in determining preferences. In addition, he found that gifted children were considerably more mature in their play interests than their nongifted age-mates. Furthermore, gifted children expressed greater interest in less active types of play (i.e., cards, puzzles, checkers, chess) and less social play activities; in fact, Terman concluded that the difference between the gifted and control groups on sociability was large enough to be significant. Additionally, Terman found that gifted children as a group possessed significantly more knowledge about games and play activities, indicating that their advantage in play knowledge paralleled their advantage on the Stanford Achievement Test.

Parents and teachers also provided information about the play behaviors of the gifted children. Their reports showed that the gifted played alone more often than controls, although the difference was small (about 10% fewer gifted played with other children "very much" compared to controls). Both parents and teachers also reported that larger percentages of gifted children tended to prefer to play with older children compared to controls. Teachers reported that 9.1% of controls preferred to play with older children, compared to 25.1% of the gifted by teacher report and 34.6% of the gifted according to parent report. Terman speculated that the preference for playing with older children on the part of gifted children might be due to the then popular practice of accelerating the gifted in school; in fact, over 80% of his sample had skipped at least one grade level. In addition, he proposed that gifted children preferred older playmates due to the tendency for mental ages to seek their own level.

Terman also examined the interests of gifted compared to control children. Gifted children were found superior to nongifted children in their level of intellectual and social interest, but equivalent with respect to interest in play. Parent and teacher ratings of various traits falling into seven groups (intellectual, volitional, emotional, moral, physical, social, and mechanical ingenuity) were also collected; the gifted group excelled on all traits except the last. To summarize, Terman's data refuted the writings of Lombroso and stereotypes that were popular during that era that gifted children develop their intellectual interests at the expense of their social and activity interests.

Terman's (1925) findings did not completely alter the popular image of gifted individuals. Current researchers continue to mention stereotypes of gifted individuals, including that of the gifted as the "oversensitive, unbalanced genius" (see Pendarvis et al., 1990), as socially inept (Pendarvis et al., 1990), as prone to interpersonal isolation (Austin & Draper, 1981; Gallucci, 1988; Janos & Robinson, 1985; Solano, 1987), and as likely to have emotional problems (L. E. Brody & Benbow, 1986; Freeman, 1983). Tomlinson-Keasey (1990) note the portrayal of gifted adolescents in popular films as "nerds" who lack appropriate social skills and prefer to spend their time pursuing obscure academic questions.

To determine whether stereotypes of the gifted as socially isolated still exist, Solano (1987) systematically varied gender and ability level (average, able, or gifted) in descriptions of hypothetical high school students. College students completed a questionnaire assessing their impressions of the hypothetical person's social and academic success. Results showed that female gifted stimulus persons were perceived as significantly less popular than average-ability and able students. Summarizing across her research with high school student, high school personnel, and college student samples, Solano concluded that the gifted continue to be stereotyped as socially isolated, although the reason for this perception could not be determined. Is this perception of social isolation due to an impression that the gifted are unlikable, or to the perception that they are uninterested in socializing with others? Solano concluded that the current stereotype of the gifted as socially isolated is more compatible with the view of the gifted as forsaking social interactions in favor of the pursuit of their work as opposed to social deviance.

Whether based in reality or in myth, several concerns have been mentioned by parents, educators, and/or researchers regarding the social and emotional functioning of gifted children. L. E. Brody and Benbow (1987) and Tomlinson-Keasey (1990) noted that parents and educators often hesitate to accelerate the grade level of gifted children due to concerns about their social and emotional development. Pendarvis et al. (1990) cited five worries voiced by parents and/or educators regarding gifted children's adjustment: (1) they may encounter difficulties in social interactions due to intellectual differences with their agemates, (2) they may experience elevated anxiety due to pressure to excel in school, (3) they may be at higher risk for dropping out of school, (4) delinquency, and (5) suicide. Freeman (1983) summarized four factors that may heighten gifted children's risk for emotional or educational problems during development: (1) heightened sensitivity of the gifted to environmental or social stimuli, (2) development by gifted children of unreal expectations for themselves ("perfectionism"), (3) heightening of "normal" sex-role problems of development, and (4) mismatch in the educational setting in terms of curriculum, teaching style, and/or learning environment. Freeman concluded that gifted children have the same emotional and educational needs for expression and exploration as other children. However, she noted that gifted children differed from other children in that their needs were more intense, and that if thwarted, gifted children would react more strongly.

Contrary to the concerns of parents and teachers and the negative stereotypes regarding the emotional, behavioral, and social adjustment of gifted children, the general conclusion drawn by many researchers in recently published studies is that gifted children and/or adolescents are at least equal, if not superior, to their nongifted cohorts in these areas (L. E. Brody & Benbow, 1986; Gallucci, 1988; Hollingworth, 1942; Lehman & Erdwins, 1981; Ludwig & Cullinan, 1984; R. M. Milgram & N. A. Milgram, 1976; Schneider et al., 1989; Tomlinson-Keasey, 1990; see also reviews by Austin & Draper, 1981; Gockenbach, 1989; Horowitz & O'Brien, 1986; Janos & Robinson, 1985; Olszewski-Kubilius et al., 1988; Pendarvis et al., 1990). Although gifted children are not immune to emotional, behavioral, or social problems, they are at a minimum no more vulnerable than other children; they are as a group predominantly well adjusted in the emotional, behavioral, and social realms. Most of these studies, however, have focused on gifted children during the school-age and adolescent periods rather than the preschool years. Three recent studies, for example, have examined adjustment during the adolescent years. Gallucci (1988) compared scores on the Child Behavior Checklist of gifted 12- to 16-year-olds participating in a residential summer camp to normative data and found no differences between the two groups. L. E. Brody and Benbow (1986) studied 13-year-old students with high SAT scores (primarily math) and found no differences between them and a comparison group of less able students in terms of self-reports of self-esteem, happiness, depression, or discipline problems. However, the gifted viewed themselves as less popular than the adolescents in the comparison group. Luthar, Zigler, and Goldstein (1992) compared 12- to 15-year-olds participating in a university talent identification program to a group matched on cognitive maturity and groups matched on chronological age. Luthar et al. reported that the gifted adolescents showed more positive psychological adjustment than the chronological age comparison groups on depression and self-image, and equal adjustment to the group matched on cognitive maturity. However, gifted females were found to have lower self-image scores than gifted males.

Studies of children of elementary school age indicate that the gifted are at least as well adjusted as their nongifted peers. Lehman and Erdwins (1981) found that gifted third graders were quite well adjusted, scoring more favorably than their nongifted age-mates on several subtests of the California Test of Personality, including sense of personal worth, social skills, sense of personal freedom, antisocial tendencies, and school relations. Janos and Robinson (1985) studied a sample of 5- to 10-year-olds who viewed themselves as "different" and found that their self-esteem, although lower than other gifted children, was still above average. Ludwig and Cullinan (1984), studying adjustment of first through fifth graders, found that gifted children showed fewer behavior problems than their nongifted classmates using teacher reports on the Child Behavior Checklist. The children studied by Luftig and Nichols (1991) consisted of fourth through eighth graders in which the gifted were participating in a pull-out education program. Utilizing peer nomination data, they concluded that gifted girls were unable to establish popularity or good social relations with nongifted peers, although gifted boys enjoyed enhanced social status. Because of the relatively low popularity and negatively perceived personality and school traits of gifted girls, Luftig and Nichols concluded that they may be an at-risk population with respect to academic achievement and personal or social adjustment. R. M. Milgram and N. A. Milgram (1976) studied fourth- through eighth-grade Israeli children using self-report measures assessing self-concept, locus of control, and anxiety. They observed that the gifted scored more favorably, that is, showed more positive self-concept, more internal locus of control, and lower levels of general and test anxiety. Unlike Luftig and Nichols, R. M. Milgram and N. A. Milgram reported that gifted girls were as well adjusted as gifted boys.

Our literature review revealed only one study of social interaction skills among preschool-aged children. Roedell et al. (1980), describing the characteristics of gifted young children, reviewed the earlier findings of Roedell on the social interaction skills of 3- to 5-year-old children with an average IQ of 138. Although comparisons to nongifted peers were not reported, Roedell et al. did report that children with higher IQs were able to generate more ideas about ways children could solve hypothetical social conflicts. However, no relation was observed between test performance and teachers' ratings of children's adjustment or observations of children's free-play behavior. Roedell et al. concluded that precocious social cognition by itself was insufficient to ensure appropriate social interaction behavior.

Thus, the exceptionality of gifted children in the intellectual realm does not appear to negatively impact their functioning in these other realms of development. Gifted children typically equal, and sometimes excel, their nongifted age-mates in terms of adjustment. Exceptions to these general findings, however, may include highly gifted children whose IQ exceeds 160 (L. E. Brody & Benbow, 1986; Hollingworth, 1942; Roedell, 1984), gifted underachievers, and possibly gifted girls (Freeman, 1983; Horowitz & O'Brien, 1986; Janos & Robinson, 1985; Luftig & Nichols, 1991; Luthar et al., 1992; Roedell, 1984).

An additional nonintellectual factor that may distinguish gifted and nongifted children is their temperament. In the Fullerton Longitudinal Study, the temperament model of Thomas, Chess, and Birch (1968), based on the New York Longitudinal Study (NYLS), was utilized. In the NYLS model, temperament is viewed as "the stylistic component of behavior—that is, the *how* of behavior as differentiated from motivation, the *why* of behavior, and ability, the *what* of behavior" (Goldsmith et al., 1987, p. 508). Nine categories of temperament were delineated by the NYLS group:

1. *Activity level*, the level, tempo, and frequency of the motor component of behavior.
2. *Rhythmicity*, the degree of regularity of biological functions (e.g., sleeping and waking, feeding).
3. *Approach or withdrawal*, the nature of the initial response to a new stimulus.
4. *Adaptability*, the successive course of the child's responses to new stimuli (i.e., slow vs. fast).
5. *Intensity of reaction*, the energy level of response.
6. *Threshold of responsiveness*, the level of extrinsic stimulation necessary to evoke a noticeable response.
7. *Quality of mood*, the amount of pleasant, joyful, friendly behavior versus unpleasant, crying, unfriendly behavior.
8. *Distractibility*, the effectiveness of extraneous environmental stimuli in interfering with or altering the course of an ongoing behavior.

9. *Attention span and persistence,* the length of time a particular activity is pursued (attention span) and the continuation of an activity in spite of obstacles to continuation (persistence).

One could hypothesize that specific dimensions of temperament in the NYLS may promote or enhance intellectual development.

Research on the relation between intellectual development and temperament is accumulating. For example, researchers have examined the correlation between intelligence and temperament, whether gifted and nongifted children differ on specific temperamental characteristics, and the role of temperament and personality variables in predicting the achievement of eminence in adulthood. The findings can be characterized as decidedly mixed.

Temperament dimensions have been used to describe the characteristics of gifted children relative to nongifted children. For example, compared to their nongifted peers, gifted children have been described as having longer attention spans, being more persistent, happy, and active (cf. Roedell et al., 1980). Matheny (1989) cites a study of limited circulation by Burk in which the temperament characteristics of 125 gifted children in nursery school through second grade were compared to normative data; gifted children were rated as more approaching, adaptable, persistent, and more positive in mood.

In a recent study of the relation between temperament and intelligence using the Louisville Twin Study data, Matheny (1989) noted recurrent positive correlations between mental test performance and the temperament characteristics of attention span/persistence, approach/withdrawal, adaptability, and mood. Specifically, children with higher mental scores were rated as more attentive to and persistent on tasks; more approaching of new unfamiliar individuals, objects, or events; more adaptable, and more positive in mood. Whether these temperament-intelligence correlations are strong enough to distinguish gifted from nongifted children during the school years has not been demonstrated, however.

There is also evidence suggesting no relation between childhood temperament and intellectual functioning. For example, Roedell et al. (1980) reported that parents of gifted children in the Seattle Project described their children as varying so widely on temperament characteristics that it was impossible to describe them as a group in terms of temperament features.

Aspects of temperament during childhood or adolescence have also been suggested as determinants of whether gifted children maintain their intellectual skills into adulthood or achieve eminence as adults. For example, using structural equation modeling, Tomlinson-Keasey and Little (1990) found that sociability of the child at age 11 years had a negative effect on intellectual skills among adults; that is, children who were popular, enjoyed good health, radiated physical energy, and maintained a cheerful and optimistic attitude were subsequently *less* likely to maintain their intellectual skills as adults. In addition, Albert and Runco (1986) and Howe (1990) write of nonintellectual factors that differentiate those who become eminent from those who do not, the former suggesting personality and family process variables and the latter qualities such as persistence and attentiveness. Decades ago, C. M. Cox (1926) noted that childhood characteristics such as persistence and intellectual energy were predictive of achievement during adulthood.

Findings from the Fullerton Longitudinal Study with respect to behavioral adjustment, social functioning, and temperamental characteristics of gifted versus nongifted children during the infancy, preschool, and early elementary school years are presented in Chapter 5. These findings will allow us to ascertain whether intellectual giftedness is related to these aspects of functioning during the early childhood years, an age period not addressed by Terman and only modestly studied since.

Home and Family Environment

The first systematic study of the families of highly intelligent people was conducted by Galton. With the publication of *Hereditary Genius* in 1869, Galton presented evidence that eminence runs in families. Moreover, Galton was convinced that genius was, to a large degree, inherited. In the United States, the well-known longitudinal study of gifted children launched in the early 1920s by Terman also shed light on the role of family factors associated with giftedness. Terman's study provided much of the descriptive data on the characteristics of families with gifted children so often cited in the literature. These two landmark studies and several others since provide extensive support for family demographic correlates of giftedness (see Barbe, 1956; Cornell, 1984; Freeman, 1979, 1991; Gross, 1993; Sheldon, 1954; Terman, 1925–1929; see also the comprehensive overview by Olszewski, Kulieke, & Buescher, 1987). A summary of previous findings are presented here along with an overview of the home and family environmental correlates of intellectual giftedness.

Consistently supported by the data is the finding that the parents of gifted children are more likely to be of higher socioeconomic status, to be high achievers who have earned college and graduate degrees, and to practice in professional occupations. For example, Terman reported that 26% of the gifted children in his sample had one or both parents with college degrees. Other researchers, including Hollingworth (1942), Sheldon (1954), Barbe (1956), and Kincaid (1969), also found more advanced educational levels in their samples of gifted children. (It should be noted that Freeman, 1979, did not find educational attainment differences in her study.) Some have noted the higher educational status of grandparents as well (Freeman, 1988; Galton, 1869; Gross, 1993). The finding that educational accomplishments of children are fostered by highly educated families is not surprising, and we would expect to see education highly valued in the homes of the gifted children in the current study as well.

One would expect higher educational accomplishments to result in higher occupational status. Indeed, Terman (1925–1929), Hollingworth (1942), Sheldon (1954), Barbe (1956), and Freeman (1979) reported that fathers of gifted children were far more likely to be classified as professionals. As found in the educational domain, grandfathers of gifted children also had occupational positions of higher status (Gross, 1993; Hollingworth, 1942; Terman, 1925–1929). Occupational status of mothers was included in several studies as well, although the number of mothers working outside the home was far less than the number of fathers. Sheldon (1954) noted that all mothers of the 28 highly intellectually gifted (IQ = 170+) children in his study had the necessary skills with which they could earn a living independent of their husbands, although less than half were employed at the time of his study. Groth (1975) found that mothers of gifted children as compared to mothers of nongifted children were more likely to be employed outside the home. The occupations of mothers of gifted children tended to be primarily in the social sciences (e.g., teaching). Freeman (1979) and Gross (1993) found higher occupational status for mothers of gifted children in their samples. Data on maternal employment need to be interpreted within the historical context during which it was collected. Maternal employment, in general, is far more frequent now than it was prior to the 1970s. Hence, early data on employment of mothers of gifted children is not necessarily representative of current trends (A. E. Gottfried, Bathurst, & A. W. Gottfried, 1994; A. E. Gottfried & A. W. Gottfried, 1994).

A phenomenon often noted in the study of giftedness is the higher selection ratio of males to females for children identified as gifted. This was true in Terman's study and in others as well (e.g., R. L. Cox, 1977; Freeman, 1979; Hollingworth, 1942; Terman & Oden, 1959). Differential sex ratios could possibly be due to ascertainment bias if subject recruitment for gifted children is based on teachers' nominations (see below). As suggested by R. L. Cox (1977), this difference may be imposed by society as opposed to any real differences in intellectual functioning. For example, males may receive more encouragement from both parents and teachers to excel academically, while females may hesitate to compete with males for fear of social reprisal. However, the recent changes in society and overt efforts to encourage young girls to actively compete with young boys academically may eradicate these sex differences in today's gifted samples. The gender differentials noted in past studies could be dated.

Several researchers have evaluated the composition of the family with respect to marital status, parents' age, number of people in the home, and birth order. When marital status is reported, the results show that the parents of gifted children have lower divorce rates than the general population (Barbe, 1956; Groth, 1975). However, our study was conducted in a different era and the incidence of divorce has increased continually over the years since the 1950s (Cherlin, 1992; Hernandez, 1988). It was of interest to evaluate whether these patterns continue to hold for gifted versus nongifted children in the 1980s and 1990s.

With respect to the age of gifted children's parents, the findings are consistent in the literature. Parents of gifted children are typically older than parents of nongifted children (Silverman & Kearney, 1988; Storfer, 1990; Terman, 1925), with mothers typically giving birth to their first child when in their late twenties. In Terman's study, the mean age of fathers and mothers was 33.6 and 29 years, respectively. Silverman and Kearney (1988) found similar demographics in their study of children with IQs in the very superior range (170+). It is noteworthy that these findings spanned several decades and seem to be immune to the effects of changing family demographics during the same period of time. A likely explanation is that postponing the birth of children to a later time allows parents to pursue and achieve higher educational and occupational status and develop greater stability, maturity, and financial security.

Gifted children typically come from small families and are often the firstborn or only child. Barbe (1956) found that approximately 64% of the gifted children in his study had no (21.8%) or one (42.6%) sibling; 52.5% were firstborns. Terman (1925–1929) reported the mode at two siblings with approximately 60% of the subjects being only children or the oldest child. Sheldon (1954) reported that the highly intellectual children in his sample tended to be firstborns or only borns. Several years later, R. L. Cox (1977) reported that nearly half of a sample of 465 gifted children were firstborns. Common explanations include the hypothesis that the first child in the family has the complete attention of his or her parents, while later borns must share their parents. As early as the mid-1800s, it was noted that men of eminence are often the eldest child (Galton, 1869). Over 100 years later, M. G. Goertzel, V. Goertzel, and T. G. Goertzel (1978) studied the biographies of several hundred eminent persons and corroborated this finding. Albert (1980), in investigating the birth order status of eminent persons, coined the term "special positions" to describe the unique treatment of these children within the family.

The early researchers such as Galton and Terman were interested in describing the characteristics of families that produce gifted children. However, demographic data provide no information about the specific features within the home that may account for the observed differences between the intellectually gifted and nongifted. More recent researchers have taken a closer look at the home and family environment of gifted children. Although there are far fewer studies in this area, results have been consistent. The homes of gifted children are child centered (Olszewski et al., 1987). Indeed, Gross (1993) postulates that the family may be the most significant factor in the development of intellectual talent. Without parental encouragement and facilitation, children who have high potential may not reach their potential. Gross did not discount the role of schools in the development of the intellectually gifted, but Gross argued that the development of exceptional ability is the result of both parental and educator support, a position taken by Colangelo and Dettmann (1983) as well. Howe (1990) also argued that children will not realize their potential without parental support. Although an advocate of effective schooling, he stated, "On its own, a school can rarely succeed in giving the intellectual nourishment that results in a child excelling at something, rather than being merely competent" (p. 124). A stimulating home environment must be accompanied by someone who is there to explain, direct, and provide feedback to children.

Children of high intellectual ability have parents who are highly involved in their children's activities and education. Their parents provide a wide range of reading materials; encourage hobbies; foster positive attitudes toward learning; model good learning attitudes; and encourage parent-child discussions (see Colangelo & Dettmann, 1983; Howe, 1990; Kulieke & Olszewski-Kubilius, 1989; Olszewski et al., 1987;

Roedell et al., 1980). In our earlier work (A. W. Gottfried & A. E. Gottfried, 1984), we examined the home and family correlates of cognitive ability in infants and preschool children and found that children with higher intellectual functioning were provided with more materials that enhance children's cognitive skills. Mothers were more involved in their activities, provided them with a greater variety of experiences, read to them more as infants, and presented them with more stimulating educational challenges. In the Gulbenkian Project carried out in England, Freeman (1979) found two major home influences associated with high IQ. The first was the provision of more learning materials (e.g., books and writing materials). The second, and necessary, component was the involvement of parents in the learning process. Parents of gifted children set examples for their children and provide an atmosphere conducive to learning. Mothers of high-IQ children exert more educational pressure on their children and are more involved in their activities and in the day-to-day functioning of their children's school. Freeman concluded that it was not enough for parents simply to provide the appropriate learning materials for children; parents must be actively involved in the learning process.

Reading activities are the most often cited parental involvement practice for educational enrichment (Colangelo & Dettmann, 1983). These include reading to children from a very young age, providing age-appropriate books that are informative and interesting, encouraging and modeling reading behavior, and helping develop a positive attitude toward learning. Freeman (1979) reported that the homes of gifted children contained far more books than did the homes of nongifted children, that these children were more avid readers than other children, and that they had a greater variety of interests.

Terman's data included the number of books read by children in his sample, and he compared those data with information from several hundred control children. By age 7, gifted children were reading an average of five books per month, whereas control-group children read very little. By age 11 years, gifted children averaged seven and one-half books per month; control-group children averaged less than four. Further, gifted children read on a broader range of topics and more often chose books about science, history, biography, travel, poetry, drama, and informational fiction. These children also pursued a broad variety of interests and hobbies. R. L. Cox (1977) noted that gifted children most often cited reading as a free-time activity. They read for entertainment and for their own special interests, which were broad and varied.

The study of family relationships and the quality of the social climate in the home has revealed differences between gifted and nongifted groups. Parents of gifted children place a stronger value on being closely involved with their children and on participation in more family activities than do parents of nongifted children (Cornell, 1984; Cornell & Grossberg, 1987; Freeman, 1979; Gross, 1993; Kulieke & Olszewski-Kubilius, 1989). More specifically, families whose activities are predominantly intellectual and cultural have children with higher intellectual functioning (Cornell, 1984; A. W. Gottfried & A. E. Gottfried, 1984). The importance of academic achievement is stressed along with a value of working hard, striving for success, and being active and persevering (Kulieke & Olszewski-Kubilius, 1989). Families of intellectually high-functioning children also experience less conflict in the home (Cornell, 1984) and report higher levels of cohesiveness (Cornell, 1984; A. W. Gottfried & A. E. Gottfried, 1984). More free expression of thoughts and feelings is also characteristic of families with higher intellectually functioning children (A. W. Gottfried & A. E. Gottfried, 1984).

Collectively, these prior studies provide a snapshot of the home environment and family life of gifted children. Clearly, it is the combination of learning materials, parental involvement, and social atmosphere that is associated with high intellectual ability. Indeed, we expected to find differences between the gifted and nongifted groups of children in our sample consistent with prior research in the demographic, environmental, and family relationships domains. While our summary of the issues included the comparison of the giftedness status groups in these domains, our focus was on the early years in development, before children were identified as gifted or nongifted.

An important question that has been inadequately addressed in the literature is whether parents are aware of their child's intellectual potential and, if so, how early do they recognize that their child is advanced intellectually? We addressed this question directly because it is relevant to the understanding of the process by which some children achieve higher intellectual status. Two earlier studies compared the ability of parents versus teachers to correctly identify intellectual giftedness in kindergarten children. In the first (Jacobs, 1971), parents of kindergarten children accurately identified 61% of the gifted children, while teachers correctly identified only about 4%. In the second study (Ciha, Harris, Hoffman, & Potter, 1974), parents of 465 kindergarten children were asked to indicate whether or not they believed their child to be gifted after they read a list of characteristics associated with giftedness; teachers were asked to nominate those children they believed to be gifted. Again, parents did better than teachers in that they correctly identified 76% of the gifted children, whereas teachers correctly identified only 22%. The findings of these two studies question the validity of teachers' nominations in the process of identifying gifted children. Based on these data, parents would be more effective than teachers in identifying gifted children, yet teachers have often been used for this purpose.

The clues that parents use to evaluate their children's potential will help us to understand how parents appraise intelligence in their children. When parents of preschoolers seeking to have their child tested for giftedness were asked to list the characteristics in their child that caused them to believe their child might be gifted, the item ranked number one was expressive or productive language, followed by memory, abstract thinking, ahead of peers, curiosity, and receptive or comprehensive language (Louis & Lewis, 1992). In the Ciha et al. (1974) study, parents of kindergartners reported advanced vocabulary, complex verbalizations, and high reading skills as the discriminating factors. The identification of language skills as one of the criteria parents use to evaluate their children's intellectual potential was common to both studies. Freeman (1991) noted that the gifted children in her study had higher reading, writing, and talking skills than nongifted children, and that their mothers were aware of these differences when their children were very young. However, the data from Ciha et al. (1974) and Louis and Lewis (1992) were collected during the preschool and kindergarten years, and Freeman's data were collected retrospectively. In the current study, we measured parents' beliefs about their children's developmental status beginning in infancy and continuing through the preschool years and thus were able to address the question of if or when parents were aware of their child's advancement potential during infancy and preschool years.

Overall, these findings support the notion that parents recognize their child's potential prior to the time that educators test for giftedness status, which is typically in the early elementary years. It may therefore follow that parents respond by providing more stimulating and academically oriented materials and activities to these children. Alternately, it is just as reasonable to suspect that highly functioning children make greater demands on their parents for stimulating activities and experiences. In fact, Freeman (1979) concluded that gifted children need more from the environment because they have the ability to take in more and to use the information more effectively. Perhaps Olszewski et al. (1987) said it best:

> The family is an interactive system where children and parents mutually influence each other. The development of a talent is a result of the delicate interweaving of many arenas such as the family history, the unique characteristics or attributes of the child in the family, and family events.... Giftedness...is both a dependent and independent variable, a cause as well as an effect. (p. 25)

There is substantial evidence that intellectual giftedness blossoms in homes where there is high family involvement, intellectually stimulating materials and experiences for the children, and a social atmosphere fostering intellectual and cultural growth. It was these findings that led us to the next logical phase in the study of the environmental correlates of intellectual giftedness: the systematic evaluation of the early environmental fabric of children who become gifted and nongifted. Specifically, we asked whether the environmental factors associated with giftedness are apparent in these children's early developmental histories, years before they are identified as gifted or nongifted. Further, we did not rely on retrospect or past memories for data collection. On the contrary, we gathered information as the children developed, having begun our investigation 7 years prior to identifying the subsample of gifted children. Thus, the present research on the early home and family environment of gifted and nongifted children represents a major contribution to this body of literature.

A comprehensive and detailed account of the early environment of children who become gifted and nongifted is presented. Both direct observation in the children's homes and indirect assessment by use of questionnaires and inventories were included. The use of indirect measurement allowed us to expand on the environmental information gathered at each assessment by tapping aspects of children's environments and provision of educationally relevant experiences not assessed in the direct observation methods. In our past research (Bathurst, 1988; A. E. Gottfried, Bathurst, & A. W. Gottfried, 1994; A. E. Gottfried, A. W. Gottfried, & Bathurst, 1988; A. W. Gottfried & A. E. Gottfried, 1984), we found indirect assessment to be a reliable and valid means of acquiring information about families. Further, we were able to gather environmental data more frequently and include a more varied set of conceptual measures than direct assessment would have allowed. The result was a comprehensive set of home and family measures gathered at systematic intervals beginning in infancy and continuing through the early elementary school years. Our measurement tools included standardized scales and person-report instruments. This multimethod approach allowed us to contrast and compare results across the many sources of data and to determine how the early home environment differs for children who become gifted or nongifted. In addition, our longitudinal design, use of repeated measures, and frequency with which we conducted assessments permitted us to track the environmental and family correlates across time, thereby allowing us to study cross-time trends (Horowitz, 1987). Thus, there was an ongoing assessment of a comprehensive array of variables, across methods and across time.

In our approach to analyzing the data for Chapter 6, we conceptualized our variables into three domains: distal (socioeconomic status, family structure, and family composition), proximal (detailed measurements of the home environment such as the cognitively enriching materials and experiences provided to children), and family relationships (quality of the social atmosphere in the home).

In summary, the present study provides a unique opportunity to investigate the relation between home environment and giftedness in the following ways: (1) onset of data collection from infancy so that the earliest aspects of the environment are measured; (2) ongoing assessment of multiple aspects of home and family environment; (3) data collected prospectively, rather than retrospectively; (4) direct observation as well as indirect assessment of the home; and (5) standardized home inventories that permit researchers to examine comparability and generalizability across research programs.

UNIQUENESS OF THE FULLERTON LONGITUDINAL STUDY

The Fullerton Longitudinal Study (henceforth referred to as FLS) provides a unique opportunity for investigating issues pertaining to the early developmental aspects of gifted IQ for several reasons:

1. Because we have studied children from infancy through the school-entry years (it is planned to study them through adolescence), we were able to conduct a reversed contingency analysis of systematically collected longitudinal data. This is not a retrospective or retrospective longitudinal study, known to be questionable with respect to developmental data (see Featherman, 1980). Neither parents nor children were questioned about past developmental events. The Fullerton Longitudinal Study is also not based on unscientifically gathered archival data. All data were collected contemporaneously, systematically, and are based predominately on objective measures. In the reversed

contingency analysis, the fundamental question is the following: given gifted or nongifted IQ at school age, what were these groups of children like in the past as they advanced in age? However, it is important to emphasize that reversed contingency analyses do not necessarily lend themselves to answering questions pertaining to predictability. They are postdictive and may be restricted to understanding history or developmental events in the past. Prediction involves a different question than asked in this book and is based on forward contingency analysis that does not necessarily have an overlapping set of conditional probabilities with the reversed contingency analysis (see A. W. Gottfried, 1973). Certainly the quality and quantity of data contained in the FLS provide a gold mine of information for the development of predictive models. However, this was not the task at hand in this book. Here, we present the early developmental characteristics of children who achieve gifted IQ scores in middle childhood. As we prospectively study our sample through time (thus far we have followed them into adolescence), we intend not only to address further developmental issues and questions, but to propose and test predictive models. However, the latter task is reserved for our future volume or publications. Long-term longitudinal research should afford us this opportunity.

2. Our sample comprises a wide range of middle-class families. Having a range of predominantly middle-class families displaces the distribution of IQ scores upward, thereby enhancing the probability of obtaining a larger number of gifted children than would be expected or found in the population at large. Additionally, the study sample was nonclinical and not at risk at the outset of investigation. The infants represented a healthy population.

3. The FLS encompasses a comprehensive array of conceptually derived measures tapping various developmental domains. The methodological framework was designed to obtain continuous and contemporaneous information through the time frame of this study. Measures were selected based on a preconceived foundation so as to answer questions and issues addressed in the various research themes running through this extensive longitudinal project. These themes include, for example, home environment and cognitive development, academic intrinsic motivation, cognitive and academic correlates of early manual laterality, temperament, parental employment and children's development, and the like (see, e.g., A. E. Gottfried, 1990; A. E. Gottfried, Bathurst, & A. W. Gottfried, 1994; A. E. Gottfried et al., 1988; A. W. Gottfried, 1984a; A. W. Gottfried & Bathurst, 1983; Guerin & A. W. Gottfried, in press-a, in press-b; Guerin, A. W. Gottfried, Oliver, &

Thomas, 1994; Kee et al., 1991). Moreover, data collection comprised both cross-context (laboratory and home) and multiple-person (child, parents, and teachers) assessments. This was included to enhance the level of confidence and generalizability of findings.

4. Quite often in research studies on giftedness, subjects are selected initially on the basis of teacher nominations and subsequently the sample is tested with psychological and/or educational tests. Based on this recruitment technique, subjects are then designated as gifted or nongifted. This procedure was characteristic of the Terman study and was subsequently criticized (and justifiably so) by Hughes and Converse (1962). However, this method of screening for gifted subjects continues in the literature (see, e.g., Heller, 1991; Schofield & Ashman, 1987). There are two major problems with utilizing this procedure. First, factors other than giftedness may enter into the teachers' nominations, resulting in ascertainment bias. For example, just as researchers have various conceptualizations of giftedness, so may teachers. Factors such as creativity or behavioral functioning may intrude on teachers' judgments as well as the child's (or possibly the teacher's) gender. In fact, in the Munich Longitudinal Study, Heller (1991) himself reported that girls were less frequently judged by their teachers to be the best in intellectual abilities despite the fact that the girls were somewhat superior to boys in academic achievement, except for math and physics. Certainly, cultural factors could be operating as well when it comes to teacher nominations. The issue of ascertainment bias is discussed further in this book. Second, if the identification or designation of gifted children occurs within the school context (e.g., teacher nominations or testing by school psychologists), there is the possibility that the labeling could have some unknown confounding effect on the research. For example, if teachers believe certain students are gifted and then nominate them for research projects (or enrichment or special programs), there could be halo effects or alterations in expectations operating, as well as modifications in the child's self-perceptions or reactions of classmates. If parents have access to their child's educational records (which they do) and know or are informed by teachers that the child has been labeled as gifted, there could be reactions of sorts from various family members as well (Colangelo & Brower, 1987). A. Robinson (1985) contends that there are a limited amount of empirical studies on the effects of labeling with the gifted and that conclusions are difficult to draw. However, she noted that "labeling carries with it more than stereotyping: It implies that some sort of differential treatment, or assistance, or adaptation of the educational system is required once the child has been identified" (p. 103). Our

point is that when designation or labeling of giftedness originates from or is based on school assessments, there is the risk that the labeling itself could alter the child's educational and family experiences in unknown directions. In the FLS, the designation of gifted or nongifted was not based on teacher nominations or school assessments. It was based on testing in the laboratory. Furthermore, parents or teachers were never informed of the group designation and, in the data coding process, subjects were identified by number and not by name. This prevented the testing staff from having cross-time knowledge of children's developmental status.

5. Throughout the course of investigation, we maintained a high rate of families continuing to participate in the study, thus precluding sample bias resulting from selected attrition factors. Hence, retention of the sample was impressively high across the numerous repeated assessments conducted from infancy through the primary school years.

6. The sample size is relatively high given its ratio to the comprehensiveness of developmental assessments. In designing a longitudinal project, the investigator must decide on having a very large sample size with less frequent testings and fewer measures or a relatively smaller sample size with more frequent testing periods and a greater number of measures. Because our interest is developmental psychology, we opted for the latter approach. Our sample size is by no means small with respect to the psychological literature. Moreover, we have an exceptionally intense and comprehensive assessment paradigm so that stability and change in child and family development could be studied across time.

7. The nongifted, or comparison, group represents the same cohort from which the gifted group emerged. It is not a control group that was constructed by matching subjects or by random selection. Problems of control or comparison groups in ex post facto situations have long been recognized in the psychological, sociological, and epidemiological literature (see Campbell & Stanley, 1963; Chapin, 1955; A. W. Gottfried, 1973; MacMahon & Pugh, 1970; Meehl, 1971). Matching with after-the-fact behavioral phenomena—for example, construction of a nongifted or control group to compare to a gifted group after the designation—may result in a number of methodological self-defeating problems (e.g., diminution of sample size, decrease of variability, increase in standard error, and breaking natural covariances such as social class and IQ). These problems were obviated in our longitudinal project. The nongifted group was not recruited, matched, randomly selected, or fabricated by any procedure on the part of the researcher. This investi-

gation involved the ongoing study of a single cohort from infancy onward without any intervention instituted whatsoever by our research team. In the developmental journey through the opening years of their lives, some children became gifted and others emerged as nongifted in middle childhood (age 8 years). Hence, the gifted and nongifted or comparison groups emanated from the same cohort selected at one temporal point and followed across time. This is a unique and important methodological asset in studying the early developmental aspects of children who later perform at the gifted or nongifted level.

2

Description of the Fullerton Longitudinal Study

SUBJECTS

The Fullerton Longitudinal Study (FLS) was launched in the fall of 1979. One hundred thirty 1-year-old children and their families were recruited from birth notifications of hospitals surrounding California State University, Fullerton. All children were born between September and December 1978. The criteria used in the selection process were that infants were free of visual and neurological abnormalities (A. W. Gottfried & Gilman, 1983), and that all infants were full term and of normal birth weight. All families spoke English. At the onset of the study, the sample comprised 52% males and 48% females. With respect to race, 117 were white, 7 Chicano, 1 Asian, 1 East Indian, 1 Hawaiian, 1 Iranian, and 2 interracial. Most (53%) of the children were firstborn; 31% of the children were second born; 16% were third or later born. The families represented a wide range of middle-class socioeconomic status as measured by the Hollingshead Four Factor Index of Social Status (M = 45.6, SD = 11.7), Revised Duncan Socioeconomic Index (M = 46.5, SD = 20.5), and Siegel Prestige Scores (M = 47.9, SD = 14.2). The age of parents averaged approximately 30 years (mothers: M = 28.6, SD = 4.2; fathers: M = 31.5, SD = 5.1). At the onset, all mothers but three (2%) had completed high school; 30% had high school degrees with no further formal education; 38% had some college; 30% had college or higher degrees. All fathers but three (2%) had completed high school; 22% had no education past high school; 30% had some college; 46% had college or higher degrees. Whereas 64% of mothers were unemployed, all of the fathers were employed. All fathers but one were employed full-time, whereas 26 of the 47 (55%) working mothers were employed full-time. At the onset of the study, all biological parents except for nine were married.

Throughout the course of investigation and numerous developmental assessments, subject return rates remained high: 99% (128), 95% (123), 94% (122), 92% (119), 91% (118), 85% (111), 81% (105), 82% (106), and 82% (107) returned at the 1.5-, 2-, 2.5-, 3-, 3.5-, 5-, 6-, 7-, and 8-year assessments, respectively. Analyses comparing the early data of children continuing in the study to those not continuing have yielded no evidence of selective attrition (A. W. Gottfried, Guerin, & Bathurst, 1989; Guerin & A. W. Gottfried, in press-a, in press-b).

A description of the sample characteristics at age 8 years is presented in Table 2.1. At age 8, the sample comprised 107 children; 58% boys and 42% girls; 92% white and 8% other ethnic groups such as Chicano, Asian, East Indian, Hawaiian, and Iranian; and 51% firstborns, 33% second borns, and 16% third or later borns. The families represented a wide range of middle-class socioeconomic status as measured by the Hollingshead Four Factor Index of Socioeconomic Status (SES) (A. W. Gottfried, 1985; Hollingshead, 1975). Other major SES indicators corroborated this appraisal. These included the Revised Duncan Socioeconomic Index (Stevens & Featherman, 1981) and the Siegel Prestige Scores (Hauser & Featherman, 1977). At the 8-year assessment, mothers averaged 36.1 years of age and fathers averaged 38.8 years of age. By the 8-year assessment, all parents, with the exception of three fathers, had graduated from high school with the majority having completed some college. There was a minor increase in parents' educational achievements by the time the children reached age 8 years. For both mothers and fathers, there was a wide range of occupations from semiskilled workers to professionals. Typically, fathers were continuously employed. However, mothers showed a dramatic increase in employment status from 36.2% when the children were age 1 year to 71.9% when the children were age 8 years. At age 8 years, 87% of mothers were married; however, between the ages of 1 and 8 years, 20% of the children had experienced the divorce of their biological parents. The majority of families had two children (58%) and two parents (88%) living in the home, either biological or stepparents, when the children were age 8.

Table 2.1. Demographic Characteristics of FLS Sample at Age 8 Years

Variable	Mean (SD) or frequency[a]
Sex	
Male	62
Female	45
Ethnicity	
White	98
Other	9
Birth order	
Firstborn	55
Second born	35
Third or later born	17
SES	
Hollingshead Four Factor Index of Social Status	49.8 (9.1)
Mothers' education	14.5 (2.0)
Below high school	0
High school-no college	29
Some college	38
College graduate-no postgraduate	24
Postgraduate	16
Fathers' education	
Below high school	3
High school-no college	14
Some college	32
College graduate-no postgraduate	29
Postgraduate	28
Mothers' employment status	
Employed	77
Unemployed	30
Fathers' employment status	
Employed	97
Unemployed	3
Marital status of mother	
Married	93
Living together, unmarried	1
Separated	1
Divorced	12
Number of children in home	
1	14
2	62
3 or more	31
Number of adults in home	
1	10
2	87
3 or more	10

[a]In cases where the number of subjects does not total 107, data were missing.

MEASURES AND PROCEDURES

Table 2.2 displays a summary of the measures used and ages when they were administered. Well-known standardized scales and inventories were used whenever available. In some instances (e.g., home and family assessment), we developed our own instruments in order to capture a more comprehensive picture of the children's environment. Details of the measures employed throughout this developmental study are described in the chapters.

The schedule for the FLS developmental assessments was as follows. Beginning at age 1 year, children were tested in the laboratory every 6 months until they reached 3.5 years of age. Thereafter, children were tested yearly in the laboratory at ages 5, 6, 7, and 8 years. Laboratory visits averaged 1.5 to 2.0 hours in length and consisted of a battery of individually administered tests given to the children. Parents completed surveys and questionnaires during the laboratory visit. All tests were administered to the children in the same sequence to avoid error variance due to potential test order effects. Home visits were conducted when the children were 15 months (1.25 years), 39 months (3.25 years), and 8 years of age. Home assessments lasted a minimum of one hour.

Table 2.2. Summary of Measures Utilized in the Fullerton Longitudinal Study from Ages 1 through 8 Years

Measure	Age(s) administered[a]
Cognitive measures	
• Bayley Scales of Infant Development	1, 1.5, 2
• McCarthy Scales of Children's Abilities	2.5, 3, 3.5
• Kaufman Assessment Battery for Children	5
• Wechsler Intelligence Scale for Children-Revised	6, 7, 8
• Wechsler Adult Intelligence Scale Vocabulary & Block Design subtests	3[b]
• Test of Early Language Development	3.25
• Corman & Escalona Object Permanence Scale	1, 1.5
• Recognition Memory (visual, tactile, and cross-modal)	1, 1.5, 2, 2.5, 3
Developmental inventories and rating scales	
• Parent/Child Rating Scale	1, 1.5, 2, 2.5, 3
• Bayley Behavior Record	1.5, 2, 2.5, 3, 3.5, 5, 6

Table 2.2. (*continued*)

• Minnesota Child Development Inventory	2.5
• Minnesota Preschool Inventory	5
Educational achievement and motivation measures	
• Kaufman Assessment Battery for Children Achievement Scale	5
• Wide Range Achievement Test-Revised	6
• Woodcock-Johnson Psycho-Educational Battery	7, 8
• Educational History Questionnaire	5, 7, 8
• Young Children's Academic Intrinsic Motivation Inventory	7, 8
• Academic Anxiety and Perception of Competence Inventories	7, 8
Temperament inventories	
• Infant Characteristics Questionnaire	1.5
• Toddler Temperament Scale	2
• Colorado Child Temperament Inventory	3.5
• Behavior Style Questionnaire	3, 3.5, 5
• Middle Childhood Temperament Questionnaire	8
Child behavior checklists	
• Eyberg Child Behavior Inventory	3.25
• Preschool Behavior Questionnaire	3.5
• Child Behavior Checklist-parent version	4, 5, 6, 7, 8
• Child Behavior Checklist-teacher version	6, 7, 8
Social functioning inventories	
• Preschool Interpersonal Problem-Solving Scale	3.5
• Vineland Adaptive Behavior Scales	5, 8
Home and family environment inventories	
• Hollingshead Four Factor Index of Social Status	1, 1.5, 2, 2.5, 3, 3.5, 4, 5, 6, 7, 8
• Social History Questionnaire	1, 1.5, 2, 2.5, 3, 3.5, 5, 6, 7, 8
• Home Observation and Measurement of the Environment	1.25, 3.25, 8
• Purdue Home Stimulation Inventory	1.25
• Variety of Experiences Checklist	3, 5
• Home Environment Survey	5, 7, 8
• Child's Requests for Activities	8
• Family Environment Scale	3, 5, 7, 8
• Family Inventory	8

[a]Age reported in years; months converted to decimals.
[b]Administered to mothers at the 3-year assessment.

Information from children's teachers was collected when children were 6, 7, and 8 years of age. Parents gave forms to teachers to complete; teachers returned completed forms directly to the laboratory via mail. An additional assessment was conducted at age 4 years for the Child Behavior Checklist-parent version, because at that age this inventory becomes age appropriate. At this time, the forms were mailed to parents. The Child Behavior Checklist was also administered at each subsequent laboratory assessment.

DESIGNATION OF GIFTEDNESS

The IQ score obtained with the Wechsler Intelligence Scale for Children-Revised (WISC-R) at the 8-year assessment was used to create the gifted and nongifted groups. There were many reasons for our selection of IQ. Giftedness is defined by Gagne (1985) as being above average in ability, with intellectual ability being one of the areas. Historically, IQ has been used as a measure of intellectual ability (Pendarvis et al., 1990). We needed an index that would provide a reliable, valid, and relatively stable measure by which to delineate contrasting groups for research purposes. Although we recognize the emergence of new measures of cognition to assess intelligence, a criticism of the new methods is that they lack the psychometric criteria of reliability and validity (Reschly & Wilson, 1990). It was our view that IQ provided a reliable and valid operational definition of intellectual performance. The availability of a longitudinal history of children's intellectual ability from infancy through childhood using standardized measures provided a unique opportunity to examine the developmental characteristics of IQ in our sample across the years.

Aside from its availability in our research program, IQ continues to be used pervasively in schools as one criterion for the assessment of giftedness (Klausmeier, Mishra, & Maker, 1987; Pendarvis et al., 1990). A score two standard deviations above the mean has been typically used to define giftedness (Pendarvis et al., 1990). In the Wechsler manuals (Wechsler, 1974, 1991), scores of 130 and above are classified as "very superior." IQ has had a history of strong relationships to other criteria, such as achievement, and often serves as an indication of academic ability (Pendarvis et al., 1990). Further, the Gifted and Talented Children's Education Act of 1978 (PL95-561) defines one aspect of giftedness as intellectual ability.

High psychometric scores, typically using a cutoff at two standard deviations above the mean, are used extensively in the research literature to identify intellectually gifted groups. If another form of talent is being studied, the strategy is typically the same, and scores are cut off at approximately two standard deviations above the mean on whatever particular test is used in the research (e.g., Benbow & Arjmand, 1990). Hence, our use of IQ provides a method consistent with other literature on the gifted and allows for further generalizability to a longitudinal study of young children.

We used a Full Scale IQ score of 130 from the WISC-R as the cutoff value for designating a child as gifted. Of the 107 children tested at age 8 years, 20 placed in the gifted range and 87 did not. It was the comparison of these two giftedness status groups that was the focus of this research project. The average IQ for the 20 gifted children was 137.8 ($SD = 5.6$) with scores ranging from 130 to 145. The average IQ score for the 87 nongifted children was 110.9 ($SD = 10.2$) with scores ranging from 84 to 128.

Four children in the nongifted group had IQ scores within one standard error of measurement (3.19 IQ points [Wechsler, 1974]) of the cutoff value of 130, that is, IQs between 127 and 129. In order to evaluate the potential misclassification of these children, we examined their 6- and 7-year WISC-R Full Scale IQ scores. Three of the four did not obtain an IQ in the gifted range at ages 6 and 7 years. One child had a gifted IQ at age 7, but not at age 6. We deemed these four children as intellectually nongifted. In summary, we believe our overall error rate in group assignment was minimal, and we had a high degree of confidence in the integrity of the gifted versus nongifted status group designation.

The WISC-R was chosen to assess IQ in our research project because it is a major intelligence test that has been used extensively in the fields of psychology and education. Moreover, it is widely used in both research and applied settings. This test has well-established psychometric properties such as known probability distributions, reliability, and validity. The age of 8 years was selected as the designation year because of the predictive value of the test scores at that age to the subsequent school years (Brody, 1992; McCall, 1977).

DATA ANALYTIC STRATEGY

The focus of this book is the comparison of gifted and nongifted children from infancy through the early elementary years across a broad array of developmental domains and the home and family environment. Given the enormous body of data resulting from 10 assessment periods on the numerous variables across these areas, it was necessary to develop a strategy to guide the analyses of data and presentation of results. In the following sections, we explain our conceptualization of the data analyses and statistical issues pertinent to these longitudinal data and present our general analytic/tactical strategy. The importance of having a data analytic strategy has been recently discussed by Cronbach (1991).

Data Analysis

The principles guiding our analyses were simplicity, interpretability, and power. We used the most powerful analysis that was appropriate and interpretable for each group comparison. We opted for higher Type II errors (i.e., failing to find statistical differences when the populations do in fact differ) and lower Type I errors (i.e., finding statistical differences when they do not exist in the population). The result of this approach was that if we were to err, it would be on the side of conservativeness. A variety of descriptive and inferential statistics were used. Unless otherwise noted, the level of confidence (alpha) was set at .05 for all analyses. The analyses fell into the five categories described below.

Single Measure, Single Time

In the first category, the most simple case, analyses involved comparing gifted and nongifted groups on a single dependent variable measured at a single point in time. Independent groups t tests, chi-square analyses, and proportions tests were used as appropriate to the scale of measurement. For example, an independent groups t test was used to compare the gifted and nongifted groups on the Test of Early Language Development overall score (an interval scale), which was administered only once at the age of 3.25 years. The assumption of homogeneity of variance was evaluated for each t test with alpha set at .01. In the few cases where this assumption was violated, the more stringent separate variance estimate was utilized and the statistics are reported for the adjusted degrees of freedom. When no violation existed, the pooled variance estimate was used. If the data were extremely skewed causing a serious violation of the assumption of normality, as in the distribution of behavior problems, a nonparametric statistical test (Mann-Whitney U) was substituted for the more common parametric test (t test). For frequency data, chi-square tests were employed. When contingency tables were larger than 2 × 2, we used Pearson's chi-square statistic. For 2 × 2 tables, we used the Yates correction for continuity. Proportions tests involved calculating *z* scores for the difference between proportions and determining the probability of obtaining such a score using normal curve probabilities.

Same Measure Repeated over Time

The second category of analyses involved comparing the two groups on repeated measures of the same variable. For example, intellectual status was measured at each of the 10 assessment periods. To analyze data conforming to this structure, we used repeated-measures ANOVA. In each analysis, we examined the interaction of Giftedness Status × Age. With one exception, as reported in Chapter 3, none of the interactions were significant. Therefore, these nonsignificant interaction results are not reported in the chapters. The only instance when the interaction was significant was in the analysis of Giftedness Status × Age with intelligence as the dependent variable (see Chapter 3). Following the significant interaction, we computed independent groups *t* tests at each point in time, correcting for the familywise error rate of .05 by using Holm's sequential Bonferroni procedure as described by Seaman, Levin, and Serlin (1991) and Seaman (personal communication, July 13, 1992). In this procedure, the pairs of means are ordered hierarchically from the largest to the smallest difference. The alpha level (.05 in all cases) is divided by the number of tests to be conducted. The first test is carried out with the adjusted alpha. The second and subsequent tests are conducted with the number of tests minus 1, 2, and so on until nonsignificance is reached. At that point, no further tests are conducted. For example, if there are 10 comparisons to be made, the first is conducted with alpha equal to .00500, the second with alpha equal to .00556, the third with alpha equal to .00625, and so forth. This procedure provides a compromise between the conservative and liberal approaches to post hoc testing. Finally, because the main effect of age was not inherently of interest, these results are not reported either.

Multiple Measures, Single Time

The third category involved comparing the gifted and nongifted groups on multiple dependent variables that were assessed at only one point in time, such as with the subscales of the Kaufman Assessment Battery for Children. In this test, there are two cognitive indexes: Simultaneous Processing and Sequential Processing. A more powerful test can be conducted by simultaneously comparing the groups across both dependent variables. Data such as these were analyzed using a one-way MANOVA. Following a significant multivariate *F* statistic, univariate *F* tests were examined, correcting for familywise Type I error rate as described above. Multivariate *F* statistics are reported in the text; univariate *F* statistics are reported in tables.

Multiple Measures Repeated over Time

The fourth category involved comparing the two groups on multiple dependent variables that were collected over multiple assessment periods. For example, WISC-R Verbal IQ and Performance IQ were measured at three different ages. Doubly multivariate data, that is, multiple dependent variables measured two or more times, were analyzed with a repeated-measures MANOVA. As in the prior case, a more powerful test of the hypotheses of interest can be achieved when combining dependent variables. If the multivariate *F* was significant, the univariate *F*s for each of the dependent variables were evaluated for significance. The *p* value was adjusted using Holm's sequential Bonferroni procedure described previously. Interactions between giftedness status and age were examined; however, none were significant and, hence, are not reported. As previously noted, the main effect of age was not of interest; therefore, these statistics are not reported either. Again, multivariate *F*s are presented in the text; univariate *F*s are presented in tables.

Planned Comparisons

The final category comprised planned comparisons. In cases where prior research governed the direction of expected differences, one-tailed *t* tests were conducted. For example, specific scales of the Home Observation and Measurement of the Environment inventory have been shown to positively correlate with cognitive ability; hence, gifted children were predicted to have higher scores than nongifted children on certain scales. The benefit of conducting planned comparisons is the increase in power while holding familywise Type I error rates at acceptable levels. For a complete discussion, see Maxwell and Delaney (1990) and Toothaker (1991).

Statistical Issues

Size of Sample

The size of the FLS sample comprising the gifted and nongifted groups was 107. Thus, the sample size was large enough to support the use of multivariate statistics when appropriate. We were confident that the sample size was sufficient to reject a false null hypothesis, thereby providing adequate power to statistically detect reliable differences between the groups.

Relative and Absolute Group Size

Gifted IQ (i.e., IQ ≥ 130) is found in the top 2.28% of a theoretically normal random distribution. Therefore, we expected the sizes of the gifted and nongifted groups to differ considerably. Moreover, because giftedness is found in higher proportions in the middle- and upper-middle-class segments of the population, we anticipated that a greater number of children in our sample would be identified as gifted than found in the population at large. As indicated above, the sample at 8 years comprised 20 gifted and 87 nongifted children. Because of the inequality in group sizes, we evaluated the effect that unequal group sizes would have on inferential statistics. Several analyses were conducted in BMDP 2V (Dixon, 1992), which has the capability to adjust the analyses for group size. In no case were the results of the unadjusted analyses different from the results of the adjusted analyses. Therefore, we concluded this was a minor concern with respect to planned comparisons and repeated-measures ANOVA (Tabachnick & Fidell, 1989). In some cases, however, a number of our analyses required MANOVAs, and the small *n* in the gifted group was an issue because it is necessary to have more cases than dependent variables in every cell (Tabachnick & Fidell, 1989) or risk low power and untestable hypotheses. This small *n* impacted analyses involving a large number of subscales. For example, there are 10 WISC-R subscales that were measured at three points in time. This resulted in 30 dependent variables in the MANOVA, but only 20 subjects in gifted-group cells. Our solution was to run subsets of the WISC-R subscales separately; that is, we analyzed the five verbal and five performance subscales separately at each age. This resulted in five dependent variables for each analysis, which was an acceptable number. This analytic strategy was used whenever necessary due to group size restrictions.

The absolute size of the gifted group (n = 20) precluded any meaningful test of hypotheses regarding sex differences. There was not a sufficient number of subjects to further divide the group by sex and still adhere to the analytic strategy developed for this book. Furthermore, we would have been concerned about the reliability of the findings with such small cell sizes. Therefore, sex differences were not examined.

Missing Data and Missing Subjects

Occasionally, a child was unable to complete an assessment (Bathurst & A. W. Gottfried, 1987a) or missed an assessment. Consequently, there are varying *N*s across measures. This is not uncommon in longitudinal research. Our strategy for dealing with missing data was to utilize the listwise option on all statistical analyses. Missing data were not estimated or replaced. The n is shown on each table or reported in the text for each analysis.

Outliers

Extreme values can be a serious problem in hypothesis testing whether using univariate or multivariate tests (Tabachnick & Fidell, 1989). Our data were thoroughly screened and examined for both univariate and multivariate outliers. We found few. Because of the rarity of outliers, we concluded that they did not impact our analyses, and hence, no adjustments were made to the data.

Number of Measures and Type I Error Rates

Given the comprehensiveness of each assessment and the number of times the children were evaluated, the number of variables to be analyzed was very large. We realized the risk of Type I error (i.e., erroneously detecting differences in the sample that are not reflected in the population) would be elevated if not controlled. To reduce this risk, we carefully considered each research question and evaluated the most appropriate method by which to analyze the data. Our primary guide was provided by Hertzog and Rovine (1985) and the decision tree they presented for repeated-measures designs. For example, when we had *a priori* hypotheses, we conducted planned comparisons. When we had multiple dependent variables, we conducted multivariate tests, followed by post hoc procedures that would maintain an acceptable familywise error rate, that is, Holm's sequential Bonferroni procedure (Games, 1990; Seaman et al., 1991; Toothaker, 1991).

Repeated Measures

Given the longitudinal nature and goals of this unique study, we had several measures that were repeatedly administered over time. For example, intelligence and demographic data were collected at each assessment. The cross-time data were therefore not necessarily independent, but were likely to be correlated instead. This condition results in a mixed model with one between factor (Giftedness Status) and one within factor (Age). Sphericity (or circularity) is assumed among the repeated measures. It is highly likely, however, that the correlations between ages close in time are greater than those more distant. (For example, IQ at 8 years of age is more highly correlated with IQ at 7 years of age than with IQ at 6 years of age.) Because violations of homogeneity of covariance such as that described inflate the Type I error rate, a viable alternative is to adjust the degrees of freedom for the hypotheses tests by employing Huynh-Feldt or Greenhouse-Geisser estimating procedures (Games, 1990; Hertzog & Rovine, 1985; O'Brien & Kaiser, 1985). An index of sphericity—epsilon—is computed and the degrees of freedom of the mean square ratios are adjusted accordingly. We tested for violations of the symmetry assumption and adopted the following guidelines for values of epsilon (Hertzog & Rovine, 1985): (1) epsilon $\geq$ .90: trivial or no violation; mixed-model F test was used (Hotelling's T^2); (2) epsilon > .50 < .90: violations exist; adjusted degrees of freedom test was used (Huynh-Feldt or Greenhouse-Geisser). There were no cases where epsilon was less than .50.

A related concern with the use of repeated measures is the time interval between assessments (Hertzog & Rovine, 1985). In our longitudinal design, the amount of time between consecutive measurements of a given construct varied. For example, intelligence was assessed at half-year intervals from 1 through 3.5 years and at 1-year intervals beginning at 5 years of age. To address the issue of unequal assessment intervals, we conducted several analyses using BMDP 2V (Dixon, 1992), which allows specification of unequal spacing. We compared the results adjusting for unequal intervals with those not adjusted. In all cases, differences were negligible, and in no case were conclusions altered.

Conceptually Similar Measures

The question of how to treat conceptually similar measures (e.g., intelligence) that were assessed across the 7-year span using different instruments due to developmental appropriateness presented a challenging dilemma that has been heretofore unaddressed in the literature. The construct of intelligence provides an excellent example of this issue. Specifically, should we treat the Mental Development Index of the Bayley, the General Cognitive Index of the McCarthy, the Mental Processing Composite of the KABC, and the Full Scale IQ of the WISC-R as the same construct and therefore analyze them as repeated measures? Alternatively, should each scale be treated as a conceptually different construct and therefore analyzed separately? Similar concerns were raised for other variables such as achievement, temperament, and home environment measures. We adopted the following strategy. In cases where there was a standardized scale available with a known population variance and a common metric, we opted for treating the measures as repeated (e.g., intelligence). If we were operating without a known population variance (e.g., home environment measures), each scale was analyzed separately or converted to a common metric (i.e., *z* scores).

Statistical Controlling of Variables

We pondered the issue of whether to control for certain variables. For example, socioeconomic status (SES) is a common measure that is expected to covary with other variables such as intelligence and home environment. Often, researchers choose to control for SES when groups are compared by partialling out variance accounted for by this variable. However, covariate analyses are inappropriate when groups are not randomly assigned (Overall & Woodward, 1977), as is the case in the present research. Moreover, we are working with naturally occurring covariances. That is, giftedness occurs more frequently in higher-SES groups. We would be disrupting what occurs naturally if we used statistical controls that, in turn, may spuriously alter our findings and affect generalizability of our conclusions. Our approach was to allow the variables to naturally covary and not to institute statistical controls.

3

Intellectual and Cognitive Functioning

ISSUES

In this chapter, we address the intellectual and cognitive differences that emerge in the course of early development of children who become intellectually gifted or nongifted. Several central issues and questions were examined:

1. If differences exist during infancy or the preschool periods between the designated groups, when do these differences emerge, and do the differences maintain continuity thereafter? If differences are present during infancy, are they found on psychometric and/or Piagetian-type sensorimotor scales, on measures of recognition memory (i.e., visual, tactual, and cross-modal), or in language development (receptive and expressive skills)?
2. Is there a characteristic developmental pattern for children who become gifted; that is, do the children who become gifted have common ontogenetic age changes in intellectual performance, or are the cross-time or age-related changes individual?
3. During infancy and the preschool period, are there signs or indicators of potential intellectual giftedness that may serve to identify those children who later exhibit gifted IQs during the early school years?
4. Do differences in the summary IQ scores reflect differences across the various specific cognitive domains as well? In other words, the issue of globality versus specificity of intellectual giftedness in the course of development is addressed.

5. Despite relative differences in the level of intellectual performance between gifted and nongifted children, are there differential patterns or profiles of cognitive abilities between the groups during the preschool and school entry years? Is there a pattern of cognitive abilities characteristic of intellectually gifted children? This pertains to a pattern not across the ages but at a given age or period.

6. The final issue addresses how cognizant parents are of differences in the development of children who become gifted or nongifted. Additionally, if differences are recognized by parents, how early are these differences recognized and in what specific developmental domains? As noted in Chapter 1, the literature comprising retrospective anecdotal reports of parents of gifted children suggests that such children are advanced, particularly in language skills, during the early years. In the course of investigation, we gathered ongoing contemporaneous information, not retrospective reports, from each parent on how they perceived their child's development compared to others of the same age across various skills.

DESCRIPTION OF MEASURES

During infancy, preschool, and the early elementary school years, intelligence tests were administered. A variety of assessments appraising cognitive functioning in infants were employed. Two types of intellectual measures were administered during infancy: psychometric and Piagetian-type scales. Infants were tested on the Mental scale of the Bayley Scales of Infant Development (Bayley, 1969) at 1, 1.5, and 2 years. The Bayley was selected primarily because it is the most extensively standardized and researched psychometric assessment of sensorimotor intelligence. The Mental Development Index (MDI) was used in all analyses. At 1 and 1.5 years, object permanence was assessed using the Corman and Escalona (1969) Piagetian scale. Object permanence was assessed because, according to Piaget (1954), it represents the basis of epistemological construction and the most important accomplishment during the sensorimotor period. The scale yields a single score indicating the highest level passed in the object permanence ordinal progression.

In addition to the Bayley and object permanence, more contemporaneous assessments deriving from the experimental literature were incorporated into the cognitive test battery. Measures of recognition memory of objects' shapes, both within and across the visual and somesthetic (i.e., tactual) sensory modalities, were based on the paired-comparison technique. The recognition memory tasks included tactual-visual cross-modal, visual intramodal, and tactual intramodal procedures, which were administered at 1, 1.5, 2, 2.5, and 3 years. The assessment relies on infants' differential responsiveness to novel and familiar stimuli. Evidence of memory is indexed by a differential preference that significantly departs from chance expectation (i.e., 50%). Beyond 2.5–3 months of age, infants reveal a proclivity to respond to novel over familiar stimuli (Rose, A. W. Gottfried, Melloy-Carminar, & Bridger, 1982). The actual procedure involves two stages: a familiarization period and a subsequent recognition test phase. In the former, the infant is familiarized (either visually or tactually) for an accumulated temporal period of designated length. Various time intervals were employed. However, the familiarizations were reduced with age because of the rapidity of information processing as infants and young children advance in chronological age. During the test phase, both the novel and familiar stimuli are presented simultaneously and the infants' visual or tactual responses are recorded. The researcher recording the behavior during the test phase has no knowledge of which object is familiar or novel so as to prevent any biasing. The stimuli used were designed by A. W. Gottfried and employed in several published studies by A. W. Gottfried and Rose. They are typically based on the dimensionality of open–closed and/or linear–curvilinear types. In the present investigation, a composite score based on the novelty percentages for each task was derived and used in the analyses (results remain invariant whether arcsine transformations on the novelty percentages are employed or not). The paradigm used to assess these recognition memory skills has been well documented in the developmental literature. (For further discussion of the cross-modal and intramodal recognition memory technology and the developmental issues upon which it is based, as well as photographs of stimuli used in experiments, see Brown & A. W. Gottfried, 1986; A. W. Gottfried et al., 1989; A. W. Gottfried & Rose, 1980; A. W. Gottfried, Rose, & Bridger, 1977; Rose, Gottfried, & Bridger, 1983; Rose et al., 1982; Rose & Ruff, 1987.)

A direct appraisal of language skills was conducted during the infancy period. A separate scale or measure was not employed. The assessment of receptive and expressive language development was achieved by analyzing the language items on the Bayley at ages 1, 1.5, and 2 years. Language items administered at each assessment were extracted and categorized into the receptive or expressive domains. This was a conceptual and not an empirical analysis (e.g., factor analysis). These two domains were selected because they (1) have long been considered to represent theoretically important and distinct language abilities (Huttenlocher, 1974; Nelson, 1973); (2) are easy to assess, identify, and distinguish; and (3) are also included in the Test of Early Language Development and the Minnesota Child Development Inventory, both of which were used in this longitudinal investigation during the preschool years (see below), thereby permitting us to explore whether differences were present during the early years between those children who became gifted or nongifted. Lastly, it is obvious and well established that receptive abilities emerge before expressive or production skills (Bates, O'Connell, & Shore, 1987). However, because evidence shows that word comprehension begins around 9 or 10 months with considerable variability thereafter in the rate at which receptive vocabularies expand (Bates et al., 1987), and because a major transition in infants' language comprehension skills occurs between 9 and 17 months of age (Oviatt, 1980), we were able to determine whether the gifted group was advanced compared to the nongifted group in this specific cognitive ability during this early period of language development. As noted, the initial assessment was at 1 year of age. For purpose of presentation, the exact items and their placement within the particular language category will be displayed in the results section.

During the preschool period, children were administered the McCarthy Scales of Children's Abilities (McCarthy, 1972). This test was selected because it is a well-known assessment of cognitive or intellectual functioning during the preschool years that provides information on separate abilities relevant to success at school entry (A. S. Kaufman & N. L. Kaufman, 1977; Massoth, 1985; Massoth & Levenson, 1982). Additionally, the separate abilities allowed us to determine the level of achievement within each area as well as examine differential patterns across abilities between the gifted and nongifted groups. The McCarthy was administered at 2.5, 3, and 3.5 years and comprises six indexes: Verbal, Quantitative, Perceptual-Performance, Memory, Motor, and a General Cognitive Index (GCI) based on a summation of the first three indexes. The Test of Early Language Development (TELD) (Hresko, Reid, & Hammill, 1981) was given to the children at the 3.25-year home assessment. The TELD assesses various aspects of language development relating to expressive and receptive form and content. The total number of items passed on the scale sequence was employed for analyses as well as performance in the overall receptive and expressive language domains.

At age 5 years, children were tested on the Kaufman Assessment Battery for Children (KABC) (A. S. Kaufman & N. L. Kaufman, 1983). The test yields several indexes: Simultaneous Processing, Sequential Processing, and a Mental Processing Composite Score (MPS) based on these two indexes. Additionally, there are nonverbal and achievement indexes; results involving the latter will be addressed in the chapter on school functioning. At ages 6, 7, and 8 years, children were administered the Wechsler Intelligence Scale for Children-Revised (WISC-R) (Wechsler, 1974). This well-known test of intellectual performance comprises 10 subtests resulting in Verbal and Performance IQs, and a Full Scale IQ score.

Concurrent with direct psychological assessments, parents completed rating scales and inventories from infancy through school entry. At ages 1, 1.5, 2, 2.5, 3, and 3.5 years, mothers rated their children in the areas of intellectual, verbal, social, and motor development. Each mother rated her child's development compared to other children of the same age on a Likert scale ranging from 1 ("below average") to 5 ("above average") in each of the developmental domains. Mothers filled out the Minnesota Child Development Inventory (MCDI) (Ireton & Thwing, 1972–1974) at age 2.5 years and the Minnesota Preschool Inventory (MPI) (Ireton & Thwing, 1979) at age 5 years. These scales have proven to be valid measures of children's current and predictive developmental status in this longitudinal study (A. W. Gottfried, Guerin, Spencer, & Meyer, 1983, 1984; Guerin & A. W. Gottfried, 1987). A number of studies have provided data supporting the screening efficiency of the Minnesota inventories in both nonclinical and clinical or at-risk populations (e.g., Bryne, Backman, & Smith, 1986; Colligan, 1976, 1977; Dean & Steffen, 1984; Eisert, Spector, Shankaran, Faigenbaum, & Szego, 1980; Garrity & Servos, 1978; Ireton & Thwing, 1979; Ireton, Thwing, & Currier, 1977; Saylor & Brandt, 1986; Shoemaker, Saylor, & Erickson, 1993; Sturner, Funk, Thomas, & Green, 1982; Ullman & Kausch, 1979). Hence, there is considerable evidence that the MCDI and MPI are sensitive standardized parent report measures of variation in children's development. However, their effectiveness in discerning children who are developmentally advanced or gifted from those who are not has never been empirically tested. The MCDI comprises 320 empirically derived age-related items describing children's development. The items are grouped to form eight developmental scales: Gross Motor, Fine Motor, Expressive Language, Comprehension-Conceptual (receptive language skills), Situation Comprehension, Self Help, Personal Social, and a General Development scale that is composed of the most discriminating items from the seven other scales. The MPI consists of 150 items assessing seven developmental areas: Self Help, Fine Motor, Expressive Language, Comprehension, Memory, Letter Recognition, and Number Comprehension. The mother's task for both the MCDI and MPI is to respond "yes" or "no" to each of the statements pertaining to whether her child attained a particular developmental skill. The scale score was the number of skills accomplished (as indexed by number of yes responses in each developmental area).

RESULTS

Patterns of Group Differences

To determine if and when differences emerge in the children's intellectual performance, a 2 × 10 (Giftedness Status × Age: 1 through 8 years) repeated-measures ANOVA was conducted on the intelligence index scores (i.e., Bayley MDI, McCarthy GCI, KABC MPS, WISC-R Full Scale IQ). We realized that a significant difference would exist at age 8 because of our designation of the groups. However, the omnibus test was the preferred choice because of its power and ability to detect interactions. This analysis was based only on children completing all 10 testings. A main effect of Giftedness Status was found ($F(1, 76) = 50.77$, $p < .001$). The gifted children scored significantly higher than nongifted children across the entire time frame. The Giftedness Status × Age interaction was also significant ($F(9, 684) = 6.78$, $p < .001$). As revealed by post hoc tests, the differences between gifted and nongifted children were significant at 1.5 years and every age thereafter. These results are presented in Table 3.1.

We also analyzed the intellectual indexes separately by developmental period (infancy: ages 1, 1.5, 2 years; preschool: ages 2.5, 3, 3.5 years; early school years: ages 6, 7, 8 years). The KABC was not included because it was used at only one age. These additional analyses were conducted because the omnibus analysis included the 8-year data, the year at which the children were assigned to the designated status groups. It is possible that the nonoverlapping distribution of IQ for the groups at 8 years may be sufficiency powerful to carry the omnibus test, causing the group main effect. By conducting the analyses within the developmental period, we were able to exclude the effect of the 8-year data. Additionally, these latter analyses allowed us to examine the group by age interaction within each developmental period. The results within

Table 3.1. Comparisons of Means between Gifted and Nongifted Children: Developmental and Intelligence Quotients

	Giftedness status		
Age in years	Gifted	Nongifted	*t* test
Bayley Scales of Infant Development			
1.0	116.4 (12.2)	113.1 (9.8)	1.16
1.5	126.2 (15.7)	114.1 (1.7)	3.23*
2.0	135.4 (11.6)	113.4 (18.3)	4.67*
McCarthy Scales of Children's Abilities			
2.5	125.3 (11.4)	109.2 (12.5)	4.76*
3.0	118.2 (10.2)	107.5 (11.7)	3.43*
3.5	122.7 (5.2)	112.5 (9.9)	4.07*
Kaufman Assessment Battery for Children			
5.0	127.0 (9.2)	111.2 (11.0)	5.43*
Wechsler Intelligence Test for Children-Revised			
6.0	130.6 (7.0)	113.1 (9.6)	7.03*
7.0	133.4 (9.1)	114.0 (10.2)	7.12*
8.0	137.7 (6.0)	112.4 (9.9)	9.96*

Note. Standard deviations in parentheses. $n = 17$ for gifted; $n = 61$ for nongifted.
*$p < .05$ with Bonferroni correction.

each developmental period corroborate the overall findings presented here (see also 2 × 3 analyses of raw scores below).

Figure 3.1 displays the pattern of intellectual performance of the gifted and nongifted children from age 1 through 8 years. As can be seen in this graph, the nongifted group reveals a relatively flat profile across the age span studied. There is relatively little cross-time variability, with vacillations in mean performance confined to the upper average IQ range. In contrast, the means of the gifted group are always above those of the nongifted group (statistically different at 1.5 years and thereafter) with mean performance levels generally in the superior range. Furthermore, the gifted group exhibits marked variability. This was particularly evident during the infancy and elementary years, when the developmental trajectories of the gifted group revealed increasing divergence compared to their nongifted cohort.

Although both groups showed a downward shift during the preschool period, this by no means signifies an attenuation of intellect. The reasons underlying this downward shift are unknown; however, we surmise that numerous factors may be operating. Contributing factors,

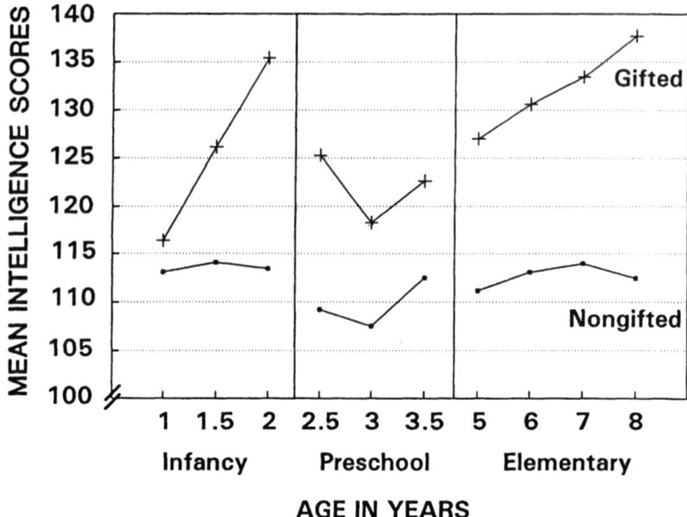

Figure 3.1. Mean intelligence scores for gifted and nongifted children from age 1 through 8 years of age.

for example, could be developmental changes in temperament characteristics (Guerin & A. W. Gottfried, in press-a), untestability during the preschool years (Bathurst & A. W. Gottfried, 1987a), preschool entry and associated separation issues, toilet training, or the behavioral constellation of the "terrible twos." Psychometric factors may also be responsible for the observed decline during the preschool period. Specifically, the McCarthy has been found to underestimate overall intellectual performance during the preschool years (Gregory, 1992; Roedell et al., 1980). This underestimate may be particularly true for highly intelligent children. A rationale behind this is that for a child to obtain an exceptional score on the GCI, he or she must achieve relatively high scores across the Verbal, Quantitative, and Perceptual-Performance indexes. Low performance on just one index could preclude the child from obtaining a score at the superior level. At the time we were selecting our psychometric intelligence measure during the preschool period, there were limitations in availability of tests. The Stanford-Binet was being revised, with the Stanford-Binet: Fourth Edition not available until 1986. The norms of the Wechsler Preschool and Primary Scale of Intelligence were outdated, with the revision not published until 1989. We opted at the time

(1981–1982) for an established scale with relatively contemporary norms that would also furnish information on various major cognitive skills. Hence, we selected the McCarthy Scales of Children's Abilities, which proved to be informative in addressing the developmental issues investigated.

With respect to the shifts in intellectual scores for both groups (as noted when moving across panels in Figure 3.1), it is noteworthy that we are plotting longitudinal data from a single cohort on cross-sectional norms across various intelligence tests. The shifts from one panel to another could be a function of differential normative characteristics across the population of the tests employed. By the same token, shifts within the same panel could be due as well to nuances in the cross sections making up the standardization population of the given test. Lastly, because statistical regression can be bidirectional, that is, going back in time as well as forward (Humphreys, 1985), it is possible that the divergent patterns of the intellectual indexes for the gifted and nongifted groups across time could to some extent be a function of statistical retrogression (i.e., finding regression toward the mean when examining the data in reversed age order).

Because IQ is not a developmental concept, but rather a statistical abstraction (i.e., a quantity or score relative to others of the same chronological age), a more precise picture of each group's actual intellectual development (i.e., absolute quantity) can be obtained by examining the raw scores separately for each test. Raw scores provide a way to examine children's actual intellectual development or progress without normative transformations. The raw scores are displayed in Figure 3.2. (The KABC could not be used in this analysis because it was administered only at age 5 years.) Examination of the data clearly reveals that both groups show increases in their mental growth as would be expected in the course of normal development. Furthermore, this is how mental age scales are designed. However, beginning at age 1.5 years, the children who became gifted passed a greater number of items (or obtained higher raw scores). These differences were statistically confirmed by three separate ANOVAs, one for each test used repeatedly: Bayley at 1, 1.5, and 2 years; McCarthy at 2.5, 3, and 3.5 years; WISC-R at ages 6, 7, and 8 years. Each analysis was a 2 × 3 (Giftedness Status × Age) repeated-measures ANOVA on the raw scores. A main effect of Group was found for the Bayley ($F(1, 103) = 23.95, p < .001$), the McCarthy ($F(1, 85) = 29.39, p < .001$), and the WISC-R ($F(1, 99) = 113.97, p < .001$). An interpretation of these data is that children who become gifted exhibit a more rapid

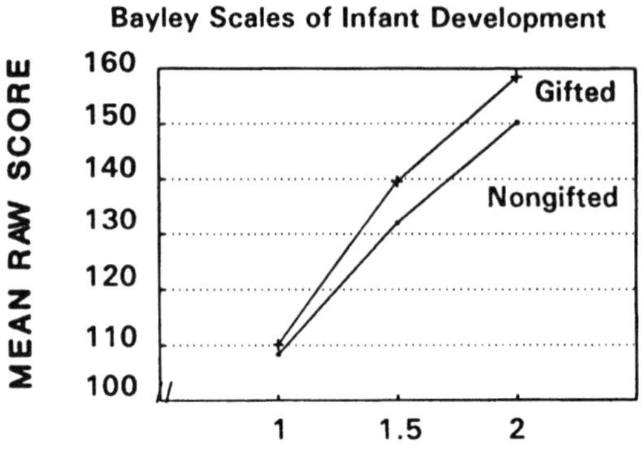

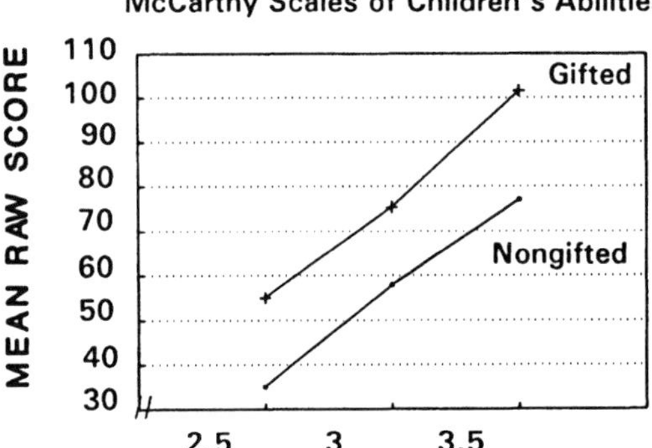

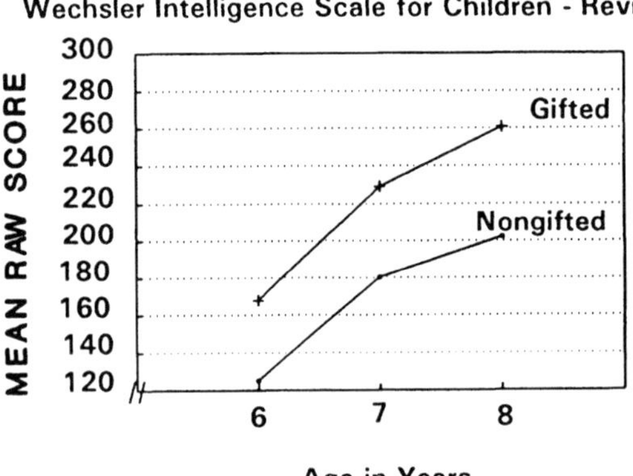

Figure 3.2. Comparison of mean raw scores of gifted and nongifted children for each of the intelligence measures at each developmental period (infancy: Bayley; preschool: McCarthy; school entry: WISC-R).

pace of early mental development (i.e., on the Bayley), and their superiority compared to nongifted children emerges as early as infancy. Hence, continuity of superior performance characterizes the intellectual development of gifted children as a group during the early years. It is interesting to note that our longitudinal findings during the early years dovetail with those of Baldwin and Stecher (1923) of the historic University of Iowa Studies in Child Welfare. These researchers conducted consecutive testings of intellectually superior and average boys and girls from ages 5 through 16 years, as shown in Figure 3.3. As can be readily seen, the gifted children as a group maintained their intellectual advantage compared to the average children across this considerable age span, indicating developmental stability of group differences. However, cross-time stability of individual differences is another issue (see below). Taken together, these two longitudinal studies demonstrate that gifted and nongifted children develop at different levels from infancy through adolescence.

The finding that gifted and nongifted children develop at different levels should not be interpreted to mean that there are quantitative differences between these groups simply because the basis of distinction rests on a psychometric appraisal. Data show that variation in psychometrically measured intelligence implies differences in cognitive development and functioning (Carter & Ormrod, 1982; Keating, 1975, 1976). Researchers had school-age children tested on psychometric instruments, which provided the classification of gifted/bright or average, and also gave them Piagetian tasks to assess concrete and formal operations. Results showed that the gifted/bright children, compared to the average children, were more advanced in their cognitive reasoning as indexed by a further progression within stages and more rapid transition from concrete to formal operations. Hence, gifted/bright children in contrast to average children (with age correction) are more advanced in their reasoning within the Piagetian theoretical framework. However, the implications of the findings go beyond this as indicated by Keating (1976):

> Since, according to Piaget, cognitive development proceeds as an interaction of the organism and the environment, the brighter individual would be at an advantage in moving through the successive stages more quickly. This would be so because the bright child would be involved in more varied and interesting interactions with the environment, generating a greater quantity of useful information, and would also be able to make effective use of the information generated. That is, the "self" enriches the cognitively relevant environment. (p. 98)

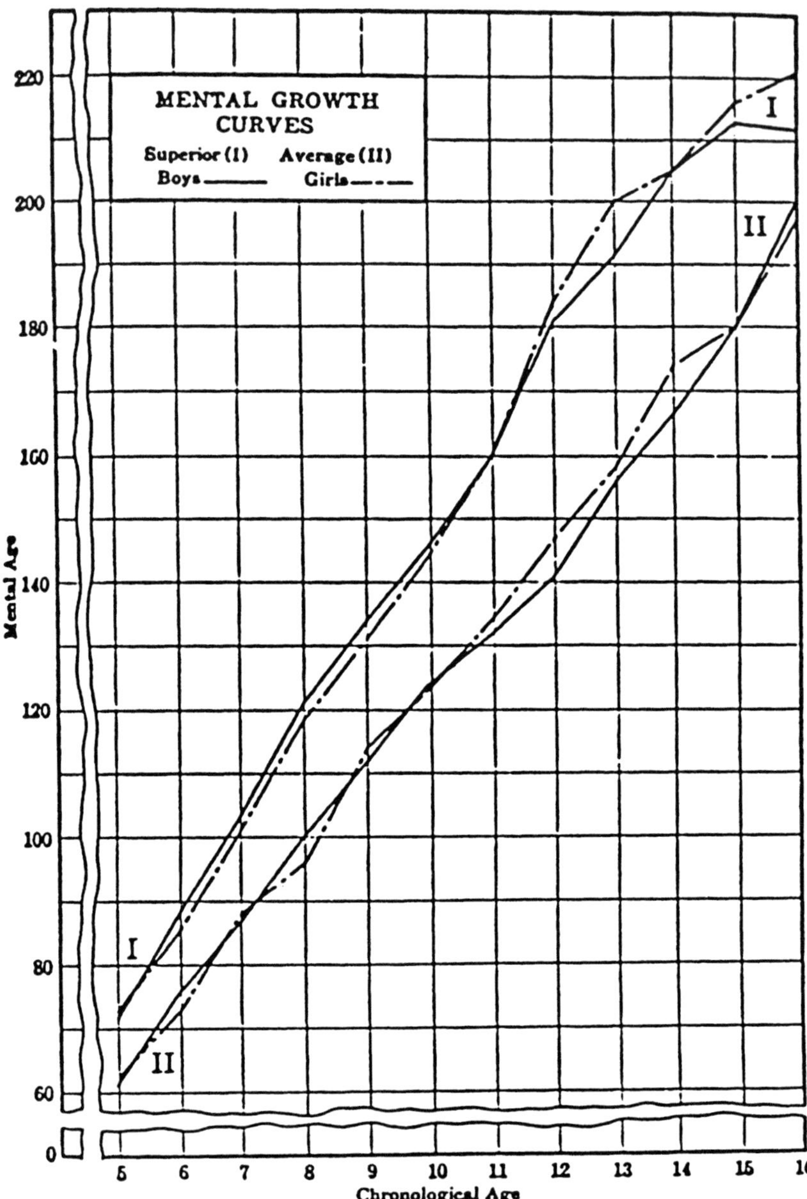

Figure 3.3. Mental age curves based on consecutive testings of superior and average boys and girls from age 5 years through age 16 years (Baldwin & Stecher, 1923; reprinted with permission from University of Iowa).

Individual Case Profiles

The pattern for gifted children as a group may not be representative of cross-time individual patterns. To determine whether there is a unique or characteristic pattern for children who become gifted, we examined individual case profiles. The intellectual indexes for each of the 20 gifted children from ages 1 through 8 years are presented in Figure 3.4. Examination of these graphs shows considerable variability in performance across time between children as well as within each child's developmental profile. There is no ontogenetic age pattern characterizing the intellectual performance of gifted individuals; that is, each child displays a unique course of intellectual performance as he or she progresses toward giftedness at age 8. As can be seen, there are as many individual patterns as there are children. Development toward gifted intellectual performance appears to be highly individualistic. The implication of these data is that while one may develop a psychological theory or conceptualization of how children become gifted, it may not be possible to formulate a theory as to how an individual child becomes gifted; the intellectual development of gifted children as a group does not represent how an individual child becomes gifted. The observed intraindividual variability patterns across time raise the issue of stability of gifted IQ from middle childhood through adolescence. Will these children at age 8 years maintain their gifted IQ status through the remaining childhood years? We intend to address this issue as we continue to follow these children through adolescence.

In scrutinizing these data of individual children, however, we observed an interesting phenomenon: a high number of infants scored exceptionally high (≥ 130) on the Bayley between 1 and 2 years of age. During infancy, 90% (18/20) of the gifted children displayed a Bayley MDI of 130 or greater on at least one of the three assessments (1, 1.5, 2 years). In contrast, only 20.7% (18/87) of the nongifted group achieved a score of this magnitude during infancy. This was statistically significant (χ^2 (1, N = 107) = 31.96, p < .001). Thus, children who became gifted during childhood were more likely to achieve an exceptionally high level of sensorimotor intellectual performance at one point or another during infancy, thereby providing an early indication or cue of potential for superior intellectual performance. This finding is intriguing in view of the fact that infant measures of sensorimotor intelligence have been known to lack long-term predictive validity. However, previous conclusions have been based upon static time analysis (or scores aggregated across time), that is, correlations with one point in time with some later

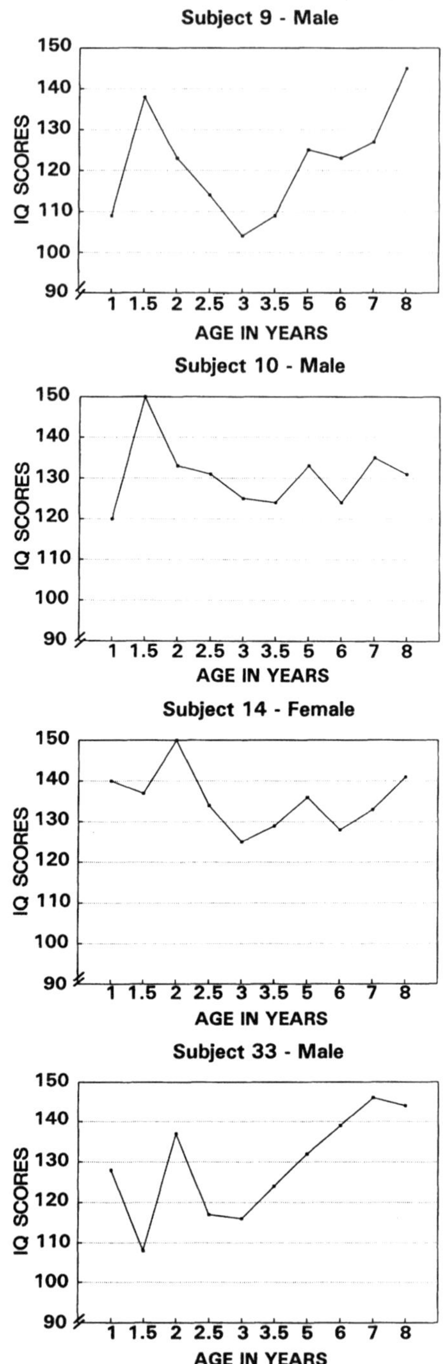

Figure 3.4. Individual case profiles of the gifted children's intelligence scores from 1 year through 8 years of age.

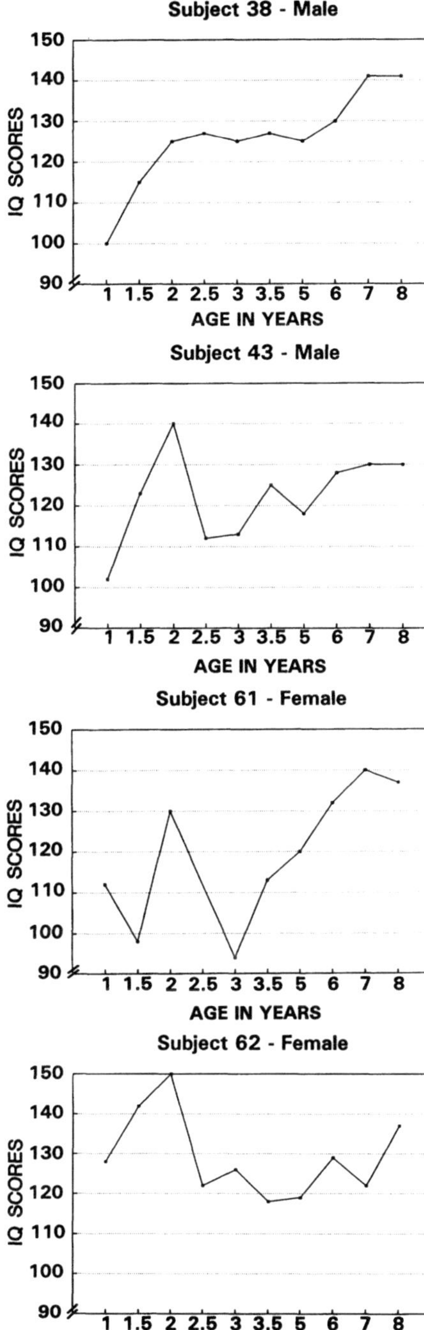
Subject 38 - Male
150
140
130
120
110
100
90
IQ SCORES
1 1.5 2 2.5 3 3.5 5 6 7 8
AGE IN YEARS
Subject 43 - Male
150
140
130
120
110
100
90
IQ SCORES
1 1.5 2 2.5 3 3.5 5 6 7 8
AGE IN YEARS
Subject 61 - Female
150
140
130
120
110
100
90
IQ SCORES
1 1.5 2 2.5 3 3.5 5 6 7 8
AGE IN YEARS
Subject 62 - Female
150
140
130
120
110
100
90
IQ SCORES
1 1.5 2 2.5 3 3.5 5 6 7 8
AGE IN YEARS

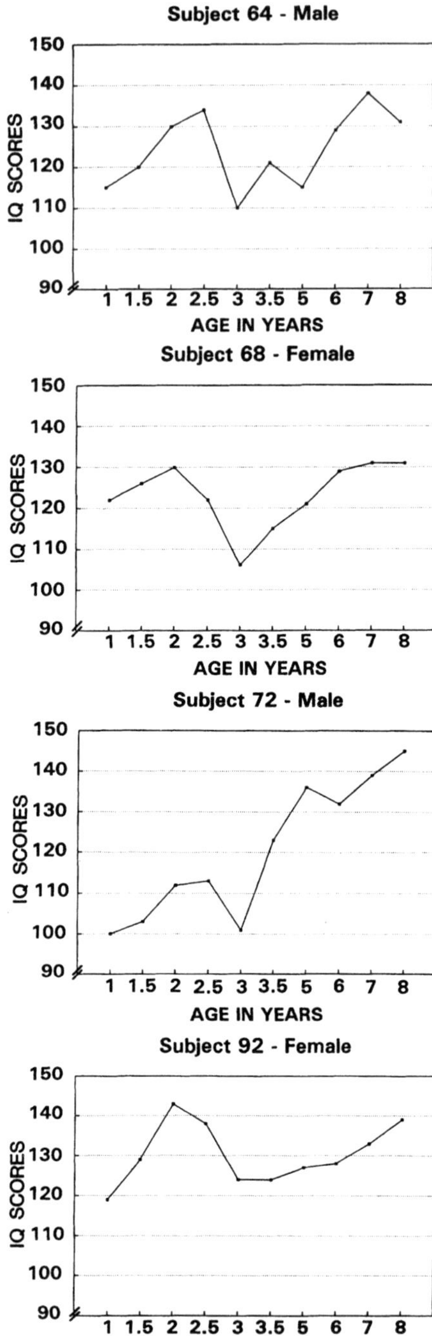

Figure 3.4. *(Continued)*

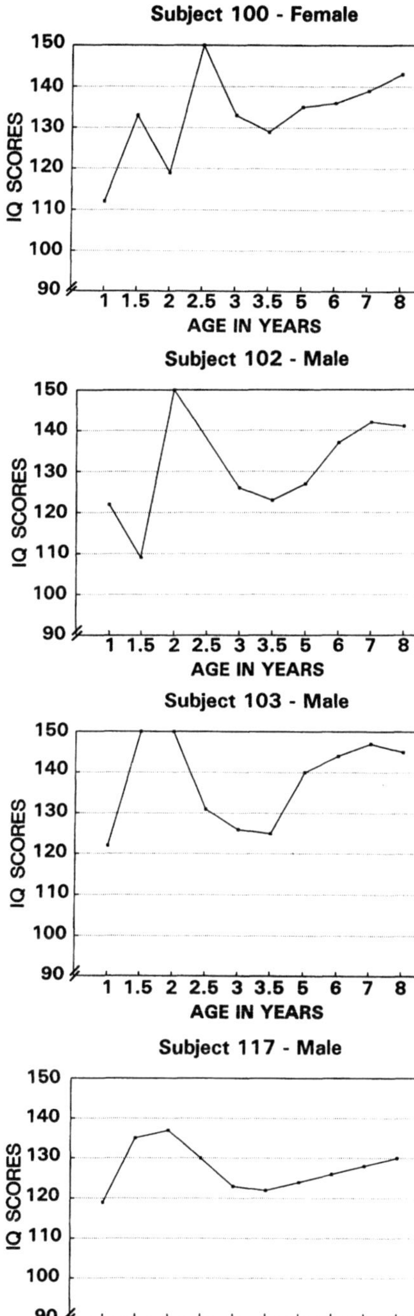
Subject 100 - Female
Subject 102 - Male
Subject 103 - Male
Subject 117 - Male
IQ SCORES
150
140
130
120
110
100
90
1 1.5 2 2.5 3 3.5 5 6 7 8
AGE IN YEARS

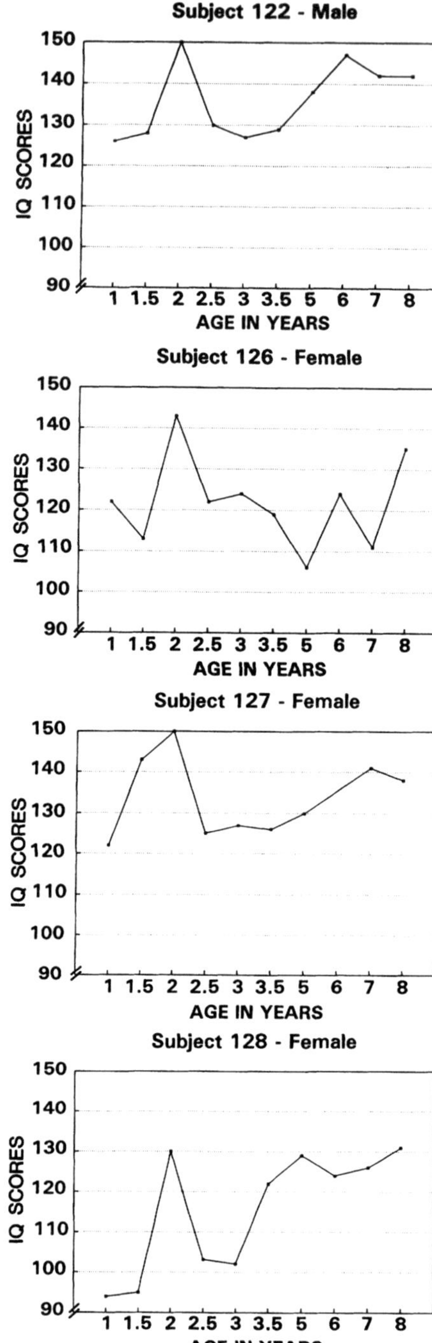

Figure 3.4. *(Continued)*

criterion age. Thus, cues lurking in the course of development toward giftedness may be found not at one fixed period (i.e., age), but, rather, within a time-frame analysis.

A comparable analysis was conducted on the McCarthy GCI data during the preschool period (2.5, 3, and 3.5 years). It is important to keep in mind that the McCarthy may not be a very sensitive instrument for detecting giftedness because, as noted above, it underestimates overall intellectual or cognitive status. In fact, as shown in the middle panel of Figure 3.1, scores were lower relative to the adjacent periods. The percentage of gifted children who received a GCI of 130 or greater at any of the three McCarthy assessments was 40.0% (8/20); the comparable value for the nongifted was only 3.4% (3/87). This resulted in a significant chi-square value (χ^2 (1, N = 107) = 19.76, $p < .001$). Similar to the aforementioned findings on the Bayley, children who become gifted compared to nongifted are significantly more likely to also reveal exceptionally high performance on the GCI of the McCarthy, even though it tends to underestimate overall intellectual functioning.

Further analyses were conducted by examining the number of children in each group who achieved one or more scores at or above two standard deviations above the mean (this represents the top 2.28% of a normal distribution of scores on each of the four cognitive scales of the McCarthy: Verbal, Quantitative, Perceptual, Memory). The percentage of gifted and nongifted children scoring within this upper percentile range on these four subscales at 2.5, 3, and 3.5 years was 50.0% (9/18) versus 15.3% (11/72), 30.0% (6/20) versus 6.2% (5/81), and 35.0% (7/20) versus 8.2% (7/85), respectively. All three chi-square tests were significant; χ^2 ranged from 7.09 to 8.14 with one degree of freedom and *N*s ranged from 90 to 105 (all *p*s < .01). Moreover, it is interesting to note that gifted children at each of the three ages had scores above this cutoff across a greater number of the cognitive scales. For example, at age 2.5 years, 77.7% (7 of the 9 gifted children who had elevated scores) of the gifted children had elevated scores on three of the scales, compared to none of the nongifted children. The frequency of elevated scores in the gifted group was distributed more or less equally across the four cognitive scales. There was no pattern in the distribution of elevations. These findings are in accord with the "best performance" concept advocated by Roedell et al. (1980) that gifted children could possibly be identified by exceptional performance in one or more specific realms. Rather than identify giftedness by the child's average or overall performance across an array of tasks, these researchers have adopted the philosophy that the most meaningful, that is, advanced or exceptional, performance area should be employed. Hence, an individual domain of developmental acceleration could prove to be more significant in the designation of gifted than the use of composite scores. However, the Seattle investigators acknowledge that the validity and utility of this concept remains to be proven.

Our data reveal that children with gifted IQs have an overall higher level of cognitive functioning than that of nongifted IQ children as a group. However, as individuals, gifted IQ children show divergence in their spectrum of intellectual exceptionality (defined by scores equal to or in excess of two standard deviations above the mean in specific domains or skills). They did not all show exceptionality in the same cognitive realms or academic subject areas (see Chapter 4).

Another interesting finding emerging from the McCarthy data pertained to the untestability of children during the preschool period. In our longitudinal investigation, Bathurst and A. W. Gottfried (1987a) studied the significance of unresponsiveness or uncooperative behavior of children in standardized developmental assessments (specific to the McCarthy) during the preschool years. We found that the untestable children when compared to testable children were significantly lower on a wide range of abilities at all ages from age 1 to 6 years. Although the untestable children scored relatively lower on an array of skills and test-taking behaviors, there was a pervasive pattern of lower performance, particularly in language and social skills. Thus, we compared the proportion or percentage of children in the gifted and nongifted groups who were untestable at 2.5, 3, and 3.5 years. (One gifted and one nongifted child were not classified as testable or untestable because each missed one assessment during this time frame.) Succinctly, 5% (1 out of 19) of the gifted children were untestable, whereas 22% (19 out of 86) of the nongifted children were untestable during this time frame. The .17 difference between these proportions was significant ($p < .05$). These data reveal that children who become nongifted exhibit a rate of untestability during the preschool years over fourfold that of children who become gifted. Gifted children are highly unlikely to be untestable in standardized intelligence testing situations. These findings, in conjunction with our findings in Chapter 4 involving children's test-taking behaviors, imply that gifted children are more adept in, oriented to, or motivated in cognitive test-taking situations or demands. Hence, responsiveness to or cooperativeness in testing situations (i.e., the dimension of testability/untestability) during the preschool years may serve as an additional signifier or cue in the developmental course of giftedness or nongiftedness.

Globality versus Specificity

While differences were found at 18 months and thereafter on the overall indexes of intellectual performance, we focus now on differences between the gifted and nongifted groups on specific cognitive skills (or subtests). Although specific cognitive skills correlate positively with each other, there is still a degree of specificity operating. This is even the case during infancy; for example, psychometric sensorimotor tests correlate with Piagetian measures of sensorimotor intelligence (A. W. Gottfried & N. Brody, 1975). This phenomenon is well established during childhood as well as adulthood (E. Brody & N. Brody, 1976; N. Brody, 1992). There is a tendency for a child who does well on one type of cognitive task to do well on another. However, a child who is highly advanced in one type of cognitive skill does not necessarily excel in another type of cognitive skill. To this issue we now turn in our comparison of the gifted and nongifted groups.

As noted above, significant differences between gifted and nongifted children were found on the summary score index of the Bayley at 1.5 and 2 years. For object permanence at 1 and 1.5 years, a 2 × 2 (Giftedness Status × Age: 1 and 1.5 years) repeated-measures ANOVA showed no differences between the gifted and nongifted groups ($F(1, 103) = 0.55, p > .05$). Similarly, there were no differences between the groups on the visual and tactual memory and cross-modal tasks at 1 through 3 years as tested with a 2 × 5 (Giftedness Status × Age: 1, 1.5, 2, 2.5, and 3 years) MANOVA on cross-modal, visual, and tactual memory task (multivariate $F(3, 45) = 0.01, p > .05$). The gifted children did not exhibit significantly more novelty preference than the nongifted group. Thus, during infancy, differences between the groups were found only on the general psychometric sensorimotor scale.

From the Bayley, we extracted items pertaining to language development. This provided a direct assessment of receptive and expressive or production language abilities during the infancy period. Thus, we were able to determine if differences exist in this important realm of development between those children who eventually became gifted from those who did not. Our conceptual categorization of the items from the Bayley scale is presented:

The Bayley 12-month language items are as follows:

Receptive	*Expressive*
84 Listens selectively to familiar words	5 Says "da-da" or equivalent
89 Responds to verbal request	101 Jabbers expressively
94 Inhibits on command	106 Imitates words
117 Shows shoes or other clothing, or own toy	113 Says 2 words
126 Follows directions, doll	124 Names 1 object
128 Points to parts of doll	127 Uses words to make wants known

The 18-month Bayley language items included:

Receptive	*Expressive*
117 Shows shoes or other clothing, or own toy	101 Jabbers expressively
126 Follows directions, doll	106 Imitates words
128 Points to parts of doll	113 Says 2 words
131 Finds 2 objects	124 Names 1 object
132 Points to 3 pictures	127 Uses words to make wants known
133 Broken doll: mends marginally	130 Names 1 picture
139 Points to 5 pictures	136 Sentence of 2 words
140 Broken doll: mends approximately	138 Names 2 objects
144 Discriminates 2: cup, plate, box	141 Names 3 pictures
148 Points to 7 pictures	145 Names watch, 4th picture
152 Discriminates 3: cup, plate, box	146 Names 3 objects
153 Broken doll: mends exactly	149 Names 5 pictures
158 Understands 2 prepositions	150 Names watch, 2nd picture

The 24-month Bayley language items comprised:

Receptive	*Expressive*
117 Shows shoes or other clothing, or own toy	124 Names 1 object
126 Follows directions, doll	127 Uses words to make wants known
128 Points to parts of doll	130 Names 1 picture
131 Finds 2 objects	136 Sentence of 2 words
132 Points to 3 pictures	138 Names 2 objects
133 Broken doll: mends marginally	141 Names 3 pictures
139 Points to 5 pictures	145 Names watch, 4th picture

140 Broken doll: mends approximately
144 Discriminates 2: cup, plate, box
148 Points to 7 pictures
152 Discriminates 3: cup, plate, box
153 Broken doll: mends exactly
158 Understands 2 prepositions
162 Concept of 1
163 Understands 3 prepositions

146 Names 3 objects
149 Names 5 pictures
150 Names watch, 2nd picture

In order to determine whether there were differences between the gifted and nongifted children on the receptive and expressive items of the Bayley, a 2 × 3 (Giftedness Status × Age: 1, 1.5, and 2 years) MANOVA was conducted using both dependent variables. The three-way interaction was significant (multivariate $F(4, 100) = 20.66$, $p = .001$). The univariate tests showed that the three-way interaction held for both dependent variables. Therefore, we conducted three follow-up analyses, one at each age. These post hoc comparisons were three MANOVAs with giftedness status as the independent variable and the two language scales as the multiple dependent variables. The means, standard deviations, and univariate F results are shown in Table 3.2; a plot of the group differences at each age can be seen in Figure 3.5. At age 1 year, the multivariate test revealed significant differences for receptive language, but not for expressive language (multivariate $F(2, 102) = 3.77$, $p < .03$). This is not surprising, because receptive ability precedes expressive language skills and expressive skills are just emerging at this time. For the receptive language scale, the gifted children passed 58% of the items, whereas the nongifted children passed 52% of the items. At 1.5 years, the differences were significant for both receptive and expressive language (multivariate $F(2, 103) = 6.76$, $p < .002$). Again, the gifted children passed significantly more items than the nongifted children. For receptive language, gifted children passed 52%, whereas nongifted children passed 38%; for expressive language, gifted children passed 70% compared to 49% for nongifted children. The effect was again significant at 2 years of age (multivariate $F(2, 102) = 10.92$, $p < .001$). The gifted children passed significantly more items than nongifted children for both dependent variables. For receptive language, gifted children passed 89% and nongifted children passed 70% of the items. For expressive language, gifted children passed 98% and nongifted children passed 80% of the items.

Whether these particular results in language development account for the overall Bayley differences is difficult to know. It may very well

Table 3.2. Comparisons of Means between Gifted and Nongifted Children: Receptive and Expressive Language Items from the Bayley across Ages 1, 1.5, and 2 Years

	Giftedness status		
Scale	Gifted	Nongifted	Univariate *F*
1 year			
Receptive	3.5 (.7)	3.1 (.6)	6.62*
Expressive	2.9 (1.1)	2.6 (.6)	1.80
1.5 years			
Receptive	6.8 (3.0)	4.9 (2.7)	7.41**
Expressive	9.1 (3.4)	6.4 (2.8)	13.66***
2 years			
Receptive	13.3 (1.5)	10.5 (2.5)	21.99***
Expressive	9.8 (.5)	8.0 (2.3)	11.19***

Note. Standard deviations in parentheses. $N = 105$. Number of items on each scale are: 1-year receptive = 6; 1-year expressive = 6; 1.5-years receptive = 13; 1.5-years expressive = 13; 2-years receptive = 15; 2-years expressive = 10.
*$p < .05$. **$p < .01$. ***$p < .001$.

be the case. However, the findings are significant not only because they confirm the retrospective anecdotal reports of parents of gifted children as reported in the introduction, as well as our findings (to be reported below), but because they reveal that children who become gifted are advantaged in their very early development in the ability to comprehend and express themselves linguistically. Certainly this has paramount cognitive and social implications. Oviatt (1980), who studied comprehension skills in infants between 9 and 17 months, noted: "During the rapid comprehension development,... language becomes a powerful tool for focusing infants' attention and one that caretakers capitalize on to create new learning opportunities" (p. 105).

During the preschool period, the issue of generality was evaluated by examining the five specific subscales of the McCarthy as well as the TELD. For the McCarthy, a 2 × 3 (Giftedness Status × Age: 2.5, 3, and 3.5 years) MANOVA using the standard scores of the five scales of the McCarthy as the dependent variables yielded a significant main effect for Group (multivariate $F(5, 78) = 8.13$, $p < .001$). Table 3.3 displays the means, standard deviations, and univariate *F*s for each McCarthy scale combined across time. Across the preschool period from 30 to 42 months, the gifted group outscored the nongifted group on the Verbal,

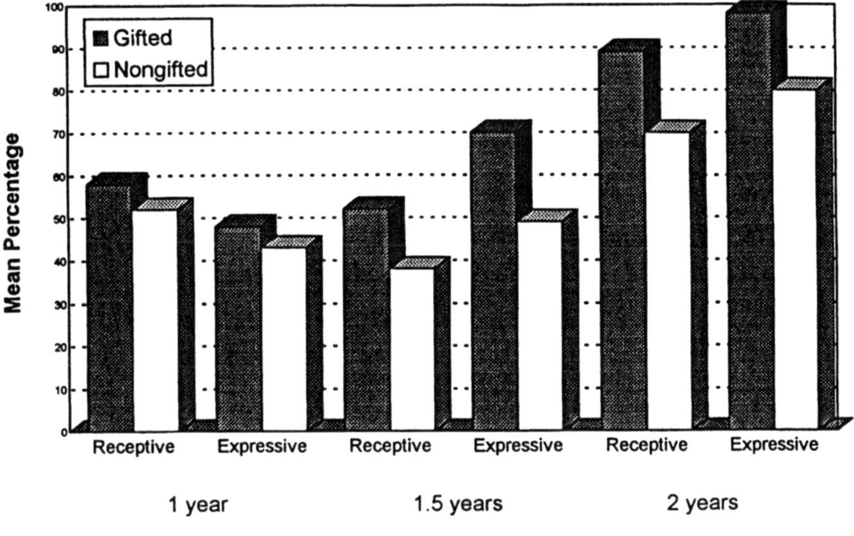

Figure 3.5. Comparison of receptive and expressive language skills of gifted and nongifted children during infancy.

Perceptual-Performance, Quantitative, and Memory scales, but not on the Motor scale.

The Test of Early Language Development was also administered during the preschool period (3.25 years). The results of the independent t test on the overall score are in accord with the differences found on the McCarthy Verbal scale in that the gifted group ($M = 12.7$, $SD = 4.9$) was significantly more advanced on this global measure of language development than the nongifted group ($M = 9.2$, $SD = 5.0$; $t(101) = 2.71$, $p < .01$). We sought to determine whether there were differences in the specific receptive and expressive domains, as we found on the Bayley items. A repeated-measures MANOVA using the receptive and expressive subscale scores of the TELD as dependent variables revealed a significant difference between the gifted ($M = 6.33$ and 6.64 for these two subscales, respectively) and nongifted group ($M = 4.58$ on both subscales; $F(1, 101) = 8.77$, $p < .01$). These findings are consistent with those found on the Bayley language analyses as well as those to be reported on the MCDI expressive and receptive or comprehension

Table 3.3. Comparison of Raw Score Means between Gifted and Nongifted Children: Subtests of McCarthy Scales of Children's Abilities

McCarthy scale	Giftedness status		Univariate F
	Gifted	Nongifted	
Verbal	64.6 (7.1)	56.5 (7.9)	20.72***
Perceptual-Performance	59.7 (6.3)	52.8 (6.9)	22.68***
Quantitative	62.9 (6.1)	55.2 (8.5)	19.84***
Memory	62.5 (8.6)	55.9 (8.1)	14.10***
Motor	53.5 (8.0)	51.1 (7.4)	2.36

Note. Standard deviations in parentheses. $N = 84$.
***$p < .001$.

language scales (see below). However, with respect to the specific issue at hand, the overall findings show that there is generality of superior performance during the preschool period in children who become gifted versus nongifted. Furthermore, the results are restricted to cognitive measures and do not extend to motor skill tasks.

The two psychometric instruments used during the early school ages were the KABC administered only at age 5 and WISC-R at ages 6, 7, and 8. For the KABC, a one-way MANOVA with Giftedness Status as the between-subjects factor and KABC subtests as the multiple measures showed a significant difference between the gifted and nongifted groups (multivariate $F(3, 101) = 12.45, p < .001$). As shown in Table 3.4, the gifted group scored higher on both processing subscales (Sequential and Simultaneous) as well as the Nonverbal subscale.

As for the WISC-R Verbal IQ and Performance IQ scores, a significant main effect resulted, with the gifted group scoring significantly higher than nongifted at all ages as shown by a 2 × 3 (Giftedness Status × Age: 6, 7, and 8 years) MANOVA (multivariate $F(2, 98) = 55.46, p < .001$). Two further analyses concerning the generality of effect across the verbal and performance subtests were also conducted. A 2 × 3 (Giftedness Status × Age: 6, 7, and 8 years) MANOVA using the WISC-R subtests of the Verbal scale (Information, Similarities, Arithmetic, Vocabulary, and Comprehension) was performed. There was a significant overall effect for Group (multivariate $F(5, 95) = 17.16, p < .001$). The same analysis was conducted for the performance subtests (Picture Completion, Picture Arrangement, Block Design, Object Assembly, Coding), resulting in a significant effect for Giftedness Status (multivariate $F(5, 95) = 14.00, p < .001$). Across all 10 subtests of the verbal and performance

Table 3.4. Comparison of Means between Gifted and Nongifted Children: Subscales of the KABC

	Giftedness status		
KABC subscale	Gifted	Nongifted	Univariate F
Sequential Processing	117.3 (10.5)	105.0 (11.2)	19.93***
Simultaneous Processing	127.2 (7.5)	112.3 (11.3)	31.91***
Nonverbal	124.8 (9.5)	111.2 (10.9)	26.37***

Note. Standard deviations in parentheses. $N = 105$.
*** $p < .001$.

subscales, the gifted group scored significantly higher than the nongifted group. The group means, standard deviations, and univariate Fs are shown in Table 3.5 for the Verbal and Performance IQ scores and the 10 subtest scale scores.

These findings imply that gifted IQ means generalized high intelligence (see also Humphreys, 1985). Intellectually gifted children are cognitively well rounded; that is, they are cognitively adept. The gifted group was significantly elevated above their nongifted peers on all cognitive skills, certainly by preschool, and through the school-entry years. We anticipate that these findings will be maintained thereafter as well.

While the aforementioned analyses addressed the issue of differences in elevation across various cognitive skills, they do not address the question as to whether the *patterns* in intellectual performance across areas are similar or different between the groups. In other words, do gifted and nongifted groups share the same profile across various cognitive skills, and if so, is this characteristic in the course of development? Profile analysis is a repeated-measures ANOVA where the dependent variables are treated as the within factor. Nonparallel profiles would be indicated by a significant interaction.

To determine whether the profiles between the gifted and nongifted groups were different on the four cognitive scales of the McCarthy test during the preschool period, profile analyses were conducted at each of the three ages. The results of these analyses revealed that, in each case, the profiles were parallel (largest $F(3, 86) = 1.27, p > .05$). The profiles of the gifted and nongifted groups, with means collapsed across age, are presented in Figure 3.6.

Profile analyses were also conducted for the five subtests of the WISC-R Verbal scale and the five subtests of the WISC-R Performance scale at each of the three ages. On the verbal subtests, none of the analyses

Table 3.5. Comparison of Means between Gifted and Nongifted Children: Subscales and Subtests of the Wechsler Intelligence Scale for Children (Revised)

	Giftedness status		
WISC-R	Gifted	Nongifted	Univariate *F*
Verbal IQ	132.1 (10.1)	109.5 (11.3)	85.40***
Performance IQ	129.5 (7.5)	111.9 (10.9)	61.03***
Verbal subtests			
Information	15.3 (2.0)	11.2 (2.4)	64.63***
Similarities	15.9 (2.6)	12.3 (3.0)	45.82***
Arithmetic	14.3 (2.3)	11.2 (2.6)	38.27***
Vocabulary	16.0 (2.2)	11.8 (2.9)	59.68***
Comprehension	14.1 (2.6)	11.5 (2.7)	25.16***
Performance subtests			
Picture Completion	13.8 (1.9)	11.7 (2.4)	19.81***
Picture Arrangement	14.9 (2.1)	12.9 (2.5)	18.12***
Block Design	15.4 (2.3)	11.6 (2.4)	56.35***
Object Assembly	14.5 (2.5)	11.6 (2.5)	30.48***
Coding	12.4 (2.1)	10.9 (2.8)	9.11**

Note. Standard deviations in parentheses. $N = 101$.
**$p < .01$. ***$p < .001$.

revealed reliable differentiating patterns. Profile analyses for the performance subtests revealed significant interaction effects at ages 6, 7, and 8 years ($Fs(4, 97–102) = 2.83$ to 3.00, all $ps < .05$). The magnitude of the differences between the giftedness status groups differs as a function of the subtests. Across the ages, the only consistent distinction was that the difference in magnitude was largest on the Block Design subtest. It is interesting to note that this subtest possesses the highest internal consistency and test-retest stability coefficients among the WISC-R performance subtests. Profiles for the verbal and performance sets, with means collapsed across age, are presented in Figures 3.7 and 3.8, respectively.

We conclude that the difference between gifted and nongifted groups is one of elevation or superiority in intellectual performance and not one of differential patterns. It is our interpretation that intellectually gifted children are developmentally advanced or advantaged by their level of development and not distinguished by their pattern of intellect. The consistently and markedly higher elevations of the gifted children were more striking than any deviations in relative differences of

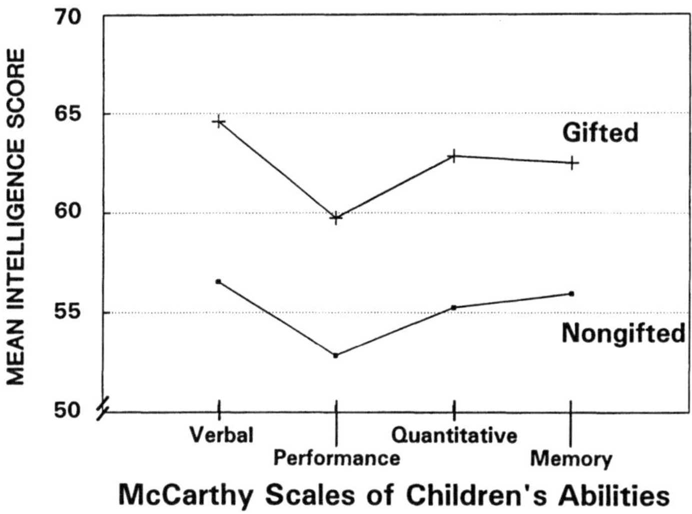

Figure 3.6. Mean intelligence scores for gifted and nongifted children for the subscales of the McCarthy averaged across 2.5, 3, and 3.5 years of age.

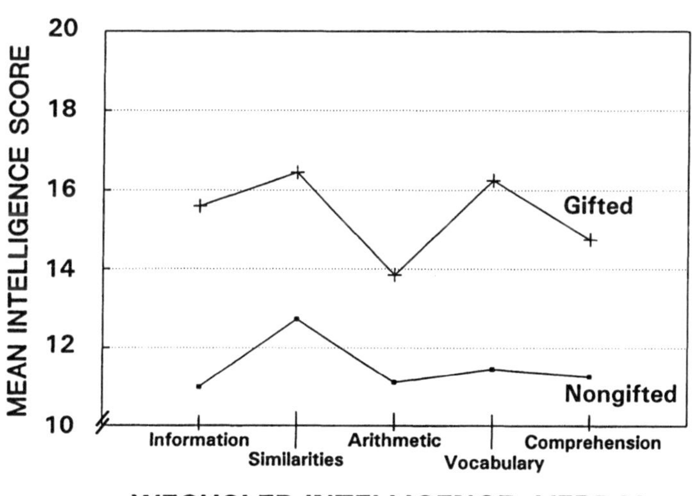

Figure 3.7. Mean intelligence scores for gifted and nongifted children for the verbal subtests of the WISC-R averaged across 6, 7, and 8 years of age.

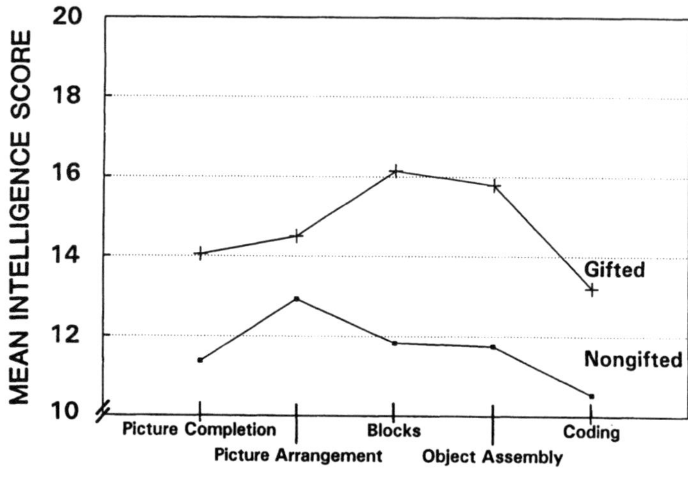

Figure 3.8. Mean intelligence scores for gifted and nongifted children for the performance subtests of the WISC-R averaged across 6, 7, and 8 years of age.

subscales. The profiles were essentially parallel and do not represent a unique profile of giftedness. The fact that the profiles were not substantially different indicates that they may more accurately represent the profiles of predominantly white, middle-class children of average to above-average intelligence during the preschool and early elementary school years. It is interesting to note the similarity between our McCarthy profiles and those found by Lesser, Fifer, and Clark (1965) for their white children on verbal, quantitative, and perceptual/spatial skills. Whether patterns of intellectual performance are identical between gifted and nongifted children in other cultural or racial groups (as our data suggest for white children) remains to be determined (see Saccuzzo, Johnson, & Russell, 1992). However, the delineation of differential patterns may only be accomplished by comparing profiles of both gifted and nongifted children within diverse racial or ethnic groups.

Parental Assessments

In contrast to the above data, which are based on objective developmental tests, the data in this section rely on parents' appraisals of their children's development during infancy and the preschool period. The central issue addressed here is whether parents are perceptive of differences in the early development of children who become gifted or nongifted.

Every 6 months from ages 1 to 3.5 years, each mother rated her child's functioning compared to other children of the same age in four areas: intelligence, verbal, social, and motor. Higher ratings (scale 1 to 5) indicated more advanced functioning for the designated age. A 2 × 6 (Giftedness Status × Age: 1, 1.5, 2, 2.5, 3, and 3.5) MANOVA with these four repeated measures as dependent variables yielded a significant effect for Giftedness Status (multivariate $F(4, 91) = 4.58, p < .001$). The mean ratings given by parents of children who become gifted or nongifted are displayed in Figure 3.9. In line with the significant main effect for Giftedness Status, parents of children who become gifted rated their children as functioning at higher developmental levels. Significant univariate effects were found for the dimensions of intelligence, verbal, and social functioning. No statistically significant difference emerged for motor skill functioning.

Parent assessments of their children's development were also evaluated with the MCDI and MPI, two standardized inventories of children's development. Parents' responses on the MCDI, which was completed at 2.5 years, were analyzed using a one-way between-subjects MANOVA. The two giftedness status groups were compared on seven MCDI scales: Gross Motor, Fine Motor, Expressive Language, Comprehension-Conceptual, Situation Comprehension, Self Help, and Personal Social. The General Development scale was not included in this analysis because it comprises items from the other seven scales. Results showed a significant effect for Group (multivariate $F(7, 84) = 4.17, p < .001$). As shown in Table 3.6, parents of gifted children reported significantly higher scores on the Expressive Language, Comprehension-Conceptual, and Fine Motor scales. The overall General Development scale was analyzed separately because it is a composite of items from the other scales. A t test showed that parents reported the general development scores of gifted children to be higher than nongifted children ($t(90) = 4.25, p < .001$).

An analysis of the MPI responses, completed by mothers at the 5-year assessment, also showed that gifted children were reported to be performing higher on the scales assessing the cognitive skills of Expressive Language, Comprehension, Memory, and Letter Recognition, as displayed in Table 3.7 (multivariate $F(7, 95) = 4.50, p < .001$). A significant

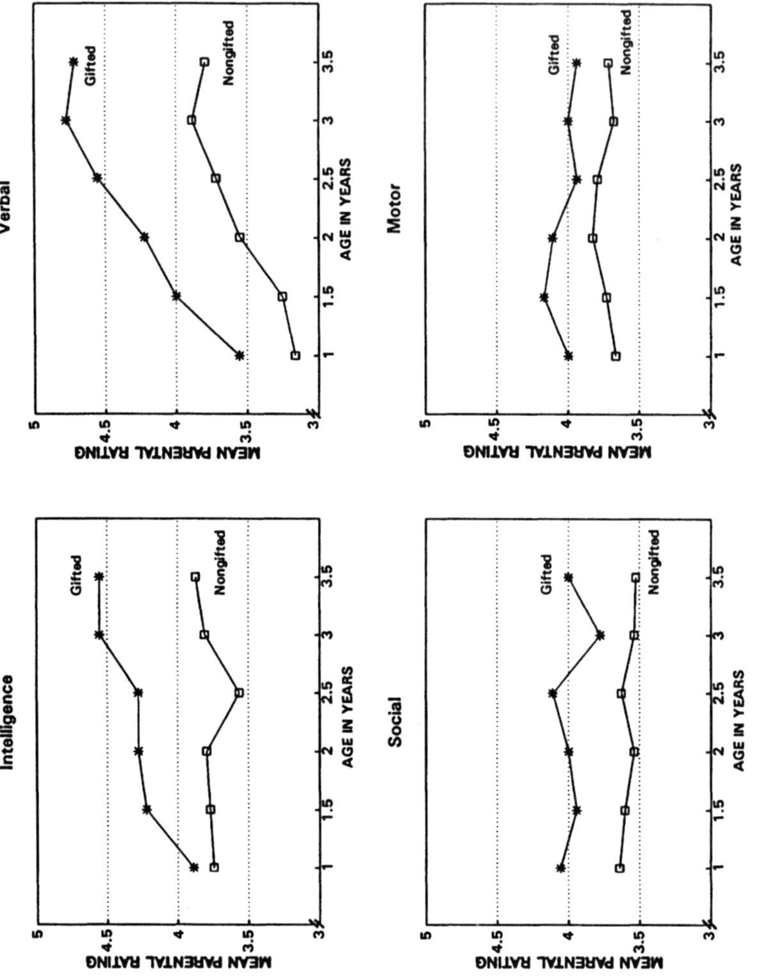

Figure 3.9. Mothers' ratings of gifted and nongifted children at ages 1 year through 3.5 years in four areas: intelligence, verbal, social, and motor.

Table 3.6. Comparison of Means between Gifted and Nongifted Children: Subscales of the Minnesota Child Development Inventory (MCDI)

MCDI subscale	Giftedness status: Gifted	Giftedness status: Nongifted	Univariate F
Gross Motor	27.7 (2.1)	27.2 (2.3)	0.50
Fine Motor	32.8 (2.0)	31.4 (2.1)	6.48*
Expressive Language	51.5 (2.3)	45.2 (5.5)	22.35***
Comprehension-Conceptual	46.8 (5.3)	36.9 (9.4)	18.57***
Situation Comprehension	33.3 (4.2)	31.5 (4.1)	2.58
Self Help	25.1 (4.9)	23.9 (4.4)	0.97
Personal Social	28.4 (3.1)	27.3 (3.5)	1.74

Note. Standard deviations in parentheses. $N = 92$.
$^{*}p < .05$. $^{***}p < .001$.

difference did not emerge on the number scale; this is due to a ceiling effect for the gifted children.

These findings suggest that parents of children who become gifted or nongifted are accurate in their ratings of their children's functioning and that parents are perceptive of their children's developmental position as early as infancy. This is supported by both the absolute (actual mean level) and relative levels (gifted vs. nongifted) of their ratings, and also by the correspondence of their ratings with the objective developmental test data presented above. The early advancement in verbal skills

Table 3.7. Comparison of Means between Gifted and Nongifted Children: Subscales of the Minnesota Preschool Inventory (MPI)

MPI subscale	Giftedness status: Gifted	Giftedness status: Nongifted	Univariate F
Self Help	15.8 (2.0)	15.8 (2.6)	0.02
Fine Motor	16.7 (0.6)	15.2 (1.8)	12.31***
Expressive Language	17.7 (0.6)	16.5 (1.6)	9.29**
Comprehension	33.1 (0.8)	29.1 (3.7)	23.12***
Memory	14.0 (0.8)	12.4 (2.3)	8.52**
Letter Recognition	7.0 (0.0)	5.6 (1.6)	16.80***
Number Comprehension	7.7 (0.8)	7.3 (1.3)	1.40

Note. Standard deviations in parentheses. $N = 103$.
$^{**}p < .01$. $^{***}p < .001$.

is particularly interesting because such findings have been documented in the retrospective anecdotal reports of the parents of gifted children in several studies as well as in the objective contemporaneous analyses conducted in this longitudinal investigation. Advancement in language development in the gifted compared to the nongifted group was found from infancy onward and on all of the objective developmental tests administered in this study, that is, the Bayley items, McCarthy, TELD, and WISC-R. The fact that parents perceive differences in intelligence is also in accord with the body of objective psychometric testing in this study. Gifted children were perceived as advanced in social functioning when rated by parents, but not on the social skill items of the MCDI. However, advancement in social competence skills was also found in our study on the Preschool Interpersonal Problem-Solving test as well as the Vineland Adaptive Behavior Scales administered during the early elementary grades. These results are presented and discussed further in Chapter 5. The lack of difference found on the parent ratings of motor skills is in accord with the findings found on the McCarthy motor scale. Note that the MCDI and MPI discriminate between fine and gross motor skills whereas the McCarthy does not. Differences were found on the fine motor, but not gross motor, skill scales of the MCDI and MPI. The findings of differences in fine motor skills in these latter two scales may reflect an element of perceptual-cognitive functioning in the fine motor tasks. In view of the fact that there is a general or global advantage in cognitive skills in the development of children who become gifted, the fine motor tasks may be tapping this quality which may not be the case in gross motor functioning which may rest more heavily or exclusively on coordination or neuromuscular development. The difference between copying a pattern versus simply hopping on one foot illustrates this point. In summary, the parents in our study were cognizant of their children's developmental status and their reports or perceptions were in accord with objective developmental testing. Parents' views of their children's development may be an important ingredient in the developmental outcome of children, whether gifted or nongifted.

SUMMARY

1. Differences in level of intellectual performance between the gifted and nongifted children emerged on the psychometric testing at 1.5 years and maintained continuity thereafter. However, the earliest

difference was found on receptive language skills at age 1 year. Differences in receptive and expressive language skills were consistently found from infancy onward. This was found on the objective assessment as well as on contemporaneous parent ratings. No differences were found on object permanence or on the recognition memory tasks (cross-modal, visual, or tactual memory).

2. There is no characteristic pattern of intellectual performance across time. Each child revealed a unique ontogenetic age pattern. As noted, there are as many patterns as there are children, and the individuality of their course of development is what is characteristic of these children. No individual pattern characterized the group pattern and vice versa—the group pattern was not representative of the individuals contained within.

3. There were reliable signs of potential intellectual giftedness in the course of early development. In addition to advanced early language development, almost all infants who eventually became gifted exhibited a developmental index of 130 or greater between 1 and 2 years of age. As preschoolers as well, these children were significantly more likely than preschoolers who did not become gifted to reveal a general cognitive index of 130 or greater between 2.5 and 3.5 years of age. On specific cognitive domains of verbal, quantitative, perceptual-performance, and memory, they were also significantly more likely to have at least one or more index at or above the 97th percentile. Lastly, a significantly lower proportion of gifted children were untestable as compared to the children who did not become gifted. This specific finding, which is in line with results in Chapter 4, indicates that children who become gifted are more strongly geared toward orienting themselves to cognitive testing situations.

4. Gifted IQ implies generalized high intelligence. Gifted children were superior across an array of cognitive tasks beginning as early as the preschool period. Gifted children tend to be cognitively well rounded or adept. Globality rather than specificity in cognitive performance characterizes intellectual giftedness.

5. Gifted and nongifted children did not differ substantially in their profiles of cognitive or intellectual abilities. In other words, there was no particular pattern characteristic of either group. The emerging patterns (i.e., during the preschool years) in our study were characteristic of predominantly middle-class, white children performing at the average or above levels of intelligence. Hence, we found no characteristic pattern of intellectual performance characterizing gifted children. The differences we found reside in the rate of development (during infancy)

as well as the level of performance thereafter. Gifted children progress at a higher intellectual level. They are advanced in their cognitive development or reasoning.

6. Parents of infants and preschoolers who become gifted were cognizant that their children were advanced compared to children of the same age. This was noted particularly in children's intellectual or general developmental status and verbal skills, although differences were also found in social functioning, fine motor skills, and letter recognition skills.

4

Education, Achievement, and Motivation

ISSUES

This chapter presents findings concerning important aspects of the educational histories, achievement, classroom performance, and motivation of the gifted and nongifted children. The issues addressed in this chapter were based on our conceptualizations as well as several raised in the literature reviewed in Chapter 1. These include:

1. Are there differences between gifted and nongifted children in their chronological age at the time of kindergarten entry? The literature reviewed suggests that gifted children tend to be younger than nongifted children in the same grade level. In this study we examined children's age at kindergarten entry, and also their grade levels at subsequent ages.

2. Are there any differences between gifted and nongifted children in the types of schools attended? This issue emerged not from the literature per se, but because private education has become more prevalent in recent years. We wanted to determine if gifted children tended to be in one type of school more frequently than another.

3. From ages 5 through 8, do gifted and nongifted children differ in their achievement? If differences occur, are these generalizable across achievement area (subject areas), source of information (actual testing vs. teacher and parent report), and type of achievement score (percentile, standard score, ratings)? The body of literature on the superior academic achievement of gifted children during the school years provided the foundation for examining

achievement of young children who are subsequently identified as gifted. The diversity of achievement information in the present study provided a robust look at this issue.

4. Examining intrachild achievement patterns, do gifted children evidence extremely superior achievement scores across subject areas and over time? Our interest was to determine the extent of individuality or similarity of achievement patterns with regard to academic subject areas during these early years. Is there a consistent pattern across gifted children, or do individual patterns of higher and lower achievement across subject areas tend to be more typical of the gifted?

5. Do gifted and nongifted children differ in their classroom behavior and other aspects of school functioning? Whereas the gifted are expected to excel in their academic achievement, is this also likely to be true regarding their classroom behaviors? Arguments for gifted children being either better or more poorly adjusted to school than nongifted children could be advanced. To the extent that the gifted child's needs are met or not met in the school environment, their adjustment could be affected accordingly. Examining classroom adjustment in the present study adds to the total picture of academic performance in gifted and nongifted children.

6. Are there differences between gifted and nongifted children in their academic intrinsic motivation? Gifted children were expected to be more intrinsically motivated than nongifted children. The literature reviewed in Chapter 1 supports this expectation. We expected that gifted children, who experience more academic mastery, would evidence more academic intrinsic motivation.

7. Are gifted and nongifted children different in their perception of academic competence and academic anxiety? The literature reported in Chapter 1 supports the expectation that gifted children will evidence more positive perceptions of academic competence and lower academic anxiety compared to nongifted children.

8. Are there differences between the gifted and nongifted groups on behaviors indicative of cognitive mastery motivation from infancy through age 6? This study provides the first look at mastery motivation in gifted and nongifted children from infancy onward. Together with the data on academic intrinsic motivation, the data provide a longitudinal, developmental account of mastery and intrinsic motivation pertaining to cognitive and academic tasks.

DESCRIPTION OF MEASURES

Educational History

Information regarding children's age at kindergarten entry was collected at the 5-year assessment through a questionnaire administered to the parent who accompanied the child to the lab (almost always the mother). At the 7- and 8-year assessments, data concerning the child's current grade level were obtained. The type of school the child attended was surveyed at age 7. Categories included public, private nonreligious, and private religious. Because the children in our study attend many different schools, and because schools differ in their policies regarding identification and provision of programs for the gifted, we felt that whether or not the child was in a special program would be an unreliable indicator of his or her giftedness. Hence, such data will not be presented.

Achievement

Achievement tests were individually administered to each child at ages 5 through 8. At age 5, the Achievement scale of the Kaufman Assessment Battery for Children (KABC) (A. S. Kaufman & N. L. Kaufman, 1983) was administered. This scale consists of knowledge in naming well-known faces and places, arithmetic, riddles, and reading/decoding. Standard scores are computed with a population mean and standard deviation of 100 and 15, respectively.

At age 6, the Wide Range Achievement Test-Revised (WRAT-R) (Jastak & Wilkinson, 1984) was administered. Academic performance in the areas of reading, arithmetic, and spelling are appraised. Standard scores for the WRAT-R are 100 and 15 for the mean and standard deviation, respectively.

The Woodcock-Johnson Psycho-Educational Battery (Woodcock & Johnson, 1977) was administered at ages 7 and 8. Children's achievement in reading, mathematics, and academic knowledge (science, social studies, humanities) was assessed. Percentile scores comparing children with their appropriate grade population were analyzed.

Teachers' and parents' ratings of child achievement were gathered from the teacher and parent versions of the Child Behavior Checklist, respectively (Achenbach, 1991a, 1991b). Teachers' and parents' ratings were on a 5- and 4-point scale, respectively, with higher scores corresponding to higher achievement. On the same checklist, teachers also rated children on the sufficiency of their school functioning in four areas:

how hard working they are, how well behaved they are, how much they are learning, and how happy they are. Ratings varied from 1 to 7, with higher scores corresponding to more positive ratings.

Academic Intrinsic Motivation

At ages 7 and 8, children's academic intrinsic motivation was measured with the *Young Children's Academic Intrinsic Motivation Inventory* (YCAIMI) (A. E. Gottfried, 1990). This instrument measures enjoyment of learning, an orientation toward mastery, curiosity, persistence, task endogeny, and learning challenging, difficult, and novel tasks (A. E. Gottfried, 1990). The YCAIMI, a downward extension of the *Children's Academic Intrinsic Motivation Inventory* (CAIMI) (A. E. Gottfried, 1986a), is a reliable and valid self-report scale in which children rate their agreement or disagreement, on a 3-point scale, with statements such as "I like learning new things in reading." The content of the items on the YCAIMI was derived from the CAIMI but reworded for young children. In addition, the number of items was reduced, and the response format was simplified to be appropriate for young children. At age 7, the areas of reading and math were assessed with 10 items in each area, yielding a score in reading, math, and a total score consisting of the sum of the reading and math area. At age 8, the inventory was enlarged to a total of 39 items in reading (12 items), math (12 items), school in general (12 items), and a scale dealing with the enjoyment of school work as related to difficulty (3 items). In order to facilitate comparability with the age-7 YCAIMI, scores used for analyses at age 8 were reading, math, and a total consisting of the sum of all four age-8 subscales. For each scale, the totals were divided by the number of items comprising that scale to obtain averages, which ranged from 1 to 3. Higher scores correspond to higher academic intrinsic motivation. These averages were used in the analyses.

Academic Anxiety and Perception of Competence

At ages 7 and 8, children were asked to rate their anxiety and perception of competence on a 3-point scale, with higher scores indicating greater anxiety and greater perception of competence, respectively. At age 7, children rated their anxiety in reading and math (e.g., "I worry about reading (math) tests") with three items in each area. At age 8, anxiety items were presented for reading, math, and school in general (three items each). For perception of competence, children responded to two items at age 7: "I do well in reading (math)"; and to three items at age 8: "I do well in reading (math, school in general)." At ages 7 and 8, total anxiety and perception of competence scores were computed, and these were used in the analyses in addition to the reading and math scores.

Cognitive Mastery Motivation

The Bayley Infant Behavior Record (Bayley, 1969) was administered from ages 18 through 72 months. Henceforth we will refer to it as the Bayley Behavior Record (BBR) because we extended its use beyond the infancy period. Ratings on the BBR reflect the child's behavior during the administration of a standardized test, and are made by the test administrator. Only items that met our criterion of 85% interobserver reliability were retained for analysis (Bathurst & A. W. Gottfried, 1987a). Also, some items were inappropriate at certain age levels. The items that were included are:

Item	*Ages*	*Scoring*
Examiner orientation	1.5–3.5 yrs	1 (avoidance) to 5 (inviting)
Goal directedness	1.5–6 yrs	1 (no directed effort) to 9 (compulsive absorption with a task until it is solved)
Object orientation: Responsiveness	1.5–3.5 yrs	1 (does not look at or indicate interest in objects) to 9 (reluctantly relinquishes test materials)
Object orientation: Play	1.5–3.5 yrs	Plays imaginatively with materials: 1 (yes) 2 (no)
Attention span	1.5–6 yrs	1 (fleeting attention) to 9 (long-continued absorption with a toy, activity, or person)
Fearfulness	1.5–3.5 yrs	1 (accepts entire situation with no evidence of fear) to 9 (strong indication of fear of the strange)
Cooperativeness	1.5–6 yrs	1 (resists all suggestions or requests) to 9 (very readily and enthusiastically enters into suggested games or tasks)
Emotional tone	1.5–6 yrs	1 (child seems unhappy throughout) to 9 (radiates happiness)
Energy	1.5–3.5 yrs	1 (low level) to 9 (high level)
Activity	2.5–6 yrs	1 (stays quiet in one place) to 9 (hyperactive—cannot be quieted for sedentary tests)

Reactivity	2.5–3.5 yrs	1 (unreactive—seems to pay little heed to what goes on) to 9 (very reactive—every little thing seems to stir him/her up)
Deviant behavior	1.5–3.5 yrs	1 (yes) 2 (no)

RESULTS

Educational History

The numbers of children in the gifted and nongifted groups who entered kindergarten at age 5 are presented in Table 4.1. A chi-square analysis indicated that the gifted children were significantly more likely to enter kindergarten at a younger age than nongifted children (χ^2 (1, N = 104) = 4.23, p = .04). Of the 20 gifted children included in this analysis, 90% entered kindergarten at age 5. Of the 84 nongifted children, 63% entered kindergarten at age 5. This is particularly important because the birth months of the entire sample fall between September and early December 1978, and children entering kindergarten at age 5 would be among the youngest in their class since the cutoff date for public school entry in California is generally within the initial week of December. Hence, our data are consistent with the Terman data in that the gifted children tended to enter school at a younger age than nongifted children. A child who is subsequently identified as gifted is likely to be displaying school readiness earlier than nongifted children.

At age 7, children were either in grade 1 or 2. A chi-square analysis was conducted on the number of gifted and nongifted children in each grade level. A significant difference again emerged between the gifted

Table 4.1. Kindergarten Attendance at 5 Years: Gifted versus Nongifted Children

Kindergarten attendance at age 5	Giftedness status	
	Gifted	Nongifted
Yes	18 (90%)	53 (63%)
No	2 (10%)	31 (37%)

Note. Column percentages in parentheses.

and nongifted (χ^2 (1, N = 106) = 8.1, $p < .01$). For the gifted, 18 (90%) of 20 children were in the second grade; for the nongifted, 45 (52%) of 86 were in the second grade. Interestingly, the number of nongifted children in the higher grade placement was lower than the number who had entered kindergarten at age 5, whereas for the gifted children, the same number was in second grade as had entered kindergarten. According to the teachers' reports gathered on the Child Behavior Checklist, eight of the nongifted children were known to have repeated an earlier grade, and none of the gifted children were known to have repeated a grade. Results for grade placement and repeating grades were virtually identical at age 8. In sum, the gifted children were significantly more likely to enter school at a younger age, and were not retained in a grade through age 8. Nongifted children were significantly less likely to enter school at age 5, and were significantly more likely to repeat a grade between ages 5 and 8.

At age 7, parents reported on whether their children were enrolled in a public school, private religious, or private nonreligious school. A chi-square analysis was conducted to determine if gifted and nongifted children differed with regard to their school type. The results were nonsignificant (χ^2 (1, N = 106) = 5.4, p = .07), indicating no significant differences in the types of schools the gifted and nongifted attended.

Achievement

Comparisons between the gifted and nongifted children's achievement test scores from ages 5 through 8 are presented in Table 4.2. Analyses differed depending on whether there was one or multiple subtests, and whether the same achievement test was repeated across time. For the KABC, a t test was used to compare the gifted versus nongifted since there was only one score at a single point in time; for the WRAT-R, a single-factor (Giftedness Status) MANOVA was used to analyze the three subtests (Reading, Math, Spelling); and for the Woodcock-Johnson, a 2 × 2 (Giftedness Status × Age: 7 and 8 years) repeated-measures MANOVA was used with Age as the repeated factor, and the three subtests (Reading, Math, Knowledge) were the dependent variables.

Results showed highly significant differences across all measures and subtests. Across all measures, the mean of the gifted group exceeded that of the nongifted group by at least one standard deviation (using the standard deviation of our sample combined across giftedness status). On the KABC, the significant t value is reported in Table 4.2. For the

WRAT-R, giftedness status was significant (multivariate $F(3, 98) = 15.14$, $p < .001$), indicating that across all three subtests, gifted children had significantly higher scores. For the Woodcock-Johnson, giftedness status was significant (multivariate $F(3, 100) = 12.24$, $p < .001$), also showing that the gifted children had higher scores on all three subtests, and at ages 7 and 8. For each subarea on the WRAT-R and Woodcock-Johnson, a univariate F test was conducted showing that each of these was significant, and these are presented in Table 4.2.

Comparisons between the gifted and nongifted children's achievement as rated by their teachers and parents are presented in Table 4.3. Teachers' and parents' ratings were analyzed with separate 2 × 3 (Giftedness Status × Age: 6, 7, and 8 years) repeated-measures MANOVAs in which Age was the repeated factor. For teachers' ratings, reading and math were the multiple dependent measures, and for parents' ratings, reading, math, writing, and spelling were the multiple dependent meas-

Table 4.2. Comparisons of Means between Gifted and Nongifted Children: Achievement Tests

	Giftedness status		
Achievement	Gifted	Nongifted	Univariate F
5 years			
KABC[a]	125.2 (7.9)	108.7 (9.9)	6.95***
6 years			
WRAT-R[a]			
Reading	119.5 (16.7)	96.9 (13.6)	38.9***
Spelling	114.5 (11.1)	94.9 (13.4)	34.6***
Arithmetic	114.6 (8.0)	97.5 (14.8)	23.9***
7 and 8 years			
Woodcock-Johnson[b]			
Reading	87.9 (16.3)	62.1 (24.5)	21.3***
Math	90.7 (10.2)	68.0 (23.4)	22.8***
Knowledge	90.5 (9.7)	62.6 (24.3)	27.8***

Note. Standard deviations in parentheses. KABC = Kaufman Assessment Battery for Children; WRAT-R = Wide Range Achievement Test-Revised; Woodcock-Johnson = Woodcock-Johnson Psycho-Educational Battery. *N*s = 105, 102, and 104 for analyses with the KABC, WRAT-R, and Woodcock-Johnson, respectively.

[a]Standard scores analyzed. t test reported for KABC because there is no repeated measurement on this test.

[b]Percentiles analyzed.

***$p < .001$.

ures. For both teachers' and parents' ratings, a significant multivariate main effect was obtained for Giftedness Status ($F(2, 56) = 7.59, p < .01$ and $F(4, 75) = 4.37, p < .01$, respectively). Univariate F tests were all significant and are presented in Table 4.3.

Profile analysis was conducted for the WRAT-R and Woodcock-Johnson to determine if the differences between the gifted and nongifted groups were related to specific subject areas. Profile analysis is conducted using repeated-measures ANOVA in which the subscales of the measure are treated as the repeated factor and Giftedness Status is the between-groups factor. A parallel profile was obtained as indicated by a nonsignificant interaction between the repeated and giftedness status factors. Hence, the differences between the gifted and nongifted children were the same across the subject areas.

Overall, these data reveal consistent group differences, as early as age 5, in achievement as measured by different tests, as reported by teachers and parents, and across all measured subareas. At an early age, the gifted group is distinguishable from the nongifted group in this way.

Individual achievement patterns were examined as well. An important issue concerned the likelihood of obtaining an extremely superior achievement test score given one's giftedness status. An extremely superior achievement test score was defined as a score at or above 130

Table 4.3. Comparisons of Means between Gifted and Nongifted Children: Teacher and Parent Ratings of Achievement across Ages 6, 7, and 8 Years

	Giftedness status		
Achievement	Gifted	Nongifted	Univariate F
Teachers' ratings			
Reading	4.27 (.6)	3.43 (.9)	15.3***
Math	3.93 (.8)	3.46 (.7)	9.2**
Parents' ratings			
Reading	2.85 (.4)	2.39 (.7)	13.1***
Math	2.74 (.4)	2.41 (.5)	10.8***
Writing	2.65 (.5)	2.27 (.6)	9.4**
Spelling	2.75 (.4)	2.40 (.7)	7.4**

Note. Standard deviations in parentheses. Teachers' and parents' ratings were obtained from the teacher and parent versions of the Achenbach Child Behavior Checklist, respectively. *Ns* = 59 and 80 for teacher and parent ratings, respectively.
**$p < .01$. ***$p < .001$.

on the KABC and WRAT-R, corresponding to the definition of giftedness used in this study, which is the second standard deviation or above. For the Woodcock-Johnson the 97th percentile and above was used since 97.5 is the specific percentile at the second standard deviation and the latter value was unavailable. Moreover, using the 97th percentile is consistent with procedures used by the researchers at the Center for Talented Youth, Johns Hopkins University, to identify talented youth in their national search (Center for Talented Youth, 1993).

Chi-square tests were conducted to determine if giftedness status was significantly associated with achieving a superior score. Separate analyses were conducted for the KABC, WRAT-R, and Woodcock-Johnson.

In the first analysis, chi-square tests were conducted for the following: (1) KABC: a score of 130 or greater; (2) WRAT-R: at least one of the three subscale scores at 130 or greater; and (3) Woodcock-Johnson: at least one of the six subscale scores (three at ages 7 and 8) at the 97th percentile or greater. Results were highly significant, with chi-square values presented in Table 4.4. Across all three tests, the gifted children were significantly more likely to obtain extremely superior scores. There was no particular subject-area pattern obtained for the Woodcock-Johnson; superior scores occurred evenly across all subtests. For the WRAT-R, however, seven of the eight superior scores were in reading.

Table 4.4. Associations between Giftedness Status and Attainment of Extremely Superior Achievement Test Scores

Extremely superior score	Giftedness status		
	Gifted	Nongifted	χ^2
KABC			
Yes	8 (40%)	2 (2%)	
No	12 (60%)	80 (98%)	21.58***
WRAT-R			
Yes	8 (42%)	4 (5%)	
No	11 (58%)	77 (95%)	16.76***
Woodcock-Johnson			
Yes	14 (70%)	16 (19%)	
No	6 (30%)	68 (81%)	18.03***

Note. Column percentages in parentheses. $df = 1$ for all analyses.
***$p < .001$.

A second analysis was conducted to determine if giftedness status was significantly associated with scoring between the 90th and 96th percentile range. It was our judgment that the 90th percentile and above is indicative of high academic achievement because it includes the upper 10%. For the KABC and WRAT-R, a score of 120 was set as the cutoff (in the normal distribution a percentile of 90 is equivalent to a standard score of 120), and this cutoff was similar to the percentile range reported in the KABC and WRAT-R manuals (Jastak & Wilkinson, 1984; A. S. Kaufman & N. L. Kaufman, 1983). For the Woodcock-Johnson, the cutoff score was the 90th percentile. In these analyses, a child would have had to achieve a single score between 120 and 129 for the KABC, at least one of the three scores between 120 and 129 on the WRAT-R, or at least one of the six scores between the 90th and 96th percentile on the Woodcock-Johnson.

Chi-square analyses were conducted for each test separately. For the KABC, giftedness status was significantly associated with being in the range extending from 120 to 129 (χ^2 (1, N = 102) = 10.83, $p < .01$). For the WRAT-R, χ^2 (1, N = 100) = 13.78, $p < .001$). However, there was no significant association between giftedness status and scores in the 90th through 96th percentile on the Woodcock-Johnson (χ^2 (1, N = 104) = 5.43, $p > .05$) (Bonferroni corrected alpha). Hence, gifted children showed a very early pattern of both extremely high and high academic achievement at ages 5 and 6. At ages 7 and 8, gifted and nongifted children were not significantly different regarding scoring between the 90th and the 96th percentile, but gifted children were significantly more likely to score in the upper extreme of achievement.

A last analysis was conducted examining the association between giftedness status and obtaining multiple scores at these high and extremely superior levels. This was conducted only for the WRAT-R and the Woodcock-Johnson because these tests had multiple subscales. For the WRAT-R, there was no instance in which a child had all three scores at 130 or higher, and only one child achieved two scores at 130 or higher. Hence, achieving multiple extremely superior scores was rare on this test. The association between giftedness status and achieving multiple scores at or above 120 was tested. This was also of relatively low incidence, with only six and four children of the gifted and nongifted groups, respectively, scoring two out of three scores in that range. The chi-square test was not significant (χ^2 (1, N = 100) = .93, $p > .05$).

For the Woodcock-Johnson, there were six scores to use across ages 7 and 8. Six different patterns were examined: three out of six scores falling at or above the 97th percentile; five or six out of six scores falling at or above the 97th percentile; three out of six scores falling between the 90th and 96th percentile; five or six of the six scores falling between the 90th and 96th percentile; three out of six scores falling between the 90th and 99th percentile; five or six of the six scores falling between the 90th and 99th percentile. The rationale was to examine patterns for which half were at the cutoffs, and to examine the more extreme pattern in which almost all subtests were at that level. Results for all analyses examining three out of six subtests were significant as reported in Table 4.5, indicating that giftedness status was associated with obtaining these patterns. Again, the finding is particularly clear for the pattern pertaining to scores above the 97th percentile. Almost all children who had three of the six scores at that cutoff were gifted. However, across all analyses, a gifted child was more likely to evidence a pattern of three out of six scores in the specified ranges.

The analyses examining the incidence of five or six subscores falling at the specified ranges showed an extremely low incidence. For the 97th percentile and above, only three of the gifted and one of the nongifted had such a near-perfect pattern; for the analyses examining scores between the 90th and 96th percentiles, only two gifted and one nongifted child obtained five or six scores in that range. None of the chi squares for these analyses was significant. However, in examining the entire range extending from 90th to 99th percentile, giftedness status was significantly associated with obtaining five or six scores as reported in Table 4.5, which revealed that of the 17 children who had this pattern, 13 of them were gifted. Hence, if a child evidences a pattern of high achievement across subtests, and across age, there is an increased likelihood that the child is intellectually gifted.

In examining each child's pattern on the Woodcock-Johnson, it was apparent that the patterns were all different and showed no clearcut subject-area concentration. While the WRAT-R did show a concentration of extreme scores in reading, this was not replicated at ages 7 and 8, and it is impossible to determine if this concentration was due to age or the test itself. Therefore, it seems that it is more important to examine *any* extremely high score, rather than an extreme score in a particular subject area, as a sign of potential intellectual giftedness in children.

What do these patterns indicate? First, and foremost, much prior to children's identification as gifted in our study, and by schools in general, the achievement of gifted children was more likely than that of nongifted children to fall in the extremely high range. At ages 5 and 6, almost half of the gifted children scored at 130 or above on the KABC and WRAT-R. At ages 7 and 8, 70% of the gifted had at least one score

Table 4.5. Associations between Giftedness Status and Attainment of Multiple High and Extremely Superior Achievement Test Scores: Woodcock-Johnson

	Giftedness status		
Achievement test score	Gifted	Nongifted	χ^2
97th to 99th percentile: 3 out of 6 scores			
Yes	10 (50%)	2 (2%)	
No	10 (50%)	80 (98%)	31.37***
90th to 96th percentile: 3 out of 6 scores			
Yes	6 (30%)	7 (8%)	
No	14 (70%)	77 (92%)	27.73***
90th to 99th percentile: 3 out of 6 scores			
Yes	16 (80%)	12 (14%)	
No	4 (20%)	72 (86%)	32.47***
90th to 99th percentile: 5 or 6 out of 6 scores			
Yes	13 (65%)	4 (5%)	
No	7 (35%)	80 (95%)	38.57***

Note. Column percentages in parentheses. $df = 1$ for all analyses.
***$p < .001$.

at or above the 97th percentile, whereas only 19% of the nongifted group fell in that range. Moreover, 50% of the gifted had half of their scores in the extremely superior range, whereas only 2% of nongifted children had such a pattern. The gifted were also significantly more likely to have five or six subtests on the Woodcock-Johnson fall above the 90th percentile, with 65% of the gifted, and only 5% of the nongifted showing this pattern. Hence, it can be concluded that overall, the gifted show a strong pattern of high and superior achievement across measures and subtests.

However, the conclusion needs to be elaborated. There were five gifted children who showed no score in the extremely superior range although they did have scores between either 120 and 129 or the 90th to 96th percentile. Further, there was no specific age at which high and extremely high achievement patterns occurred except that the incidence of extreme scores increased across ages 7 and 8. If a particular age had been chosen at which to examine the occurrence of extremely superior scores, not all of the gifted children would have obtained that criterion. Over a 3-year period, 75% of the gifted scored at that level at least once. Hence, while it is highly likely that a child who is later identified as intellectually gifted will evidence at least one achievement test score in the extremely superior range, there is no specific age or subject area characteristic of this occurrence. For identification purposes, it would be wise to examine children's early achievement test histories over time to search for a single incidence of extreme scoring as an indication of potential intellectual giftedness. These scores may occur as young as age 5 on highly reliable and valid measures as used in this study.

Theoretically, these data indicate the uniqueness of each gifted child. Our findings are consistent with those of Roedell et al. (1980) in that not all gifted children evidenced superior achievement, although as a group the gifted are significantly stronger in achievement. Further, these results for achievement are consistent with our findings for intelligence in infancy and early childhood. In both the achievement and intellectual domains as reported in Chapter 3, gifted children are likely to evidence at least one superior score, and the group as a whole is significantly higher. Therefore, instead of expecting superior achievement or intellectual performance for the gifted at a single measurement time and measure, it may be more developmentally appropriate to adopt a repeated assessment approach.

Classroom Behavior and School Functioning

Teachers' ratings of children's functioning as gathered from their responses to the Child Behavior Checklist were analyzed with a 2 × 3 (Giftedness Status × Age: 6, 7, and 8 years) repeated-measures MANOVA in which Age was the repeated factor. Multiple dependent measures were teachers' ratings of children's behaviors in the following areas: hard working, well behaved, learning adequacy, and happiness. A significant, multivariate, main effect for Giftedness Status was obtained ($F(4,51) = 3.74, p < .01$). Univariate F values are presented in Table 4.6. Gifted children were rated as significantly harder working, better behaved, and learning more than the nongifted. However, the gifted and nongifted were not significantly different on the happiness rating. Both groups of children tended to be slightly above average in this latter rating. Regarding the other ratings, the mean for the gifted is about 6 (somewhat more than average), and the mean for the nongifted is between 4 (average) to 5 (slightly more than average).

Academic Intrinsic Motivation

Children's scores on the Young Children's Academic Intrinsic Motivation Inventory at ages 7 and 8 were analyzed with a 2 × 2 (Giftedness Status × Age: 7 and 8 years) repeated-measures MANOVA

Table 4.6. Comparisons of Means between Gifted and Nongifted Children: Teachers' Ratings of School Functioning across Ages 6, 7, and 8 Years

	Giftedness status		
Teachers' ratings	Gifted	Nongifted	Univariate F
Hard working	5.58 (1.1)	4.47 (1.6)	8.26^{**}
Behavior	5.80 (1.2)	4.62 (1.6)	9.48^{**}
Learning	6.08 (0.8)	4.89 (1.4)	13.07^{***}
Happy	5.41 (1.1)	4.92 (1.2)	3.04

Note. Standard deviations in parentheses. Ratings based on the teacher version of the Achenbach Child Behavior Checklist. $N = 56$.
$^{**}p < .01$. $^{***}p < .001$.

with Age as the repeated measure. The multiple dependent measures were Reading and Math subscales. A separate repeated-measures ANOVA, utilizing the same design, was conducted with the total motivation score as the dependent measure. Analyses were conducted on the scale averages, rather than the sum of the raw scores within the scales, because the total number of items comprising the scales differed at ages 7 and 8. A significant main effect for Giftedness Status was obtained for the subscale and the total score analyses (multivariate $F(2, 100) = 3.85$, $p = .02$, and univariate $F(1, 101) = 5.46$, $p = .02$, respectively). Univariate F tests for reading and math are reported in Table 4.7. Gifted children had significantly higher intrinsic motivation scores in reading, and for the Total score, but gifted children's intrinsic motivation for math was not significantly higher than nongifted children's.

Table 4.7. Comparisons of Means between Gifted and Nongifted Children: Academic Intrinsic Motivation across Ages 7 and 8 Years

	Giftedness status		
Motivation	Gifted	Nongifted	Univariate F
Reading	2.82 (.3)	2.62 (.4)	7.66^{**}
Math	2.66 (.3)	2.60 (.4)	.63
Total	2.74 (.2)	2.59 (.3)	5.46^{*}

Note. Standard deviations in parentheses. $N = 103$.
$^{*}p < .05$. $^{**}p < .01$.

Academic Anxiety and Perception of Competence

Findings for academic anxiety and perception of competence were consistent with those obtained for academic intrinsic motivation. A 2 × 2 (Giftedness Status × Age: 7 and 8 years) repeated-measures MANOVA was conducted on the reading and math items for anxiety and perception of competence separately. Scale averages were used. For both anxiety and perception of competence, the main effect for Giftedness Status was significant (multivariate $F(2, 100) = 6.58$ and 4.92, $p < .01$, for anxiety and perception of competence, respectively). Univariate F tests revealed significant differences between the gifted and nongifted across reading and math for anxiety, and in reading for perception of competence. The total scores for anxiety and perception of competence were analyzed with separate 2 × 2 (Giftedness Status × Age: 7 and 8 years) MANOVAs. Giftedness Status was significant in both analyses, as reported in Table 4.8. Univariate F values and group means for all analyses are reported in Table 4.8. The gifted had significantly lower anxiety, and significantly more positive perception of their academic competence, than the nongifted across all measures except perception of competence in math. Combined with the results reported for academic intrinsic motivation, the gifted children are significantly more motivated, less anxious, and perceive their academic performance more positively than

Table 4.8. Comparisons of Means between Gifted and Nongifted Children: Academic Anxiety and Perception of Competence across Ages 7 and 8 Years

	Giftedness status		
	Gifted	Nongifted	Univariate F
Academic anxiety			
Reading	1.18 (.4)	1.53 (.6)	12.37^{***}
Math	1.33 (.4)	1.63 (.6)	8.87^{**}
Total	1.25 (.3)	1.56 (.5)	11.12^{***}
Perception of competence			
Reading	2.95 (.2)	2.70 (.5)	9.41^{**}
Math	2.80 (.4)	2.64 (.6)	2.31
Total	2.88 (.2)	2.68 (.4)	7.64^{**}

Note. Standard deviations in parentheses. $N = 103$.
$^{**}p < .01$. $^{***}p < .001$.

nongifted children. However, their perceptions were stronger in reading than in math.

Cognitive Mastery Motivation: Infancy through Age 6

Examiners' ratings of each of the behaviors assessed on the Bayley Behavior Record were analyzed with separate repeated-measures ANOVAs. As not all measures were rated at each age, it was necessary to conduct analyses separately for the individual measures. The between-groups factor in each of the analyses was Giftedness Status. The repeated-measures factor was Age, with a different age span included for each measure as indicated in parentheses in Table 4.9. Univariate *F*s are reported in Table 4.9. As can be seen, the gifted and nongifted children differed significantly on several of the variables. The gifted evidenced significantly more goal directedness (task absorption), object orientation (interest in test materials), attention span (absorption in task), cooperativeness with examiner (enters into tasks enthusiastically), positive emotional tone (happiness), and reactivity to test materials. They were significantly less fearful in the testing situation. There were no significant differences in examiner orientation, energy, and activity between the gifted and nongifted. Object orientation (play) and deviant behavior were scored dichotomously. For each of these items, a 2 × 2 (Giftedness Status × Yes/No) chi-square analysis was conducted at each age it was measured. None of the analyses proved to be significant, indicating no differences between the gifted and nongifted on these measures.

These findings are noteworthy because they indicate specific behaviors that differentiate the gifted and nongifted as early as 18 months. In particular, the differences obtained for goal directedness, attention span, object orientation (interest in test materials), and reactivity provide evidence for the existence of a core of behaviors supportive of cognitive-motivational differences between gifted and nongifted children from infancy through 6 years. Other items suggest a more positive affective response to the tester and testing situation. Whereas temperamental differences between the gifted and nongifted children were not obtained on other measures in the present research, as reported in Chapter 5, the findings reported in this chapter are more specific to the testing situation rather than being indicative of more general temperamental variables. These data strongly suggest that the gifted orient

Table 4.9. Comparisons of Means between Gifted and Nongifted Children: Bayley Behavior Record

Behavior (ages assessed)	Giftedness status		Univariate F
	Gifted	Nongifted	
Examiner orientation (1.5–3.5 yrs)	3.81 (0.7)	3.43 (0.9)	5.81
Goal directedness (1.5–6 yrs)	6.08 (1.2)	5.00 (1.5)	23.16***
Object orientation (1.5–3.5 yrs)	6.62 (0.8)	5.75 (1.5)	24.13***
Attention span (1.5–6 yrs)	6.37 (1.2)	5.41 (1.6)	16.93***
Fearfulness (1.5–3.5 yrs)	1.44 (0.8)	2.05 (1.6)	7.33**
Cooperativeness (1.5–6 yrs)	6.63 (1.6)	5.51 (1.8)	17.87***
Emotional tone (1.5–6 yrs)	7.00 (1.0)	6.32 (1.5)	12.07***
Energy (1.5–3.5 yrs)	3.14 (0.7)	3.28 (0.6)	1.67
Activity (2.5–6 yrs)	5.00 (1.1)	5.06 (1.4)	.76
Reactivity (2.5–3.5 yrs)	6.26 (1.1)	5.13 (1.1)	20.61***

Note. Standard deviations in parentheses. Ages at which the items were administered are indicated in parentheses directly beneath each behavior. Items were included at ages for which they could be reliably measured. Repeated-measures ANOVAs were conducted across the ages for each item. *N*s varied from 86 to 99.
** $p < .01$. *** $p < .001$.

themselves to cognitive tasks more enthusiastically at an early age, and suggest that such behaviors may be used to identify children who readily engage themselves in such tasks. It is suggested that it is possible to identify "gifted motivational behaviors." In particular, goal directedness, attention span, object orientation, and stimulus reactivity behaviors are prime candidates for identification of such children. Moreover, these behaviors are conceptually relevant to theories of intrinsic motivation (A. E. Gottfried, 1986b), and factor analyses conducted by Matheny (1980) have identified these behaviors as a cognitive-mastery cluster.

SUMMARY

Overall, the picture of gifted children that emerges from this research is that they are not only higher on academic achievement, but also more motivationally engaged in their learning than nongifted children. Specific findings include the following:

1. Gifted children entered kindergarten at a younger age and were not retained at a later grade.
2. There were no differences between gifted and nongifted children in type of school attended.
3. The academic achievement of gifted children was significantly higher than that of nongifted children. These latter findings occur across different measures, subject areas, type of assessment, and across time from ages 5 through 8.
4. Gifted children were significantly more likely than nongifted children to obtain at least one extremely superior achievement test score between ages 5 and 8.
5. Gifted children are viewed by their teachers as significantly harder working, learning more, and better behaved than nongifted children. Gifted and nongifted children did not differ in teachers' ratings of being happy. Overall, gifted children appear to be more adapted to the demands of school than nongifted children.
6. Gifted children evidence stronger academic intrinsic motivation at ages 7 and 8 than nongifted children. Hence, compared to nongifted children, gifted children evidence stronger enjoyment of learning, orientation toward mastery, curiosity, persistence, task endogeny, and learning challenging, difficult, and novel tasks.
7. Gifted children have a more positive perception of academic competence, and lower academic anxiety, than nongifted children. Hence, gifted children are more confident in their educational accomplishments than nongifted children.
8. As early as infancy, and through the early childhood period, the gifted show significantly greater goal directedness, object orientation, attention span, cooperativeness, positive emotional tone, and responsivity to test materials.
9. It was suggested that the process of early identification of gifted children may benefit from examining motivationally relevant behaviors during testing, such as long attention span, persistence, and positive orientation toward materials, and that achievement test histories should be examined for the occurrence of at least one extremely superior score.

Our data are consistent with a body of evidence revealing that educational endeavors and academic achievement are particular strengths for gifted children. Moreover, gifted children appear to be more favorably adapted than nongifted children to the demands of the educational environment cognitively, motivationally, and behaviorally.

5

Behavioral Adjustment, Social Functioning, and Temperament

ISSUES

In this chapter, the behavioral and emotional adjustment, social functioning, and temperamental characteristics of gifted and nongifted children during infancy and early childhood are investigated to determine whether intellectual giftedness was associated with these areas. Three major issues were examined:

1. The gifted were stereotyped at the turn of the twentieth century as maladjusted; current stereotypes of the gifted continue to include an element of aberrant behavior. Therefore, the first issue addressed relates to the issue of behavioral adjustment: Is intellectual giftedness associated with increased or decreased behavioral and emotional competency during the early years of development, or is it unrelated to these aspects of functioning?

2. In Chapters 3 and 4, gifted children revealed superior performance in intellectual and academic performance during the early years. In this chapter, we examine whether these superior cognitive skills generalize to children's social functioning. Three areas of social functioning were investigated: social cognition, personal and social competence, and the nature of children's social interactions. With respect to social cognition, we examined problem solving in hypothetical interpersonal conflictual situations. The question posed is whether the social reasoning of gifted children is elevated compared to their nongifted cohort.

The next issue addressed in the area of social functioning is personal-social sufficiency. The questions investigated included the following: Do gifted compared to nongifted children differ in their personal-social sufficiency? Is it the case that gifted children are advanced in self-help responsibilities, interpersonal communication, and socialization skills?

Some have suggested that although gifted children may be able to reason at higher levels about social issues or dilemmas, their sociability or interactions as a group are indistinguishable from their nongifted peers. On the contrary, stereotypes of the gifted as socially isolated are still prevalent. Thus, a final issue addressed with respect to social functioning is whether gifted and nongifted children differ in their socialization preferences with respect to play behavior, such as playing alone or playing with older children.

3. The third major issue addressed relates to temperament. Temperament has been demonstrated to relate to teacher ratings of academic achievement and standardized achievement test scores, perhaps because certain behavioral styles facilitate the acquisition of information. Do children who become gifted exhibit similar or different temperament characteristics as a group in comparison to their nongifted peers during early development?

DESCRIPTION OF MEASURES

Behavioral and Emotional Adjustment

A variety of scales and informants was utilized to assess children's behavioral and emotional adjustment. Children's adjustment was assessed annually at ages 3 through 8 years using a combination of parent and/or teacher reports.

Eyberg Child Behavior Inventory

The 36 items on this inventory assess a wide range of parental concerns (Eyberg, 1980). The parent responds to each item using two response formats. First, the parent indicates the frequency of occurrence of each behavior on a scale from 1 ("never occurs") to 7 ("always occurs"). These ratings are summed to yield an overall *problem behavior intensity or frequency* score. Second, the parent indicates by circling "yes" or "no" whether the behavior is a problem for him or her. The "yes" responses are counted to obtain the *total problem* score. This scale was administered at the 3.25-year home visit.

Preschool Behavior Questionnaire

This behavior checklist, completed by the parent at the 3.5-year assessment, consists of 30 items. It yields scores for three scales (hostile-aggressive, anxious, and hyperactive-distractible) and a total behavior disturbed score (Behar & Stringfield, 1974).

Child Behavior Checklist

The Child Behavior Checklist is a well-known scale in the field of developmental psychopathology. Two versions of the scale were utilized: Parent Report Form and Teacher Report Form. Each version consists of 112 problem items; for each item, the respondent circles 0 ("not true"), 1 ("somewhat or sometimes true"), or 2 ("very true or often true") about the target child. Ratings are summed to yield scores representing two broadband diagnostic categories, designated as internalizing and externalizing, representing overcontrolled and undercontrolled behavioral difficulties, respectively (Achenbach, 1991a, 1991b). Also, a total behavior problem score is obtained. The Parent Report Form was administered when children were ages 4, 5, 6, 7, and 8 years. The Teacher Report Form was administered at ages 6, 7, and 8 years (once children had entered formal schooling) and is similar in format and scoring to the parent version. Although many identical items are present on both the parent and teacher report forms, there are also many unique items that relate to behaviors specific to the home and classroom settings, respectively.

Social Functioning

Social functioning was assessed in three ways: (1) by directly examining children's social reasoning skills during the preschool period, (2) through parent reports of the child's personal and social sufficiency skills at ages 6 and 8 years, and (3) by parent and teacher reports on specific items relating to children's social functioning on the Child Behavior Checklist at ages 4 through 8 years (parent) and 6 through 8 years (teacher).

Preschool Interpersonal Problem-Solving Test

This test assesses the ability of the child to generate alternative solutions to two interpersonal conflict situations, one involving a conflict with mother and the other a conflict with another child (Shure & Spivak, 1974). A higher score signifies a greater number of alternatives generated by the child. This scale was administered to children at the 3.5-year assessment.

Vineland Adaptive Behavior Scales

This established scale, which assesses personal sufficiency, social functioning, and adaptability, yields three domain scores: Communication, Daily Living Skills, and Socialization; the combination of these three scales yields the Adaptive Behavior Composite (Sparrow, Balla, & Cicchetti, 1984). These scales are standardized with a mean of 100 (*SD* = 15); standard scores were analyzed. The Vineland Adaptive Behavior Scales semistructured interview was conducted with a parent (almost exclusively the mother) when children were 6 and 8 years old.

Temperament

The temperament measures utilized in the FLS were based on the behavioral-style framework developed by Thomas, Chess, and colleagues in the New York Longitudinal Study (Thomas et al., 1968). Within this framework, temperament is defined as the *how* of behavior, as opposed to the why, the what, or the how well of behavior. Based on their interviews with parents of young children, Thomas et al. delineated nine temperament dimensions and three temperamental constellations. The "difficult" temperament constellation is perhaps the most widely used concept in the temperament literature, having at its core frequent and intense expression of negative affect (cf. Bates, 1980; Prior, 1992). Temperamental difficultness was assessed when children were 1.5 years of age; beyond the infancy period, the nine NYLS temperament dimensions served as the level of analysis. The nine dimensions in the Thomas and Chess model include activity level, rhythmicity, approach, adaptability, negative mood, intensity, distractibility, threshold, and persistence. These were described in more detail in Chapter 1.

Temperament characteristics were assessed at six points in time during the infancy, toddler, preschool, and early school years using five different temperament scales as required by age level. The temperament scales utilized possess acceptable levels of reliability (Hubert, Wachs, Peters-Martin, & Gandour, 1982). In our research program, we have found parental reports to show stability across the infant, preschool, and early elementary years and convergent validity across inventories (Guerin & A. W. Gottfried, in press-a, in press-b).

Infant Characteristics Questionnaire (ICQ)

This inventory, designed specifically to assess difficult temperament, consists of 32 items, each of which is rated by the parent on a scale from 1 (optimal temperament trait) to 7 (difficult temperament trait). Four scores, representing scales identified through factor analysis, are obtained: I. Fussy/Difficult/Demanding; II. Unadaptable; III. Persistent; IV. Unsociable (Bates, Freeland, & Lounsbury, 1979). Hubert et al. (1982) noted that the ICQ possessed high test-retest reliability for the difficult factor and an acceptable level of internal consistency. Internal reliability coefficients in our sample were .82, .67, .59, and .53, respectively. This inventory was administered when the children were 1.5 years of age.

Toddler Temperament Scale

The Toddler Temperament Scale was designed to assess temperament in 1- to 3-year-old children (Fullard, McDevitt, & Carey, 1984). Using a scale from 1 ("almost never") to 6 ("almost always"), the parent indicates for each of 97 items how often the child exhibits a given behavior. The scale yields nine temperament scores corresponding to the nine NYLS temperament dimensions. Standardization research demonstrated satisfactory reliability for the scale. Coefficient alphas ranged from .53 to .85 with a median of .72 for the nine temperament dimensions; test-retest reliabilities over a 1-month interval ranged from .69 to .89 (median $r = .81$). In this sample, coefficient alphas ranged from .48 to .86 with a median $r = .64$. The Toddler Temperament Scale was administered at the 2-year assessment.

Colorado Child Temperament Inventory

This parent report inventory assesses six temperament characteristics derived through factor-analytic methods: sociability, emotionality, activity, attention span/persistence, reaction to food, and soothability (Buss & Plomin, 1984). Thirty items are rated from 1 ("strongly disagree") to 5 ("strongly agree"). It was completed when children were 3.5 years of age.

Behavioral Style Questionnaire

This 100-item questionnaire was designed to assess temperament of 3- to 7-year-olds; it is also completed by the parent (using the same response format as the Toddler Temperament Scale) and yields scores representing the nine temperament dimensions delineated by Thomas et al. (McDevitt & Carey, 1978). In the standardization of the scale, coefficient alphas ranged from .47 to .84 for the nine dimensions (total instrument alpha = .84). For the present sample, coefficient alphas averaged separately for each of the nine dimensions across the three assessment ages (3, 3.5, and 5 years) ranged from .46 to .82 with a median of $r = .69$.

Middle Childhood Temperament Questionnaire

This questionnaire, designed to assess temperament in 8- to 12-year-olds, follows the same format as the Toddler Temperament Scale and Behavioral Style Questionnaire; the 99 items assess the nine NYLS temperament dimensions with the exception of biological rhythmicity, which was replaced with a dimension labeled predictability/quality of organization (Hegvik, McDevitt, & Carey, 1982). There is conceptual overlap between the predictability dimension and biological rhythmicity in that both assess regularity of behavior; however, predictability deals with task performance and social behavior rather than biological functioning. Coefficient alphas ranged from .71 to .87 with a median of .81 for the nine dimensions (Hegvik et al., 1982). The Middle Childhood Temperament Questionnaire was completed by a parent during the 8-year assessment.

RESULTS

Behavioral and Emotional Adjustment

There are conflicting reports in the literature as to whether gifted children exhibit superior, normal, or poorer adjustment compared to children with average intelligence. As noted in Chapter 1, early stereotypes of the gifted as emotionally unstable, socially inept social isolates have not been substantiated through empirical investigation. Nor has the notion that genius is linked to insanity. However, there are no studies of young children who become intellectually gifted. Consequently, the behavioral, emotional, social, and temperamental antecedents of children who become gifted are unknown.

Overall, our results showed that the behavioral and emotional adjustment of the gifted and nongifted groups was indistinguishable. The gifted group demonstrated neither better nor worse behavioral and emotional adjustment than their nongifted age-mates.

Behavior problems were first assessed during the preschool years using the Eyberg Child Behavior Inventory (3.25 years) and the Preschool Behavior Questionnaire (3.5 years). Although the nongifted group was scored higher by parents on behavior problem intensity ($M = 114.2$) and number of problems ($M = 5.6$) than the gifted group (Ms = 103.6 and 4.0, respectively), a one-way MANOVA with the two dependent variables indicated no overall significant difference between gifted and nongifted groups on the Eyberg Child Behavior Inventory (multivariate $F(2, 102) = 2.01, p > .05$). Burns, Patterson, Nussbaum, and Parker (1991) recently published mean intensity and problem scores for the Eyberg Child Behavior Inventory based on a large sample of parent or guardian responses collected in five outpatient pediatric clinics in four Northwestern states. Data from our gifted and nongifted groups and the Burns et al. sample are displayed in Figure 5.1. The Burns et al. sample comprised over 1,300 children brought into clinics for checkups or for a temporary or chronic illness who were not being treated for a learning disability or behavior problem. The frequency/intensity scores of all groups are similar, with the gifted group average slightly lower than that of the nonclinical group reported by Burns et al.; the average for the nongifted group was the highest of the three. With respect to the Eyberg problem scores, all group averages were again quite similar, with the gifted-group average the lowest of the three groups.

The Preschool Behavior Questionnaire contains four scales, one of which represents an overall total score. This total scale score was analyzed with a t test; the remaining three scale scores were analyzed using a one-way MANOVA with the scales as the dependent variables. Results showed that the nongifted group was rated slightly higher on all four indexes, with means on total behavior disturbed, hostile-aggressive, anxious, and hyperactive-distractible scales of 14.2, 5.6, 3.3, 2.6 for gifted children and 16.1, 6.6, 4.0, 3.2 for nongifted children, respectively. As with the Eyberg, no significant differences were detected between the

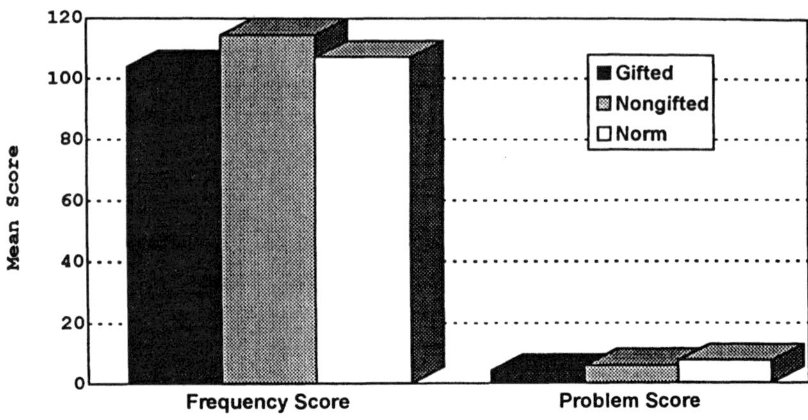

Figure 5.1. Average frequency and problem scores for gifted, nongifted, and normative groups on the Eyberg Child Behavior Inventory.

two groups (total behavior disturbed scale, $t(93) = 1.32, p > .05$; remaining three scales, multivariate $F(3, 92) = 0.88, p > .05$).

Internalizing, externalizing, and total behavior problem mean scores on the Child Behavior Checklist are displayed in Table 5.1 (parent report) and Table 5.2 (teacher report). An inspection of these data indicated that the distributions of scores for both groups were positively skewed (i.e., scores clustered at the lower end of the distributions). This would be typical and expected on a scale assessing the occurrence of psychopathology because most individuals in this study were free of behavioral and emotional problems. Due to the extremity of the skew, the nonparametric test statistic Mann-Whitney *U* was used to analyze the internalizing, externalizing, and total behavior problem scores of gifted versus nongifted groups. There was no evidence of significant group differences in behavior problems, either from parent or teacher reports (all *p*s > .05). The gifted and nongifted groups were also compared in terms of the number of children displaying scores above the clinical cutoff level (98th percentile) on the total behavior problem score at each age. Table 5.3 displays the percentage of children in the normal and clinical behavior problem ranges for the gifted and nongifted groups. As shown in Table 5.3, although the gifted group evidenced slightly lower rates of problems in the clinical range, all chi-square tests

Table 5.1. Comparisons of Means between Gifted and Nongifted Children: Child Behavior Checklist (Parent Report Form)

	Giftedness status	
Scale	Gifted	Nongifted
4 years (*N* = 92)		
Internalizing	10.7 (8.6)	12.0 (8.0)
Externalizing	10.5 (7.2)	12.7 (8.8)
Total	25.7 (15.8)	29.6 (16.7)
5 years (*N* = 102)		
Internalizing	9.1 (7.1)	9.9 (7.2)
Externalizing	7.9 (4.4)	9.3 (7.1)
Total	21.2 (12.1)	23.7 (14.3)
6 years (*N* = 99)		
Internalizing	7.1 (5.0)	7.9 (6.9)
Externalizing	11.0 (5.2)	12.8 (9.6)
Total	20.1 (10.3)	23.9 (17.2)
7 years (*N* = 106)		
Internalizing	6.9 (5.5)	9.2 (7.8)
Externalizing	10.8 (8.4)	12.4 (9.4)
Total	19.2 (13.3)	24.2 (17.9)
8 years (*N* = 104)		
Internalizing	5.4 (5.4)	7.6 (6.9)
Externalizing	8.3 (7.7)	10.1 (8.7)
Total	16.3 (13.9)	19.9 (15.9)

Note. Standard deviations in parentheses. No between-groups differences were statistically significant; all *ps* > .05.

were nonsignificant. Despite these nonsignificant differences, examination of the means reveals that without exception, behavior and emotional problem scores were consistently lower for gifted compared to nongifted children on the Parent Report Form. This was also true of the externalizing and total behavior problem scores on the Teacher Report Form. For teacher-reported internalizing problems, differences were inconsistent in terms of favoring gifted or nongifted children.

In addition to the broadband internalizing and externalizing categories, there are also eight narrow-band behavior problem scores on the Child Behavior Checklist. These scores reflect the following behavior problem categories: withdrawn, somatic complaints, anxious/depressed, social problems, thought problems, attention problems, delin-

Table 5.2. Comparisons of Means between Gifted and Nongifted Children: Child Behavior Checklist (Teacher Report Form)

	Giftedness status	
Scale	Gifted	Nongifted
6 years (N = 84)		
Internalizing	5.3 (5.6)	4.6 (4.9)
Externalizing	8.2 (7.8)	11.6 (14.2)
Total	14.7 (13.7)	17.2 (17.3)
7 years (N = 85)		
Internalizing	3.4 (3.8)	3.4 (4.1)
Externalizing	5.3 (7.3)	11.6 (15.2)
Total	9.3 10.6)	16.1 (18.8)
8 years (N = 92)		
Internalizing	4.6 (5.2)	4.5 (5.0)
Externalizing	6.3 (7.1)	11.5 (13.5)
Total	11.9 (12.1)	17.2 (16.7)

Note. Standard deviations in parentheses. No between-groups differences were statistically significant; all *ps* > .05.

Table 5.3. Percentage of Gifted and Nongifted Children Scoring in Normal and Clinical Ranges on the Child Behavior Checklist (Parent and Teacher Forms)

	Giftedness status				
	Gifted		Nongifted		
Age (yrs)	Normal	Clinical	Normal	Clinical	χ^2
Parent Report Form					
4	83.3	16.7	83.8	16.2	0.00
5	100.0	0.0	91.6	8.4	0.65
6	100.0	0.0	88.9	11.1	1.06
7	95.0	5.0	89.5	10.5	0.11
8	95.0	5.0	91.7	8.3	0.00
Teacher Report Form					
6	88.9	11.1	95.4	4.5	0.23
7	100.0	0.00	94.0	6.0	0.19
8	100.0	0.00	97.3	2.7	0.00

Note. *Ns* range from 92 to 106 for the Parent Report Form and from 84 to 92 for the Teacher Report Form. No between-groups differences were statistically significant; all *ps* > .05.

quent behavior, and aggressive behavior. Narrow-band category scores are obtained by summing the 0, 1, or 2 ratings given by respondents for the items loading on the category. In order to compare gifted and nongifted groups on these narrow-band categories, average category scores were computed for each group. These means, along with the cutoff score separating the normal range from clinical behavior problem scores for each category, are displayed in Figure 5.2 for behavior problems from 4 through 8 years (parent reports) and 6 through 8 years (teacher reports). Child Behavior Checklist norms differ slightly for boys and girls; cutoff scores displayed on these figures were averaged for boys and girls. This approach was chosen because we wanted to compare the gifted and nongifted groups on the narrow-band categories, but did not wish to base our comparison on the smaller groups that would result if data were analyzed separately for males and females. As our gifted and nongifted groups both had similar proportions of males and females (see Chapter 6), we deemed this approach acceptable for purposes of examining the relative averages of the gifted and nongifted groups to each other, as well as to the normal-range cutoff. On all figures, the results are striking in demonstrating two major findings: (1) the gifted and nongifted groups are not markedly different from each other, and (2) averages of both groups are well below the normal-range cutoff. These results extend those of the broadband categories in showing that gifted children exhibit similar levels of adjustment to those of nongifted children. On these eight narrow-band categories representing finer delineations of internalizing behavior problems (withdrawn, somatic complaints, anxious/depressed) and externalizing problems (delinquent behavior, aggressive behavior), the gifted and nongifted groups are strikingly similar.

Hence, across three different measures of behavioral adjustment (Child Behavior Inventory, Preschool Behavior Questionnaire, Child Behavior Checklist) and with both parents and teachers as informants, there were no significant differences between gifted and nongifted groups from age 3.25 years to age 8 years. Our data indicate that intellectually gifted children are neither advantaged nor disadvantaged in the behavioral and emotional adjustment realms during early childhood compared to their nongifted age-mates. Previous researchers have shown that gifted children are at least as well adjusted or evidence fewer behavioral problems than children of average intelligence. Ludwig and Cullinan (1984), who investigated teacher ratings of first- through fifth-grade gifted and nongifted children using the Behavior Problem Checklist, found that teachers reported fewer behavior problems for gifted

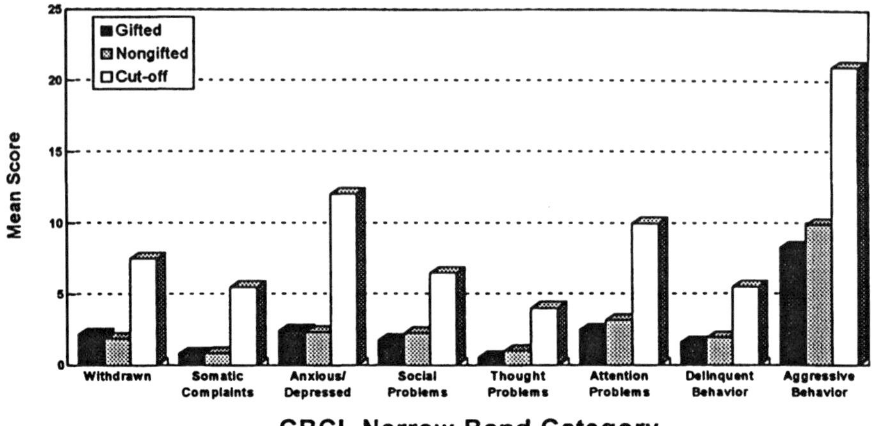

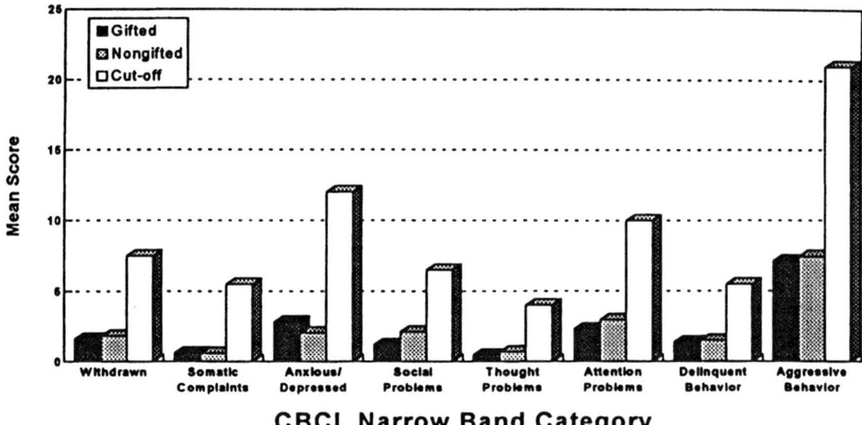

Figure 5.2. Average scores for gifted and nongifted groups and normal cutoff scores on the narrow-band categories of the Child Behavior Checklist (CBCL) Parent Report Form (4–8 years) and Teacher Report Form (6–8 years).

Parent Report - 6 Years

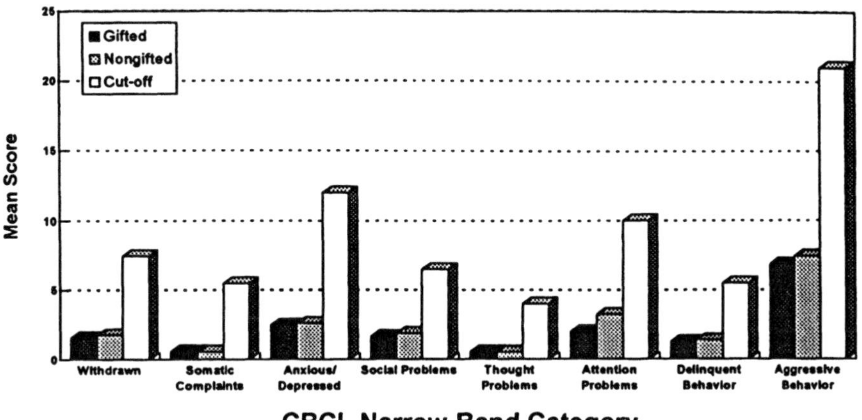

CBCL Narrow Band Category

Parent Report - 7 Years

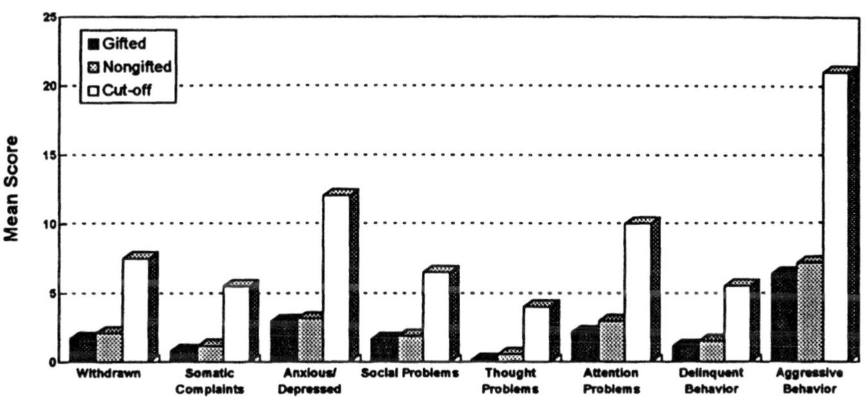

CBCL Narrow Band Category

than nongifted children. This is in line with our trend cited above, as well as with better classroom behavior of the gifted reported in Chapter 4. Lehman and Erdwins (1981) reported that gifted third graders were less aggressive and destructive and had fewer acting-out behaviors than third graders of average IQ. Studying Israeli children in grades 4 through 8, R. M. Milgram and N. A. Milgram (1976) reported less anxiety

Parent Report - 8 Years

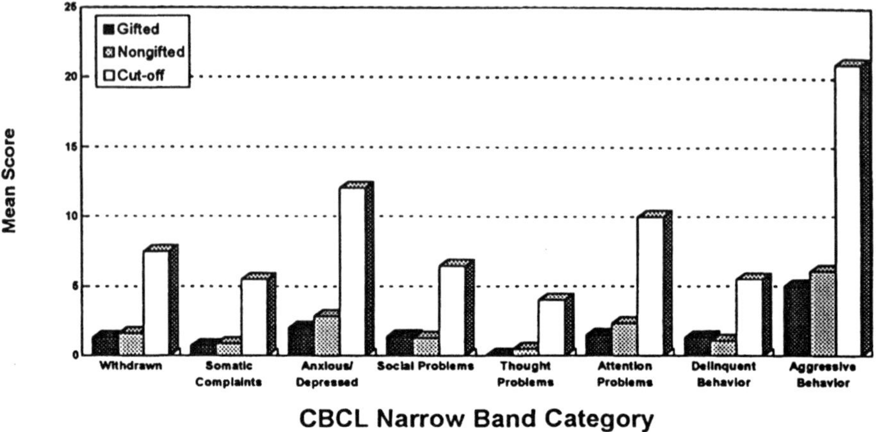

Teacher Report - 6 Years

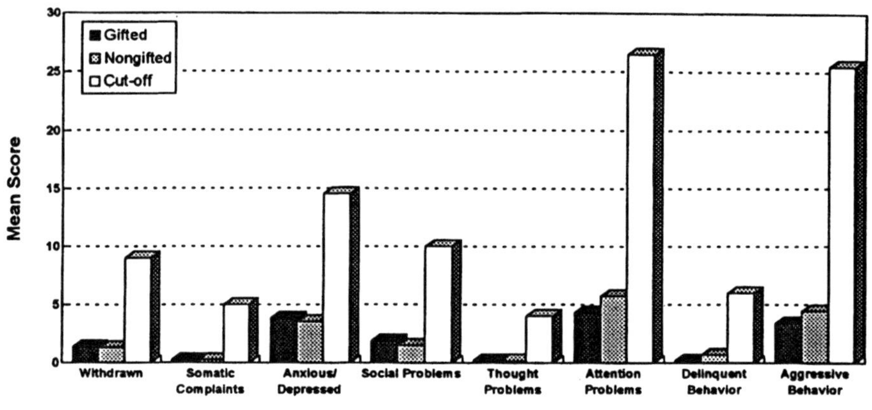

Figure 5.2. *(continued)*

and fewer indicators of psychological disturbance among gifted compared to nongifted children. Gallucci (1988) found no differences between normative data and parent, camp counselor, and teacher reports on the Child Behavior Checklist for gifted 12- to 16-year-olds. Luthar et

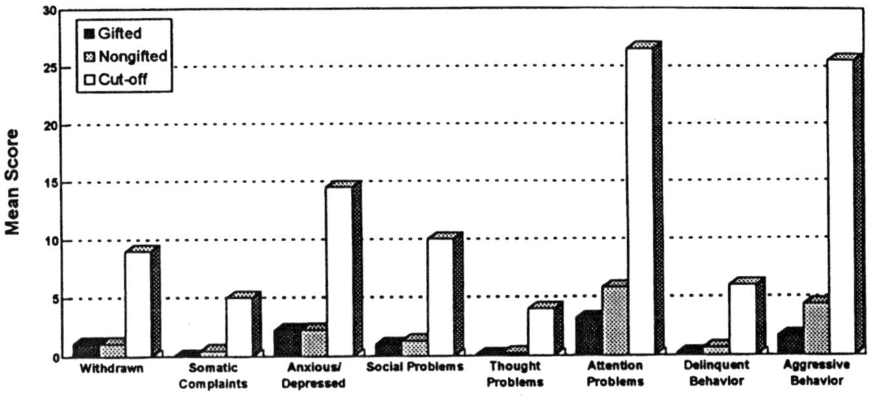

CBCL Narrow Band Category

Teacher Report - 8 Years

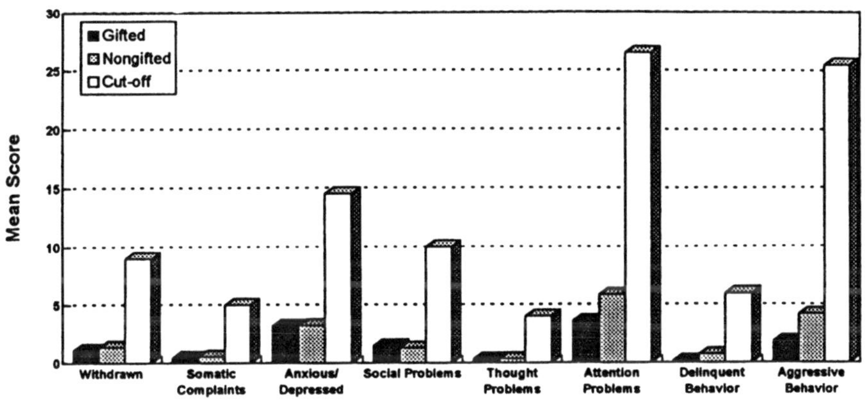

CBCL Narrow Band Category

al. (1992) reported that high-achieving gifted adolescents showed more positive adjustment than age-mates not identified as gifted.

In studies where the gifted have been found to exhibit superior adjustment, researchers have noted that the selection of research participants in the gifted group may have contributed to the findings (Ludwig

& Cullinan, 1984; Pendarvis et al., 1990). When a study involves comparing children participating in a gifted program to those in a regular educational classroom, there is the possibility of referral (identification or ascertainment) bias. Better-behaved children may be selected to participate in gifted programs. It is possible that other equally gifted children with behavior difficulties failed to be identified for participation in the gifted program. An analogous situation (although the inverse of the selection problem with respect to giftedness) has been observed in the learning disabilities field with respect to dyslexia. Children who were dyslexic and also had problem behaviors were more likely to be identified for special education programming, while dyslexics with good behavior were more likely to be overlooked (S. E. Shaywitz, B. A. Shaywitz, Fletcher, & Escobar, 1990; see also Guerin, Griffin, A. W. Gottfried, & Christenson, 1993).

Because all children in the FLS were individually assessed to determine giftedness status, selection or ascertainment bias was not operating in the formation of the giftedness groups. Moreover, the fact that our comparison group of nongifted children was not constructed, but emerged from the same cohort of children, further enhances the validity of our findings. In addition, our groups comprise students attending a variety of schools in a variety of communities. With respect to the aforementioned studies on behavioral adjustment, two studies showing superior adjustment among gifted children did involve formation of groups based on school identification procedures (Lehman & Erdwins, 1981; Ludwig & Cullinan, 1984); school selection or identification was also likely in the R. M. Milgram and N. A. Milgram (1976) study finding superior behavior among gifted children. Gallucci's (1988) sample, which did not show differences with the Child Behavior Checklist normative group, consisted of 12- to 16-year-olds attending a residential summer camp for intellectually superior children who had met the criterion for admission of a Stanford-Binet IQ score greater than 135. The intellectually and academically gifted 12- to 15-year-old adolescents studied by Luthar et al. (1992) were participating in a special summer university program. Initial selection of the group was on the basis of high SAT scores; subsequent selection criteria, if any, were not specified.

Social Functioning

In this section, we examine social functioning with regard to children's intellectual giftedness status. Three sets of data pertain to this issue. First, the social reasoning skills of the children were assessed using the Preschool Interpersonal Problem-Solving Test at age 3.5 years. Second, the children's personal and social sufficiency skills were examined using the Vineland Adaptive Behavior Scales. Finally, parent and teacher responses to specific items of the Child Behavior Checklist relating to the nature of social interactions with other children were investigated.

On the Preschool Interpersonal Problem-Solving Test, the child is asked to generate as many solutions to two social dilemmas as possible. Our results showed that the number of solutions offered by gifted children ($M = 3.9$, $SD = 2.3$) was significantly greater than the number generated by nongifted children ($M = 2.3$, $SD = 1.7$; $t(100) = 3.47$, $p < .001$). These results are in line with those of Roedell (1989), who also reported that children with higher IQs scored higher on the Preschool Interpersonal Problem-Solving Test. It is important to note, however, that Roedell also reported that this knowledge was not reflected in the children's behavior; children with higher scores did not necessarily engage in more cooperative behavior when observed in the preschool classroom.

The Vineland Adaptive Behavior Scales assess the ability to perform daily activities required for personal and social sufficiency. Gifted children were reported as significantly more mature on all scales of this test. A 2 × 2 repeated-measures (Giftedness Status × Age: 6 and 8 years) ANOVA revealed that the gifted children scored significantly higher on the overall Adaptive Behavior Composite. The means, standard deviations, and *F* statistics are displayed in Table 5.4. Gifted children also scored significantly higher on the three domain scales of Communica-

Table 5.4. Comparison of Means between Gifted and Nongifted Children: Adaptive Behavior Composite and Domains of the Vineland Adaptive Behavior Scales

	Giftedness status		
Vineland scale	Gifted	Nongifted	Univariate *F*
Adaptive Behavior Composite	111.2 (9.3)	97.1 (13.4)	24.17***
Communication Skills	119.4 (9.4)	101.2 (14.6)	33.49***
Daily Living Skills	102.8 (9.0)	96.2 (11.7)	8.34**
Socialization	102.8 (8.5)	96.8 (11.1)	7.01**

Note. Standard deviations in parentheses. $N = 99$.
**$p < .01$. ***$p < .001$.

tion, Daily Living Skills, and Socialization as revealed by a repeated-measures 2 × 2 (Giftedness Status × Age: 6 and 8 years) MANOVA (multivariate $F(3, 95) = 11.06, p < .001$).

These findings are supported by those of Lehman and Erdwins (1981), who compared 16 third graders in a gifted program to those in regular classes on personality; they also reported that intellectually gifted children were quite well adjusted. More specifically, Lehman and Erdwins found that the gifted as a group scored higher than their age-mates on sense of personal worth, social skills, and school relations.

Four items on the Child Behavior Checklist assess the nature of children's social interactions with peers and relate directly to issues discussed at length in the literature. These items, "Complains of loneliness," "Likes to be alone," "Prefers playing with older children," and "Withdrawn," were examined individually to determine whether parents and teachers reported these behaviors as more or less characteristic of gifted compared to nongifted children (see Tables 5.5 and 5.6). Due to the relatively small number in the gifted group as well as the highly infrequent rating of a "2" on these items, ratings of "1" ("somewhat or sometimes true") and "2" ("very true or often true") on the Child Behavior Checklist were combined to produce a dichotomy (behavior present or not present). Chi-square analyses were conducted for each item at each age. The results of each 2 × 2 (Giftedness Status × Behavior: Present vs. Not Present) test were consistent in that there were no significant differences between the gifted and nongifted children on these four items for ages 4 through 8 years.

On these Child Behavior Checklist items specifically relating to social isolation and a preference for socializing with older children, the gifted and nongifted were indistinguishable. All but one of the 32 chi-square tests were nonsignificant; one statistically significant difference would be expected by chance alone. There was no evidence of excessive social isolation among the gifted observed for the first item, "Complains of loneliness." This was marked "present" for a minority of both the gifted and nongifted groups, especially by teachers. No statistical differences were revealed between gifted and nongifted children, indicating that gifted children were not more likely to be socially isolated than nongifted children.

On the next item, "Likes playing alone," sizable percentages of both gifted and nongifted children were rated by parents as preferring to play alone. Chi-square tests indicated that none of the observed differences reached the .05 level of significance. Hence, gifted and

Table 5.5. Percentage of Gifted and Nongifted Children Displaying Specific Social Behaviors (Parent Report)

	Giftedness status		
Age of child (yrs)	Gifted	Nongifted	χ^2
Complains of loneliness			
4	27.8	20.3	0.14
5	31.6	21.7	0.38
6	16.7	19.8	0.00
7	15.0	17.4	0.00
8	20.0	11.9	0.35
Likes to be alone			
4	55.6	43.2	0.46
5	47.4	48.2	0.00
6	44.4	48.1	0.00
7	60.0	37.2	2.60
8	45.0	35.7	0.26
Prefers playing with older children			
4	66.7	75.7	0.23
5	47.4	63.9	1.14
6	77.8	59.3	1.44
7	65.0	55.8	0.25
8	70.0	38.1	5.43*
Withdrawn, doesn't get involved with others			
4	16.7	5.4	1.26
5	0.0	4.8	0.10
6	11.1	4.9	0.20
7	10.0	8.1	0.00
8	0.0	3.6	0.01

Note. Ns ranged from 92 to 106.
*$p < .05$.

nongifted children were equally likely to play alone according to both parent and teacher reports.

Our data from both teachers and parents do not support the view that gifted children prefer older playmates. These data are not in accord with Terman's conclusion. Terman found that teachers and parents reported a greater preference among the gifted to play with older children. There are several possibilities to account for this discrepancy. Terman's data may reflect a cohort-specific effect. Parents of today may

Table 5.6. Percentage of Gifted and Nongifted Children Displaying Specific Behaviors (Teacher Report)

	Giftedness status		
Age of child (yrs)	Gifted	Nongifted	χ^2
Complains of loneliness			
6	5.6	3.0	0.00
7	0.0	1.5	0.00
8	5.6	5.4	0.00
Likes to be alone			
6	33.3	15.2	1.97
7	27.8	9.0	2.95
8	27.8	16.2	0.63
Prefers playing with older children			
6	11.1	9.1	0.00
7	16.7	10.4	0.00
8	5.6	12.2	0.15
Withdrawn, doesn't get involved with others			
6	11.1	6.1	0.05
7	11.1	3.0	0.67
8	5.6	9.5	0.00

Note. *N*s ranged from 84 to 92. No between-groups differences were statistically significant; all *p*s > .05.

be less inclined to allow their children to play with children who are older, due to the nature of contemporary society. In the school setting, such a finding may not emerge because children spend so much time in age-graded classrooms; little opportunity may exist for cross-age play. There may also be a sentiment against accelerating the grade level of gifted children today in comparison to practices and attitudes in place during the childhood years of Terman's study. In fact, 84.9% of Terman's sample skipped at least one grade level. Finally, Terman's conclusions were based on descriptive and not inferential statistics. Thus, it is not known whether the percentages he reported were statistically different.

Finally, there were also no reliable differences between gifted and nongifted children in terms of the fourth item, "Withdrawn." This item was indicated as present by low numbers of both parents and teachers.

An additional set of questions on the parent version of the Child Behavior Checklist relate to children's social interaction and sufficiency:

(1) the child's number of friends; (2) frequency of interactions with friends; and (3) how well the child gets along with siblings, other children, parents, and how well the child plays or works by himself or herself. Chi-square analyses comparing the gifted and nongifted groups on these items at ages 4 through 8 years failed to detect any significant differences (all *ps* > .05).

Thus, gifted children enjoy the same level of social participation and involvement as their nongifted counterparts during their preschool and early elementary years. Parent and teacher reports on the Child Behavior Checklist items indicated that gifted children were not as a group more withdrawn than nongifted children, nor were they more likely to complain of loneliness or to prefer playing alone. Additionally, the gifted and nongifted groups were indistinguishable in terms of the number of friends, frequency of contacts with friends, how well they interacted with siblings, parents, and friends, or how well they played or worked alone. These findings are in accord with Terman's (1925) study showing that gifted children are not social isolates. Stereotypes that gifted children are socially inept or isolated are without foundation. Our scientific evidence shows that gifted children in the IQ range we studied are socially capable and appropriately engaged in friendships and social interactions with others.

Caveat

We detected no evidence of social disadvantage among our sample during their early development. In fact, we found our intellectually gifted children to be socially adept. However, subgroups of gifted children have been identified as at risk with respect to adjustment. Hollingworth (1942) noted that individuals who tested in excess of 160 or 170 IQ experienced difficult problems of adjustment to life. She noted that the highly gifted are not, as a group, problems for society, but rather that they suffered problems of adjustment in large part due to their deviation from the normal level of intelligence. She delineated several problems that the *highly* gifted were prone to experience:

1. *Physical disadvantages.* Due to their acceleration in school and because the highly gifted naturally choose older children as friends, they are often at a disadvantage in physical competition. Hence, they tend to choose sedentary activities or solitary, noncompetitive types of physical activities.

2. *Impaired self-confidence.* Because of age and smaller physical size compared to their grade-mates, the highly gifted are less likely to be selected for positions of leadership in school. This can lead to lowered self-confidence, feelings of social inferiority, and shyness (especially for males during adolescence).

3. *Poor adjustment to occupation.* If the highly gifted are not recognized in school and adequately challenged, they may not learn how to work hard and persevere at a difficult task. As adults, Hollingworth suggested that these individuals would tend to spread themselves too thin and/or fail to complete difficult tasks encountered in the work environment.

4. *Poor tolerance.* Because their intellectual abilities are so superior to others, Hollingworth proposed that the highly gifted may be prone to contentious or aggressive behavior.

5. *Isolation.* Hollingworth observed that children with IQs higher than 160 played little with others unless special circumstances were provided—not because the highly gifted were unfriendly, but because their interests, vocabulary and so on, were so different from those of their age-mates as to make finding a compatible playmate unlikely. She also pointed out that gifted children were more often "only" children and that they enjoyed reading as a pastime, both of which further increased the likelihood of isolation.

Hollingworth decided that the higher the IQ and the younger the child, the more difficult it was to find a suitable play companion. This trouble decreased with increasing age, because older highly gifted individuals could seek out "like-minded" colleagues. She concluded the following:

> There is a certain restricted portion of the total range of intelligence which is most favorable to the development of successful and well-rounded personality in the world as it now exists. This limited range appears to be somewhere between the range of 125 and 155 IQ... above this limit—surely above 160 IQ—the deviation is so great that it leads to special problems of development which are correlated with personal isolation. (Hollingworth, 1942, reprinted in 1976, pp. 96–97)

More recently, Roedell (1984) discussed vulnerabilities of highly gifted children, including uneven development, perfectionism, adult expectations, intense sensitivity, self-definition, alienation, inappropriate environments, and role conflict. WISC-R Full Scale IQs ranged from 130 to 145 in our study, with a mean IQ of 137.8. Hence, none of our gifted children exceeded the criterion employed by Hollingworth to be classified as "highly" gifted and all fell into what she considered to be the optimum intelligence with respect to adjustment. Our findings thus dovetail with her observations of over 50 years ago with regard to the range for favorable adjustment.

In addition to highly gifted children, there is suggestion in the literature that gifted girls may be less popular and their social acceptance may be compromised. Luftig and Nichols (1991) investigated the social status levels ascribed to 10-year-old gifted children by their nongifted age-mates. Comparing the popularity of gifted and nongifted girls and boys, they reported that gifted boys were the most popular of the four ability/gender groups, and gifted females were found the least popular. Gifted girls were generally viewed as being moody and melancholy. Luftig and Nichols proposed that gifted boys tended to at least partially mask their giftedness by being funny, vivacious, and upbeat, while girls tended to be more serious and somber, striving for academic excellence and taking their academic achievement seriously. Solano (1987), studying stereotypes of the gifted, found that female gifted persons were perceived as significantly less popular than students of average ability. Additionally, Austin and Draper (1981) concluded that gifted adolescent girls, particularly in middle-class schools, were at risk for losing social status. Finally, Luthar et al. (1992) also discussed conflicts between achievement and social acceptance faced by gifted adolescent girls. Of course, such studies raise issues as to historical and cultural specificity, as well as the operation of gender stereotype and subject selection biases. The small number of gifted girls in our study does not yield sufficient power for analysis of the data by gender. As we follow our sample through the adolescent years, we will continue to assess social and academic motivation and adjustment; case studies or other qualitative strategies may permit us to address this issue.

Temperament

To determine whether differences exist in the temperament or behavioral style of intellectually gifted children compared to their nongifted cohort, a repeated-measures MANOVA was conducted on each set of temperament scales. For those administered only once (Infant Characteristics Questionnaire, Toddler Temperament Scale, Colorado Childhood Temperament Inventory, Middle Childhood Temperament Questionnaire), a one-way MANOVA with the set of scales as the dependent measures was used. In the case of those administered more than once (Behavior Style Questionnaire), a 2 × 3 (Giftedness Status ×

Age: 3, 3.5, and 5 years) repeated-measures MANOVA was used. The number of dependent variables varied according to the inventory.

The results showed that gifted children did not differ significantly from their nongifted peers in terms of temperamental difficultness during the infancy, preschool, or early elementary period. The Infant Characteristics Questionnaire was completed when children were 1.5 years of age. This scale, which assesses aspects of temperamental difficultness, comprises four scales: difficultness, unadaptability, nonpersistence, and unsociability. The MANOVA revealed no significant differences between infants who subsequently became gifted and those who did not on these aspects of temperament (multivariate $F(4, 98) = 0.67, p > .05$). Differences also failed to emerge at age 3.5 years, when the six-factor Colorado Childhood Temperament Inventory was administered (multivariate $F(6, 29) = 0.26, p > .05$).

The next set of analyses examined whether differences existed on the nine temperament dimensions derived in the New York Longitudinal Study (activity level, rhythmicity, approach, adaptability, negative mood, intensity, distractibility, threshold, and persistence) that were assessed at five points in time (2, 3, 3.5, 5, and 8 years). No significant gifted versus nongifted group differences were detected on the Toddler Temperament Scale administered at age 2 years (multivariate $F(9, 87) = 0.77, p > .05$). Similarly, no group differences in temperament were detected on the Behavioral Style Questionnaire during the preschool years (multivariate $F(9, 73) = 1.06, p > .05$). At age 8, there was again no evidence of differences in the nine temperament dimensions of the Middle Childhood Temperament Questionnaire (multivariate $F(9, 91) = 1.61, p > .05$).

Thus, in the course of development from infancy through the early elementary years, the temperamental characteristics of gifted and nongifted children did not differ. Parents of gifted and nongifted children rated their children similarly on a variety of temperament scales administered throughout the course of study in this longitudinal project. We found no differences on temperamental difficultness, persistence, sociability, or adaptability at 1.5 years, the six temperament dimensions in the Buss and Plomin (1984) temperament model assessed by the Colorado Childhood Temperament Inventory, and on the nine New York Longitudinal Study temperament dimensions (activity, rhythmicity/predictability, approach, adaptability, intensity, mood, persistence, or distractibility) assessed at 2, 3, 3.5, 5, and 8 years of age.

Our findings elaborate and extend those reported by Roedell et al. (1980), who suggested that the setting in which observations of early personality characteristics are made may be a determinant of whether significant differences between gifted and nongifted children are detected. For example, previous descriptions appearing in the literature based on observations made during administration of standardized tests showed gifted children to exceed the nongifted in terms of characteristics such as cooperation, persistence in the face of challenging problems, enthusiasm, patience, maturity, responsiveness, and resistance to fatigue. However, as Roedell et al. pointed out, observations based on test administration sessions probably reveal little about the behavior of either gifted or nongifted in *nontest* situations. Findings from the FLS are in line with this supposition. For example, differences in temperament between gifted and nongifted children were not evident in parent reports of children's temperament. Items comprising temperament inventories typically require the parent to assess their children's behavior in natural family interactive settings as they perform a variety of activities (e.g., eating, sleeping, playing, socializing). However, ratings by the FLS staff of the gifted and nongifted children's test-taking behavior did reveal significant group differences, as discussed in Chapter 4. Gifted children were rated significantly higher than nongifted children on aspects of cognitive mastery motivational behaviors such as goal directedness, object orientation, attention span, and reactivity to test materials at ages ranging from infancy through the school-entry years. Our data on gifted children's motivational behaviors in the test setting dovetail with previous studies noting significant gifted versus nongifted group differences; however, as suggested by Roedell et al., no group differences emerged when data were collected in nontest settings. Hence, results from our study demonstrate situation specificity in human development with respect to cognitive orientation to the environment. Significant differences between gifted and nongifted children emerged as early as infancy and continued throughout early childhood for their cognitive, motivational orientation to cognitive types of activities. On the other hand, analyses repeatedly confirmed an absence of differences between the gifted and nongifted groups in the nonacademic realm with regard to temperamental variables per se. It may be that these measures in the testing situation reflect the child's propensity to become engaged in cognitive tasks and not a general behavioral or temperamental style.

Nonintellectual characteristics of gifted individuals have been considered determinants of whether gifted individuals attain eminence as adults. For example, Albert and Runco (1986) noted that fewer of Terman's gifted children attained eminence during their adult careers than would have been expected given their high IQs and cautioned against relying on cognitive factors to the exclusion of other factors such as personality and family process variables in explaining achievement. Howe (1990) also argued that nonintellectual qualities such as persistence and attentiveness play an important role in determining whether individuals achieve eminence as adults. Tomlinson-Keasey and Little (1990), reanalyzing parent and teacher ratings of personality characteristics of gifted children in Terman's study, found that childhood sociability (age 11 years) correlated negatively with intellectual superiority in adulthood.

Our data attest to an early emergence of factors that differentiated gifted children from nongifted children, but only with respect to their test-taking behavior in specific situations relating to cognitive-oriented tasks as suggested in Chapter 4. Hence, a term such as "persistence" in this context (relating to achievement in terms of academics or career success) may indeed be a cognitive-motivational variable rather than a personality characteristic; that is, "persistence" and "attentiveness" may not be temperament variables but rather cognitive-motivational variables that reveal themselves in cognitively oriented and challenging tasks. Whether these cognitive-motivational characteristics (e.g., assessed in the test setting) or the temperamental variables (i.e., based on parent reports about behavior in more natural settings), both of which were measured prospectively in the gifted children of the FLS, will differentiate those gifted children who eventually attain success during adolescence and/or adulthood from those who do not remains to be determined. As we follow our study population, we may be in a position to address this issue.

SUMMARY

1. Gifted children were comparable to their nongifted age-mates in behavioral adjustment. No significant differences in behavioral or emotional problems were detected between the gifted and nongifted children between ages 3 and 8 years on a variety of instruments that utilized parents and/or teachers as informants.

2. Our gifted group enjoyed a social life comparable to that of their nongifted peers. Gifted and nongifted groups did not differ on items assessing either social advantage (e.g., number of friends, frequency of contacts, relationships with friends, siblings, parents, or ability to play

or work alone) or problems in social interactions with peers (e.g., social withdrawal, loneliness).

3. In an assessment of social reasoning, gifted children produced a significantly larger number of solutions to hypothetical social dilemmas than nongifted children. Parents of gifted children reported more mature functioning in personal and social sufficiency for their children during the school-entry and early elementary years than did parents of nongifted children. Thus, although similar in assessments of social behavior, the social capability and social cognition of gifted children were higher than those of nongifted children.

4. Gifted and nongifted groups were remarkably similar with respect to temperamental characteristics during the infancy, preschool, and early elementary years. On five different temperament inventories administered as early as 1.5 years and through age 8, the parental ratings of the gifted and nongifted children did not differ.

5. In summary, during the preschool and early school years no evidence of behavioral, social, or temperamental disadvantage was observed when comparing the gifted and nongifted groups. Advantage in the cognitive realm was not associated with any disadvantage in the behavioral, emotional, temperamental, or social aspects of functioning. To the contrary, gifted IQ was associated with superior social reasoning and adaptive functioning during the early years. We conclude that there is no detriment for gifted children in the 130–145 IQ range.

6

Home and Family Environment

ISSUES

In this chapter, we examine the home environment and family characteristics of children who become intellectually gifted or nongifted. While differences in the home environment of gifted and nongifted children have been reported in the literature, this longitudinal study provides an opportunity to assess whether these differences are present in the early course of development and on which specific environmental characteristics.

In order to present a comprehensive and detailed analysis of the environmental characteristics, we conceptualized the measures into three levels: distal environmental variables, proximal environmental variables, and family relationship variables (A. W. Gottfried & A. E. Gottfried, 1984; A. E. Gottfried et al., 1988). Distal variables refer to the global or descriptive aspects that characterize the environment, but do not measure the specific experiences that impinge on or interact with the child that may influence development. Distal environmental variables include demographics and family structure characteristics such as socioeconomic status, marital status, and family composition or structure. For organizational purposes, we included mothers' intelligence in this rubric. Proximal variables, which focus on the process or detailed aspects of the environment, include cognitively enriching and stimulating materials and activities, variety of experiences, parental involvement, social and emotional supports, and the physical environment. Family relationships, which may also be considered proximal, were analyzed as a separate category. These included the quality of family relationships and the social climate in the home along a variety of dimensions such as the intellectual and cultural atmosphere in the home and the nature of family interactions such as cohesion and expressiveness among family members.

Because the literature clearly supports the hypothesis that gifted children have environmental advantages over nongifted children, our purpose was not to assess whether differences actually exist. Rather, our goal was to systematically investigate the specific aspects of the home and family environment that distinguish these two groups of children in the opening years of their lives before they are designated as gifted or nongifted. This systematic investigation of early environments of children who become intellectually gifted or nongifted makes this study unique in contrast to investigations that have studied the environments of gifted children after these children have been designated, identified, or labeled as gifted.

Our longitudinal study allowed us to address several issues that have not been addressed by other researchers in this field. There were two overriding issues pertaining to home and family environmental differences in the early course of development of gifted and nongifted children. First, how early in their developmental histories do we find differences between children who become intellectually gifted or nongifted, and are these differences domain specific? Second, are there developmental patterns in early environmental input; that is, is there evidence of cross-time patterns or continuity of environmental input that distinguishes gifted from nongifted children. The following specific questions were addressed:

1. Do the families of the gifted and nongifted children differ in socioeconomic status (SES) even within this predominately middle-class sample, which represents less than the full range or extreme of SES values? We used an established index to appraise family SES based on parents' educational and occupational status. We also analyzed occupational status and number of years of completed education separately for each parent in order to determine if SES differences reside in parental occupation and/or educational status. Lastly, are there differences in the occurrence of maternal employment between the gifted and nongifted groups? This latter variable was investigated because of its contemporary and controversial nature.

2. Do gifted and nongifted children's mothers differ in verbal and/or perceptual intellectual performance? We had no expectations for

this variable because no prior studies on gifted children have included an assessment of mothers' intellectual performance.

3. Are there differences in the numbers of boys and girls who become gifted? Unlike other studies where children were recruited as a result of teachers' nomination or from registries of gifted children, we followed a single cohort developmentally from infancy. This precluded potential biasing and allowed a more fair assessment of the distribution of males and females who become gifted. With respect to other demographic factors, are there differences between the gifted and nongifted groups in their parents' marital status, parents' age, number of adults or children in the home, and birth order? As for the last factor, are the gifted children more likely to be firstborns or only borns compared to nongifted children? We anticipated that our data would be consistent with the large body of literature.

4. With respect to proximal environmental variables, are there differences in the quality and quantity of home stimulation provided to gifted versus nongifted children? For example, are there differences in early cognitive enrichment, social supports, parental involvement, and educational enhancement? Based on our previous research on home environment and early cognitive development, we anticipated differences would emerge. However, we were also interested in how early in development the differences become apparent.

5. Are there differences in the educational aspirations that parents hold for children who become gifted in contrast to nongifted? More importantly, if differences are found, do they exist prior to the age at which children were designated as gifted or nongifted?

6. Do gifted compared to nongifted children place more demands or requests on parents for environmental stimulation or activities? While the literature supports the role of parental involvement in children's development, there have been no systematic investigations of the role children play in this process.

7. Are there differences in the intellectual atmosphere and social relationships in the families of gifted and nongifted children? Specifically, are the families of these groups of children different in their cohesiveness, openness, level of conflict, and means of family regulation? While the literature supports the notion that the social atmosphere in the home is an important aspect to the development of the intellectually gifted, the specific components have not been systematically studied longitudinally.

DESCRIPTION OF MEASURES

Distal Environmental Variables

These variables (with the exception of mothers' intelligence) were gathered by way of the Social History Questionnaire, which was developed by the authors and administered to parents at every assessment. This questionnaire provided a contemporaneous and ongoing appraisal of the family. Distal variables assessed with this questionnaire included socioeconomic status, which was calculated from parents' occupational status and number of years of education, parents' working status, marital status, parents' age, as well as several items pertaining to family composition. Mothers' intelligence was included in this category of variables as well.

Socioeconomic Status

Socioeconomic status (SES) was measured at each assessment using the Hollingshead Four Factor Index of Social Status (A. W. Gottfried, 1985; Hollingshead, 1975). This index is a well-established measure of SES that has been extensively used in the psychological and developmental literature. An overall family index was computed by assigning values based on an ordinal scale of the parents' occupations, if gainfully employed, and educational attainments. These values provide the data for calculation of SES (see Hollingshead, 1975). In cases where both parents were employed, data from both were entered into the computation. When only one parent was employed, SES was calculated only from that person's data.

Mothers' Working Status

Mothers' working status was measured at each assessment and dichotomously coded (working or not working). We treated mothers who were employed both part-time and full-time as one group because in our research (A. E. Gottfried, Bathurst, & A. W. Gottfried, 1994; A. E. Gottfried et al., 1988), we found that there were no differences in children's outcome measures between these two groups. We did not analyze working status for fathers because virtually all fathers were employed at each assessment.

Mothers' Intelligence

Mothers' intelligence was measured when the children were 3 years old by administering the WAIS-R Vocabulary and Block Design subtests. These subtests were chosen because vocabulary is the best single predictor of verbal intelligence, and block design is the best single predictor of performance intelligence (Wechsler, 1991). Furthermore within the group of verbal and performance subtests, the Vocabulary and Block Design subtests, respectively, have the highest internal consistency and stability coefficients and smallest standard errors of measurement. Raw scores were converted to standard scores with a mean of 10 and a standard deviation of 3 using transformation tables in the manual.

Family Characteristics

The balance of the measures in this section were included on the Social History Questionnaire, which was completed by mothers. These variables included marital status of parents, parents' ages, number of adults and children in the home, and child's birth order. Sex of the children was included in this category. Parents' ages, sex of study child, and birth order were collected at the onset of the study. The other family characteristics were collected at each assessment. We therefore had a record of changing family demographics over the entire period.

Proximal Environmental Variables

A major focus of the FLS has been on environment-development relationships. Over the course of investigation, we have employed a comprehensive set of age-appropriate scales that tap numerous aspects of the children's environment. The inventories included both standardized instruments and scales developed by the authors to assess specific characteristics of interest. Our assessments included observational or direct assessments and also nonobservational or indirect assessments of children's environments, the latter being furnished by parent reports.

Direct Observational Home Assessments

The quality of the home environment was central to our study of children's development. We therefore visited the homes of the families taking part in our longitudinal study on three occasions: when the children were ages 15 months (1.25 years), 39 months (3.25 years), and 8 years. The home visits were planned to coincide with three developmental periods: infancy, preschool, and elementary school age. Standardized instruments were administered by our staff. In all cases, the child and mother were present in the home at the time of the visit.

Home Observation and Measurement of the Environment. The Home Observation and Measurement of the Environment (HOME) (Caldwell & Bradley, 1984) inventory was selected because of its extensive use, psychometric qualities, and its relation to children's developmental outcome (A. W. Gottfried, 1984a). This inventory has three versions (infant, preschool, and elementary) and requires that an administrator visit the home of each family. Administration, which requires both direct observation in the home and semistructured interviews with mothers, was highly reliable at all three ages.

The infant version was used when the children were 1.25 years of age. This version contains 45 items divided into the following six scales: Emotional and Verbal Responsivity of Mother; Avoidance of Restriction and Punishment; Organization of the Physical and Temporal Environment; Provision of Appropriate Play Materials; Maternal Involvement with the Child; and Opportunities for Variety in Daily Stimulation.

The preschool version was used when the children were 3.25 years of age and includes 55 items divided into the following eight scales: Stimulation through Toys, Games, and Reading Materials; Language Stimulation; Physical Environment: Safe, Clean, and Conducive to Development; Pride, Affection, and Warmth; Stimulation of Academic Behavior; Modeling and Encouragement of Social Maturity; Variety of Stimulation; and Physical Punishment.

The elementary version was used when the children were 8 years of age. Fifty-nine items form the following eight scales: Emotional and Verbal Responsivity; Encouragement of Maturity; Emotional Climate; Growth Fostering Materials and Experiences; Provision for Active Stimulation; Family Participation in Developmentally Stimulating Experiences; Paternal Involvement; and Aspects of the Physical Environment. In each version, the scales sum together to form an overall total score.

Purdue Home Stimulation Inventory. The Purdue Home Stimulation Inventory (PHSI) (Wachs, 1976) was administered at the 1.25-year home visit. Whereas the HOME focuses more on the socioemotional aspects of the environment, the PHSI was devised to emphasize the physical aspects of the home. This inventory is also based on direct observation and interview. Twenty-seven items of the inventory were administered. However, only thirteen were included in the present analyses because our earlier research showed a relation between these items and children's cognitive development in the infancy and preschool years (see A. W. Gottfried & A. E. Gottfried, 1984). These items were as follows: child taken out of neighborhood, child visits neighbors, categories of training, time per day reading to child, manipulable items, ratio of rooms to people, floor freedom, number of siblings, home has restricted view of outside, noise sources, noise level, number of children's books, and access to newspapers, magazines, and books. Each item of the PHSI was analyzed separately because no subscores or overall total score are available as presented by Wachs' framework of environmental specificity (Wachs, 1992; Wachs & Gruen, 1982).

Nonobservational Assessments of the Home Environment

In contrast to the direct observational measures cited above, the variables in this category were collected by parents' written responses to questionnaires and surveys. Because specific environmental variables were found to have pervasive relations to children's cognitive development during the infancy and preschool periods (A. W. Gottfried & A. E. Gottfried, 1984), we sought to expand beyond measures of the immediate home environment and elaborate on the information gathered by the HOME and PHSI. Further, we reasoned that specific dimensions should be expanded upon in a way that would allow us to collect data indirectly through parent report at each assessment period without the necessity for home visits. In prior research (Bathurst, 1988; A. E. Gottfried, Bathurst, & A. W. Gottfried, 1994; A. E. Gottfried et al., 1988), we found parental reports to be a reliable and valid method to gather information about children's experiences and home environment. We therefore developed several questionnaires and surveys to assess specific environmental characteristics. Thus, we were able to maintain an ongoing comprehensive assessment of the children's environment, beyond observational or direct assessments.

The additional surveys included the Variety of Experiences Checklist (an assessment of children's experiences outside the home) and the Home Environment Survey (a measure of several home environmental characteristics, such as the amount of time parents spend with their children and provisions for stimulating activities and experiences in the home).

Variety of Experiences Checklist. The Variety of Experience Checklist (VEC) (A. W. Gottfried & A. E. Gottfried, 1984) was completed by mothers at the 3- and 5-year assessments. Several out-of-the-home experiences were listed and mothers were asked to check those in which the child had engaged during the last year. The experiences were grouped into three categories: types of vehicles child has traveled in (car, plane, boat, train, bus, other), types of entertainment child has experienced (TV, movie theater, circus, aquarium or Marineland, museum, amusement park, zoo or wild animal park, live theater or show, library, special lessons, other), and visits to various geographic areas (large city, mountains, desert, forest, beach or seashore, an island, a different state in the United States, other). The scale score was the total number of different experiences of the child within the year.

Home Environment Survey. Another instrument was the Home Environment Survey (HES), which was completed by mothers at the 5-, 7-, and 8-year laboratory assessments. This survey focused on cognitive enrichment and parental involvement. At each age, the items were factor analyzed for data reduction purposes. Varimax rotations were used and factors were created based on these results. Items with factor loadings of .30 or higher were retained. Items were slightly different at each age to accommodate the changing environments of children with advancement in age. At age 5 years, 12 items formed three factors: Mother Provides Educational Stimulation, Educational Attitudes, and Provision of Learning Materials. At age 7 years, 12 items formed three factors: Mother Provides Educational Stimulation, Educational Attitudes, and Mother's Time Involvement with Child. At age 8 years, 20 items formed six factors: Learning Opportunities, Reading Involvement with Child, TV Time, Mother's Time Involvement with Child, Father's Time Involvement with Child, and Academic Assistance. We decided to eliminate this last factor because it comprised only two items resulting in low internal consistency estimates, and also because one of the items, in hindsight, appeared ambiguous as to its meaning. Table 6.1 shows each factor and the items unique to that factor. Reliability and validity were thoroughly investigated by Bathurst (1988) at the 8-year assessment. Test-retest reliability coefficients were conducted on a subset of 53 respondents after an interval of 2 to 4 months. These ranged from .61 to .87 on the five scales. The HES showed strong concurrent, predictive,

Table 6.1. Home Environment Survey (HES) Scales for the 5-, 7-, and 8-Year Assessment

Age 5

Mother Provides Educational Stimulation (3 items)
1. Number of monthly trips to the library
2. Number of minutes mother reads to child each day
3. Number of minutes mother spends working with child on academic skills

Educational Attitudes (4 items)
1. Educational level child is expected to achieve
2. Child has his/her own real musical instrument
3. Amount of time child watches TV each day (–)
4. Amount of time mother watches TV each day (–)

Provisions of Learning Materials (5 items)
1. Number of activity books in the home not provided by school
2. Number of electronic teaching aids at home
3. Encyclopedia in home
4. Child receives out-of-school lessons
5. Personal computer experience at home

Age 7

Mother Provides Educational Stimulation (5 items)
1. Number of monthly trips to the library
2. Number of minutes mother reads to child each day
3. Number of minutes mother spends working with child on academic skills
4. Child has subscription to a magazine or book club
5. Number of different magazines or journals family receives monthly

Educational Attitudes (4 items)
1. Educational level child is expected to achieve
2. Child receives private lessons
3. Amount of time child watches TV each day (–)
4. Amount of time mother watches TV each day (–)

Mothers' Time Involvement with Child (3 items)
1. Hours spent taking care of and doing things with child—school day
2. Hours spent taking care of and doing things with child—weekend day
3. Discuss child's school work with child (number of days per week)

Age 8

Learning Opportunities (6 items)
1. Child has access to a real musical instrument
2. Child has own subscription to a magazine or book club
3. Child receives private lessons
4. Number of magazines or journals family receives monthly
5. Child has experience with computer at home
6. Educational level child is expected to receive

Reading Involvement with Child (3 items)
1. Number of monthly trips of child to library
2. Amount of time child reads by him/herself daily
3. Child has own dictionary

(*continued*)

Table 6.1. (*Continued*)

TV Time (3 items)
1. Amount of time per day child watches TV
2. Amount of time per day mother watches TV
3. Amount of time per day father watches TV
Mothers' Time Involvement with Child (3 items)
See age 7 items
Fathers' Time Involvement with Child
Same as for mother

and construct validity with other environmental measures and measures of achievement, intelligence, and social maturity, supporting the HES factors as theoretically meaningful. This allowed us to make *a priori* predictions about their relation to giftedness status. Specifically, we expected to find differences favoring gifted children on factors related to academic involvement of parents. Further details about the items and factor structure can be found in Bathurst (1988) and A. E. Gottfried et al. (1988).

Child's Requests for Activities. An additional set of questions were added to the HES at age 8 only. Because our research suggested that young children's differential cognitive development elicited correspondingly different levels of stimulation in the preschool years (A. W. Gottfried & A. E. Gottfried, 1984), we attempted to appraise the degree to which children make requests or demands upon parents for extracurricular activities. The intent of this variable was to capture the demandingness by children for enrichment activities with the expectation that those children who were more cognitively advanced would be more demanding for environmental stimulation. Parents completed the following question in four categories of activities: "Has your child (a) asked for lessons in the areas of music, art, dance, gymnastics, skating, etc? (b) asked to allow him or her to participate in any organized team sports such as soccer, baseball, football, etc? (c) asked to allow him or her to join any clubs or organizations such as scouts, youth clubs, etc? (d) requested to engage in any hobbies such as collections of stamps or coins, building models, etc?" Mothers listed up to three activities in each of the four areas, yielding a total possible score of 12. Higher scores mean that the child is making more requests of his or her parent. Our prior research (Bathurst, 1988) revealed that the number of activities children requested was positively related to their intelligence and achievement, and therefore, we expected this variable to be related to giftedness status as well.

Family Relationship Variables

Family Environment Scale

The Family Environment Scale (FES) (R. H. Moos & B. S. Moos, 1986) is a well-known, reliable, and valid instrument appraising the quality of family relationships. It was completed by mothers when the children were 3, 5, 7, and 8 years of age and also by fathers at the 8-year assessment. This instrument measures the social climate in the home and consists of 10 scales: Cohesion, Expressiveness, Conflict, Independence, Achievement Orientation, Intellectual-Cultural Orientation, Active-Recreational Orientation, Moral-Religious Emphasis, Organization, and Control. A. W. Gottfried and A. E. Gottfried (1984) found that the Intellectual-Cultural Orientation, Cohesion, and Expressiveness scales were positively related to early cognitive functioning. Cornell (1984) found differences between gifted and nongifted elementary-aged children on the Intellectual-Cultural Orientation, Cohesion, and Conflict scales. Hence, we analyzed only four scales. Moos and Moos conceptualized Intellectual-Cultural Orientation as the interest a family shows in political, social, intellectual, and cultural activities; Cohesion as the help and support family members show for each other; Expressiveness as openness within a family for members to express themselves; and Conflict as open expression of anger and conflict among family members.

Family Inventory. Because the FES makes no provision for computation of a total score, the Family Inventory was constructed to provide a global measure of family functioning (Bathurst, 1988). This scale incorporates items that are related to positive family functioning such as cooperation, family participation in activities, and conflict issues. Development of the Family Inventory was based on research that assessed the second-order factor structure of the FES (Bathurst & A. W. Gottfried, 1987b; Plomin & DeFries, 1985). Both research groups found two highly similar second-order factors, the first reflecting family involvement in an atmosphere promoting personal growth and the second reflecting regulation and organization of family members. The Family Inventory comprised 22 statements on which parents rated their families from 1 ("not true") to 6 ("very true"). The data were subjected to factor analysis; two factors emerged. The first was a strong general factor that comprised 16 items. It was labeled Positive Family Functioning. The second factor comprised three items and was labeled Family Regulation. The first reflects the well-functioning family that allows openness and freedom of expression as well as provision of an intellectual-cultural atmosphere marked with a lack of conflict. Higher values on this scale also represent families who enjoy doing things together and who support each other. The second reflects the amount of regulation and control within the family. The three items measure the degree to which rules and regulations are used in the family, the degree to which family members have specifically defined roles, and the degree of interdependency among family members (as opposed to independent functioning). The Family Inventory was completed by both mothers and fathers when the children were 8 years of age. Internal consistency estimates for mothers and fathers for the general factor were .84 and .85, respectively; estimates for the regulation factor were .47 and .42, respectively. The low estimates for the second factor were probably a result of the small number of items on this factor. In an earlier study (Bathurst, 1988), there was evidence of a positive relation between the first factor, and a negative relation between the second factor, and cognitive performance. Therefore, we expected to find these factors similarly associated with giftedness status.

RESULTS

The analyses in this chapter differ from preceding chapters due to our own data derived from this project that allowed us to make predictions about specific environmental variables as related to cognition. Following the decision tree of Hertzog and Rovine (1985) and the statistical strategy in this book (see Chapter 2), planned comparisons were used to test for significant differences between gifted and nongifted children's environments for specific hypothesized relationships. Data published by A. W. Gottfried and A. E. Gottfried (1984), A. E. Gottfried et al. (1988), and Bathurst (1988) provided the primary foundation for these hypotheses. It is important to note, however, that the relation between environment and development could vary across studies according to sample characteristics such as SES and ethnicity (Bradley et al., 1989; A. W. Gottfried, 1984a; A. W. Gottfried & A. E. Gottfried, 1986). For all planned comparisons, it was predicted that the environments of children who become gifted would evidence greater quality or quantity of environmental enrichment than those of children who do not become gifted.

The results are presented in the three categories in which they were conceptualized: distal environmental variables, proximal environmental variables, and family relationship variables. For ease in reading, only significant *t*, *F*, and χ^2 values are presented. Because of the number and specificity of variables in this particular chapter, nonsignificant statistical values are not reported.

Distal Environmental Variables

Socioeconomic Status

In order to address the difference for family SES between the two giftedness status groups, we employed a 2 × 10 (Giftedness Status × Age: 1 through 8 years) repeated-measures ANOVA with Giftedness Status as the between-subjects factor and Age as the repeated factor. SES was computed at each of the 10 assessment periods according to Hollingshead's coding scheme (see Hollingshead, 1975). Coupled with the uncertainty as to whether we would find a difference in this somewhat restricted range of a predominantly middle-class sample consistent with other researchers, we opted for ANOVA as opposed to planned comparisons for this variable. The results revealed that the family SES of gifted children was higher than the family SES of nongifted children across the entire assessment period ($F(1, 91) = 5.95$, $p = .017$). The mean of the gifted group was 52.8 ($SD = 10.6$), whereas the mean of the nongifted group was 46.8 ($SD = 10.2$). This relation of SES to cognitive functioning supports many findings in the psychological literature and is by no means novel. Children from relatively higher-SES families tend to have higher IQs. What is meaningful here is that, even within this predominantly middle-class sample, we detected a significant difference. The association between giftedness status and SES is sufficiently potent to be detected within a less than full range of IQ and SES variances.

Parents' Occupational and Educational Status

Because the Hollingshead is composed of two components—occupation and education—we analyzed the occupational status and educational levels separately for both mothers and fathers. For the occupational status variable, we used the scale developed by Hollingshead; persons who were unemployed were excluded from the analyses. Fathers, with few exceptions, were constantly employed. Therefore, we used the same data-analytic strategy as that imposed on the SES analysis. A 2 × 10 (Giftedness Status × Age: 1 through 8 years) repeated-measures ANOVA was conducted. There were no differences between the gifted status groups due to fathers' occupational status. However, at each age, without exception, the fathers of gifted children achieved a higher status than fathers of nongifted children. It is likely, however, that the restricted range of occupations, in the sense of Hollingshead categorization, kept the variance at a minimum, precluding the possibility of detecting statistical differences. Mothers showed a large increase in employment rate over the course of this investigation. The percentage employed ranged from 36.2% when the children were 1 year of age to 71.9% when the children were 8 years of age. The number of mothers providing data across the entire period was only 19 (2 gifted and 17 nongifted); this prohibited the use of ANOVA. Mothers would often leave and return to the work force. Therefore, we opted to conduct *t* tests at each age. For mothers, statistical significance with regard to occupational status was reached only at the 7- and 8-year periods. In both cases, the occupational status was higher for mothers of gifted children than nongifted children: At age 7 years, the mean Hollingshead status values were 6.8 ($SD = 1.1$) and 5.8 ($SD = 1.4$) for gifted and nongifted groups, respectively ($t(67) = 2.57, p = .01$). At age 8 years, the mean Hollingshead status values were 7.1 ($SD = 0.9$) and 5.7 ($SD = 1.6$) for gifted and nongifted groups, respectively ($t(72) = 3.15, p = .002$). At each age where the differences reached statistical significance, the mothers of gifted children averaged at least one category higher than the mothers of nongifted children. The mothers of gifted children were more likely to be in the categories of professionals, business owners, administrators, and managers. In fact, there were no mothers of gifted children in a Hollingshead occupational category below 5 (e.g., clerical and sales workers, owners of small businesses), whereas mothers of nongifted children did hold jobs in levels 4 and below (e.g., skilled and unskilled workers). These data at ages 7 and 8 years are consistent with our findings regarding maternal occupational status and children's cognitive development and achievement throughout childhood (A. E. Gottfried, Bathurst, & A. W. Gottfried, 1994; A. E. Gottfried et al., 1988).

We next analyzed mothers' and fathers' education. For this analysis, we used parents' actual number of years of completed education rather than the ordinal scale provided by Hollingshead. We chose this alternative to secure a more precise measure of parent education. In order to equate the values of this variable across the sample, the number of years in school was adjusted for the attained degree. For example, a high school degree was coded as 12 years and a bachelor's degree as 16 years. Therefore, if a parent took 5 years to attain a bachelor's degree, we coded the data as if it took 4 years. This adjustment provided for a more precise and consistent comparison of education attained. Because some parents were attending college, their educational attainments were gathered periodically throughout the course of investigation, specifically at the 1-, 3-, 5-, 6-, 7-, and 8-year assessments. With the same rationale used in analyzing SES, a 2 × 6 (Giftedness Status × Age: 1, 3, 5, 6, 7, and 8 years) repeated-measures ANOVA was conducted separately for each parent with giftedness status as the between-subjects variable and time as the within-subjects variable. Within this sample of relatively highly educated individuals, we found significant differences between the designated groups. Results showed that both parents of gifted children attained approximately 1.5 more years of education than the parents of nongifted children. Mothers of gifted children attained an average of 15.8 ($SD = 1.6$) years, while mothers of nongifted children attained an average of 14.0 ($SD = 1.9$) years ($F(1, 95) = 14.60, p < .001$). Fathers of gifted children attained an average of 16.4 ($SD = 2.0$) years, while fathers of nongifted children attained an average of 15.0 ($SD = 2.7$) years ($F(1, 92) = 4.97, p = .028$). Hence, the SES difference between gifted and nongifted children was primarily due to educational accomplishments as opposed to occupational status. Our findings are in line with several other studies noting such differences (e.g., Barbe, 1956; Freeman, 1979; Hollingworth, 1942; Sheldon, 1954; Terman, 1925–1929).

Mothers' Working Status

One contemporary issue is whether the employment status of mothers is related to children's development (A. E. Gottfried & A. W. Gottfried, 1988, 1994). Whereas Groth (1975) found mothers of gifted children more likely to be employed outside the home, our own contemporary research has shown that maternal employment status, per se, is not significantly related to developmental outcomes (A. E. Gottfried, Bathurst, & A. W. Gottfried, 1994; A. E. Gottfried et al., 1988; A. E. Gottfried, A. W. Gottfried, & Bathurst, in press). For the current study, we examined whether maternal employment status was associated with children's giftedness status at each age (1–8 years) using chi-square analyses. Maternal employment status (working vs. not working) was crossed with giftedness status (gifted vs. nongifted). The chi-square analyses were not significant, indicating that maternal working status and children's giftedness status are not associated. These results provide further support for the growing body of literature that finds no association between children's development and maternal employment status.

Mothers' Intelligence

To determine whether mothers' intelligence was higher in the group of gifted children, we compared the giftedness status groups on the Vocabulary and Block Design subscales of the WAIS-R. If differences emerge between the groups, one might expect the differences to favor the mothers of gifted children. However, some form of intergenerational regression effects could be operating as well, which would attenuate differences. The standard scores of the two WAIS-R subscales were analyzed using Hotelling's T^2. Results of the multivariate test showed no significant difference. Therefore, mothers' intelligence, whether verbal or perceptual, was not a discriminating factor for giftedness status in our sample. Hence, the findings show that it was neither parental occupation nor intelligence, but rather the educational achievement of parents, that was predominantly associated with differences in giftedness status of children. More important, the parents' educational achievements may serve as a marker or index variable of the family's cognitive enrichment atmosphere or curriculum in the home that, in turn, may foster and nurture the development of children who become gifted.

Family Characteristics

Additional characteristics were analyzed in order to determine if the gifted and nongifted status groups differed in this category. These variables included sex of study child, marital status of the parents, parents' ages, number of adults and children residing in the home, and birth order.

Of the gifted children, 55% (11/20) were males and 45% (9/20) were female. The comparable values for the nongifted children were 58.6% (51/87) male and 41.4% (36/87) female. The nonsignificant chi square indicated that there was no association between giftedness status and children's sex. It is interesting that in our sample we find no sex differences when so many studies of gifted children note a greater number of boys than girls (e.g., R. L. Cox, 1977; Freeman, 1979; Hollingworth, 1942; Terman & Oden, 1959). In each of these studies, subjects were recruited for their giftedness status. In our study, we began with children from the same cohort. The children who were identified as gifted at 8 years of age were not recruited because of that characteristic, but emerged from the same cohort as the nongifted children. This interpretation would suggest that ascertainment bias may well explain the greater number of boys than girls in such samples.

Marital status was recorded at each assessment and coded "married" or "not married." The code for married included cohabitation and the code for not married included those parents who were separated, even if not legally divorced. At the 1-year assessment, all gifted children had parents who were married, whereas 95.4% (83/87) of the parents of nongifted children were married. At the 8-year assessment, 90.0% (18/20) of the parents of gifted children were married, whereas 88.3% (75/85) of the parents of nongifted children were married. If parents were divorced or separated, all children resided with their biological mothers. A chi-square analysis conducted at each assessment period indicated that giftedness status and parents' marital status were unrelated. An analysis was also conducted with respect to the occurrence of divorce; that is, had the child experienced the divorce of his or her parents during the first 8 years of his or her life? Ten percent of the gifted children and 22% of the nongifted children had experienced divorce in their families by age 8 years. There was no significant association between giftedness status and the experience of divorce. These findings imply that marital stability or disruption is unrelated to intellectual differences by age 8 years. Other studies have noted differences in the rate of divorce (e.g., Barbe, 1956; Groth, 1975). However, this variable is not a static one; family structure is constantly changing. It is unlikely that a valid comparison can be made across the studies and across the different eras. More information would have to be gathered in order to begin to make sense of the meaning of this variable and implications of the results as compared to other samples.

Researchers have found that the ages of gifted children's parents are typically somewhat older than that of nongifted children's parents. In order to determine whether these differences held in our sample, planned contrasts were conducted separately for mothers and fathers. At the onset of the study, the average age of fathers of gifted children was 34.2 ($SD = 6.9$) years; the average age of fathers of nongifted children was 31.3 ($SD = 4.5$) years. This difference was significant ($t(105) = 1.76$, $p < .05$). Although the mothers of gifted children are, on the average, a half-year older than the mothers of nongifted children, this difference was not statistically significant. The average age of mothers of gifted children was 29.4 years ($SD = 4.4$) and of mothers of nongifted children was 28.9 years ($SD = 3.9$). Although Hollingworth (1942) and Terman (1925) found differences between the data from their sample and the general population for both mothers' and fathers' ages, our sample revealed a statistically significant difference only for fathers. Perhaps the more restricted age range of mothers as compared to fathers accounted for the lack of significant differences. Further, our comparison was within our sample and not to the general population. Alternatively, findings from older studies may not hold up in contemporary middle-class samples.

The number of adults and children residing in the home was recorded at the 1-, 3-, 5-, 7-, and 8-year assessments. The predominant number of families had two adults; far less had one adult or three or more adults residing in the household. Because low frequencies in cells of more than two adults in the home resulted in below-acceptable values for expected frequencies for chi-square analyses, the data were analyzed as having one adult versus two or more in the home. Across the ages, the occurrence of one adult in the home ranged from 1% to 11%, whereas the number of two or more adults in the home ranged from 89% to 99%. A chi-square analysis was conducted at each assessment period. Results indicated that giftedness status was unrelated to number of adults living in the home. Although the sample size is relatively small for these analyses, we speculate that single parenting, per se, as indexed by one adult in the home is not detrimental to the development of children who become intellectually gifted. Hence, the number of adults in the home, and possibly adult caretakers (see A. W. Gottfried & A. E. Gottfried, 1984), is not necessarily disadvantageous to the development of high intellectual performance.

In the gifted group, the percentages of families that had one, two, three, and four children in the home at 8 years of age were 25% ($N = 5$), 55% (11), 15% (3), and 5% (1), respectively. In the nongifted group, the percentages of families that had one, two, three, four, five, and nine children were 10.3% (9), 58.6% (51), 21.8% (19), 3.4% (3), 4.6% (4), and 1.1% (1). In order to assess the association between giftedness status and number of children in the home, the frequencies were coded as one, two, and three or more children in the home. This was done for two reasons: first, to keep the minimum value of expected frequencies per cell at an acceptable level, and second, to keep these analyses consistent with the birth-order analyses below. Chi-square results revealed no association between giftedness status and number of children in the home. These data, in conjunction with those pertaining to number of adults in the home, indicate that family composition is not associated with giftedness status.

Birth order was coded at the onset of the study (age 1 year). Because so few families (5) had more than three children in the home, the data were organized into the following categories: firstborn, second-born, and third- or later-born children. Among the gifted children, 80% (16/20) were firstborns, 15% (3) were second borns, and 5% (1) were third borns. In the nongifted group, 42.5% (37/87) of the children were firstborns, 36.8% (32) were second borns, and 20.7% (18) were third or later borns. Birth-order status was significantly associated with giftedness status (χ^2 (2, N = 107) = 9.22, p < .01). As clearly seen from these data, giftedness status occurred overwhelmingly more often among firstborns. These findings are in accord with our earlier analyses on birth order and early cognitive development (A. W. Gottfried & A. E. Gottfried, 1984), the several studies noting birth-order differences as summarized by Olszewski et al. (1987) and Cornell (1984), and the meta-analysis by Falbo and Polit (1986). Hence, it appears that giftedness status is not associated with family composition, but rather the child's placement in the family. The ordinality of the child among the children in the family has interesting implications for the environmental stimulation being furnished by parents (A. W. Gottfried & A. E. Gottfried, 1984).

Proximal Environmental Variables

This category was divided into two subcategories: observational and nonobservational assessments of the home environment. Inventories included in the observational category were the Home Observation and Measurement of the Environment and the Purdue Home Stimulation Inventory. Inventories included in the nonobservational category were the Variety of Experiences Checklist, Home Environment Survey, and Child's Request for Activities. Based on our research demonstrating significant and positive relationships between proximal environmental variables and cognitive functioning, it was our overall hypothesis that if differences emerged between the gifted and nongifted groups on environmental stimulation variables, they would favor the gifted children (A. W. Gottfried & A. E. Gottfried, 1984).

Direct Observational Home Assessments

Home Observation and Measurement of the Environment (HOME). The analytic strategy for the HOME scales included two types of analyses. The first was a 2 × 3 (Giftedness Status × Age: 1.25, 3.25, and 8 years) repeated-measures ANOVA for the HOME total scores. The omnibus analysis was conducted for two reasons. First, whereas we expected to find differences in specific scales favoring the gifted children, we did not necessarily expect differences in the composite total scores, although one might anticipate that the overall home environment of gifted children would be of higher quality than that of nongifted children. However, one must keep in mind that the overall home score is nothing more than an unweighted summary of the subscale scores, some for which we had no prediction. Second, we were interested in whether there was an interaction between group and age; specifically, if differences did exist, was the magnitude of these differences between groups greater at any developmental period? For this analysis, it was necessary to convert the raw scores to z scores ($M = 0$, $SD = 1$) because each version of the HOME contained a different number of items. Figure 6.1 displays the pattern of scores across the three home assessments. The main effect of group was significant: the HOME total score of gifted children was higher than that of the nongifted children ($F(1, 101) = 10.90$, $p = .001$). The mean total HOME z scores for the gifted group at 1.25, 3.25, and 8 years were .27, .66, and .72, respectively. The comparable values for the nongifted group were −.07, −.14, and −.17. These results show that during the early years, children who became gifted received a more enriched home environment overall, and the differences between the groups remained stable between infancy and early elementary years.

In Figure 6.1, we also plotted the mean z scores for the three sets of intellectual assessments (3 Bayleys, 3 McCarthys, and 3 WISC-Rs). These two sets of data allowed us a visual inspection of both the overall HOME scores and intellectual measures. These findings are quite dramatic in that they show the correspondence of the intellectual performance of the two groups with the home stimulation being provided to the children across the time frame from 1 to 8 years. Clearly, the intellectual performance of the gifted and nongifted groups from infancy through the early elementary years corresponded with the overall HOME environmental stimulation being provided by their parents across the same time frame. Levels of home environmental enrichment covary with intellectual performance of these designated groups. The data intimate a confluence of environmental stimulation and level of intellectual performance.

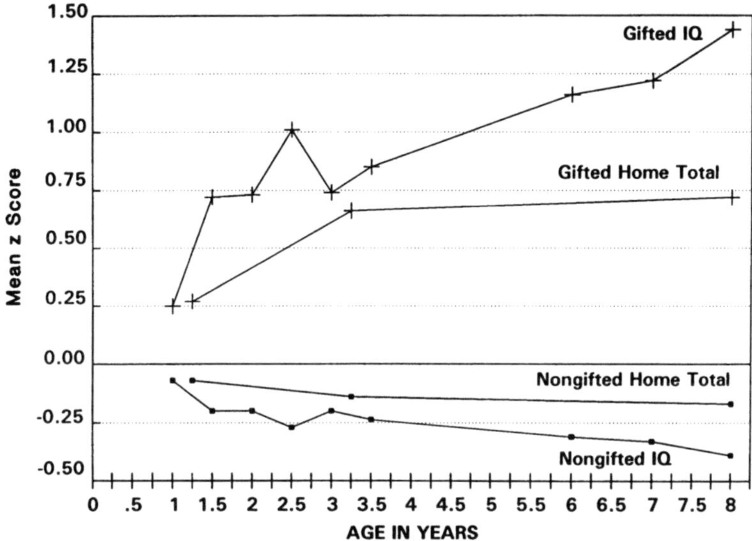

Figure 6.1. Mean z scores for gifted and nongifted children for the intelligence measures and HOME total score from age 1 year through 8 years of age.

The second strategy involved a series of planned comparisons based on specific hypotheses generated from our prior research on home environment and early cognitive development (A. W. Gottfried & A. E. Gottfried, 1984). We used one-tailed tests when we had *a priori* predictions and two-tailed tests when no predictions were put forth. Our hypotheses and the rationale for each are presented first, followed by a summary of the analyses. For the infant version of the HOME, first and foremost, we expected the Variety in Daily Stimulation to be related to giftedness status because this subscale bore the most pervasive relation to cognitive development in our earlier work. Other subscales showing a significant relation to cognitive development were Maternal Involvement with the Child, Emotional and Verbal Responsivity of Mother, and to a lesser degree, Provision of Appropriate Play Materials. Avoidance of Restriction and Punishment and Organization of Environment subscales showed no significant correlations with cognitive development. For the preschool version, the Stimulation of Academic Behavior subscale was expected to be related to giftedness status because it proved to be the most consistent in its correlation with cognitive development compared to the other preschool subscales. Variety of Stimulation; Stimulation through Toys, Games, and Reading Materials; Language Stimulation; Pride, Affection, and Warmth; and Modeling and Encouragement of Social Maturity also showed a consistent pattern of correlations with cognitive measures. The Physical Environment subscale showed a weak relation to cognitive development, and the Physical Punishment subscale was unrelated to cognitive functioning. Our expectations for the subscales of the elementary version were derived from our knowledge of the differences observed in the earlier versions. Those specific subscales involving cognitive enrichment and family involvement would be expected to relate to cognitive functioning. We would not expect the Aspects of the Physical Environment subscale to account for differences, and we had no prediction about the Emotional Climate subscale.

Table 6.2 presents the means, standard deviations, and *t*-test results for all of the subscales of the three versions of the HOME. Before proceeding with the statistical analyses, it is noteworthy that, in every instance (with the exception of Restriction and Punishment at 1.25 years), the quality and quantity of home stimulation was higher for the gifted children than the nongifted children. For the infant version, statistical analyses showed that the only scale that differentiated the groups was Opportunities for Variety in Daily Stimulation. Four of the preschool-version subscales were significant: Stimulation through Toys, Games, and Reading Materials; Language Stimulation; Stimulation of Academic Behavior; Pride, Affection, and Warmth. Five of the elementary version subscales were significant: Emotional and Verbal Responsivity; Growth Fostering Materials and Experiences; Provision for Active Stimulation; Family Participation in Developmentally Stimulating Experiences; Paternal Involvement. In no case were scales assessing the physical environment significant. Collectively, our results show that the home environments of gifted children are characterized as being more stimulating and socially responsive, and having greater parental involvement than those of nongifted children. In no instance did we find a reversal in the predicted direction; that is, nowhere did we find the nongifted group receiving a significantly greater level of home stimulation.

In summary, the preponderance of our hypotheses were supported by the planned comparison analyses. The families of gifted children provided more stimulating activities than did the families of nongifted children. Moreover, the parents were more involved with and apparently more invested in providing their children with a cognitively advantageous home environment. Whereas prior researchers found

Table 6.2. Comparisons of Means between Gifted and Nongifted Children: Home Observation and Measurement of Environment (HOME) Inventory

	Giftedness status		
	Gifted	Nongifted	*t*
1.25 years (*N* = 105)			
Responsivity	8.8 (1.4)	8.7 (1.6)	0.26
Restriction & Punishment	6.4 (1.0)	6.5 (1.1)	−0.43
Organization	5.4 (0.8)	5.2 (0.9)	0.72
Play Materials	8.7 (0.5)	8.6 (0.7)	0.37
Maternal Involvement	4.4 (1.0)	4.0 (1.2)	1.29
Variety of Stimulation	4.0 (0.6)	3.4 (1.0)	3.07**
3.25 years (*N* = 103)			
Toys, Games, Materials	9.7 (0.8)	8.9 (1.7)	3.10**
Language Stimulation	6.4 (1.0)	5.5 (1.2)	2.98**
Physical Environment	6.7 (0.5)	6.6 (0.7)	0.67
Pride, Affection, Warmth	5.5 (1.7)	4.8 (1.6)	1.73*
Academic Stimulation	4.3 (1.2)	3.3 (1.4)	3.11**
Social Maturity Modeling	3.7 (1.1)	3.4 (1.1)	1.14
Variety of Stimulation	7.2 (1.2)	6.6 (1.4)	1.49
Physical Punishment	3.5 (0.5)	3.4 (0.9)	0.62
8 years (*N* = 103)			
Responsivity	9.7 (0.5)	9.2 (1.1)	3.19**
Encourage Maturity	6.3 (1.0)	5.8 (1.3)	1.48
Emotional Climate	6.1 (1.1)	6.0 (1.2)	0.09
Materials & Experiences	6.8 (1.1)	5.9 (1.3)	2.78**
Active Stimulation	6.8 (1.0)	5.4 (1.5)	5.16***
Family Participation	5.5 (0.7)	4.6 (1.0)	4.33***
Paternal Involvement	3.2 (1.1)	2.6 (1.2)	1.98*
Physical Environment	7.6 (0.8)	7.2 (0.9)	1.39

Note. Standard deviations in parentheses. All tests were one-tailed except Restriction & Punishment and Organization at 1.25 years, Physical Environment and Physical Punishment at 3.25 years, and Emotional Climate and Physical Environment at 8 years.
*$p < .05$. **$p < .01$. ***$p < .001$.

differences in the home environment of gifted children as well, we present evidence that their homes were more stimulating from infancy onward. Furthermore, there were a greater number of significant differences emerging with advancement in age from infancy through the primary school years (see also A. W. Gottfried, 1984b). This latter observation suggests an interaction between the child and environment that complements the interaction between the child and parent as suggested by Olszewski et al. (1987). Further, the notion that gifted children receive more environmental stimulation because they process information more effectively (Freeman, 1979) and therefore assimilate more quickly is a likely conclusion to be drawn from the findings here. We presented evidence in Chapter 3 that parents recognize their gifted child's potential early in infancy. We would expect responsive parents to react by providing more stimulating environments.

Purdue Home Stimulation Inventory (PHSI). Among the 13 PHSI items at 1.25 years that bore some relationship to cognitive development in the early years (A. W. Gottfried & A. E. Gottfried, 1984), four showed significant differences between the gifted and nongifted children. First, the gifted children had fewer siblings (75% had no siblings) than the nongifted children (40% had no siblings) (χ^2 (1, N = 107) = 6.56, $p < .01$). This finding supports the preponderance of those in the literature who find there are more firstborn children in gifted groups (e.g., Barbe, 1956, 1981; Cornell, 1984; Freeman, 1979; Hollingworth, 1942; Sheldon, 1954). The literature also reveals that gifted children are more likely to be only borns as well (Hollingworth, 1942; Sheldon, 1954). The differences we found in number of children in the home at 1 year of age, which is analogous to the variable of birth-order status noted earlier, were maintained at age 8 years. Whereas 25% (5/20) of the gifted children continued to be only children at age 8 years, only 10.6% (8/87) of the nongifted children were still only children at this age. This difference was significant (χ^2 (1, N = 107) = 3.8, p = .05).

Second, gifted children were read to by parents more each day than nongifted children (t(adjusted df = 23.6) = 2.28, p = .03). The average amount of time per day parents reported reading to gifted children was 26.55 min (SD = 29.68); the corresponding figure for nongifted children was 10.59 min (SD = 21.05). What is most interesting about this finding is that it is occurring during infancy. Very early in the lives of gifted children, they receive a greater amount of exposure to parents reading to them than do children who do not become gifted. Whereas researchers as early as Terman noted that gifted children had more books and read more often than nongifted children, we have shown that this practice begins in infancy and is likely to be initiated by mothers reading to their children.

The final two items revealing significant differences from the PHSI were encouragement of self-help skills and rooms per person in the home. Children in the gifted group (35%) were more likely to receive training in dressing themselves than children in the nongifted group (11.5%) (χ^2 (1, N = 107) = 5.08, p = .024). The more rapid development of self-help skills was noted in Chapter 5 as well. What is noteworthy is that there were differences at this very young age. Why these children are ahead of their nongifted peers may be attributed to the finding that proportionally more gifted children are the firstborn in the family, and firstborn children are more likely to be independent. Finally, there was a larger room-to-person ratio in the homes of gifted children (M = 3.17, SD = .74) than in the homes of nongifted children (M = 2.68, SD = .83; t(105) = 2.45, p = .016). This latter variable is interesting in that room-to-person ratio corresponds with cognitive functioning during the adult years as well (Gribbin, Schaie, & Parham, 1980). Again, these data support the view that gifted children are receiving an intellectually more advantageous environment than nongifted children in the opening years of life.

It is impossible to determine the directionality of environmental-intellectual development from our data. While environmental input may certainly be the result of parents' efforts, it may well be the demands these children make on their parents for intellectually enhancing materials and activities (A. W. Gottfried & A. E. Gottfried, 1984). Our earlier work suggested that infants differing in cognitive development elicited correspondingly different levels of stimulation in the preschool years. Data presented below will show that gifted children place significantly more demands on their parents for extracurricular activities. Hence, the relation between intellectually gifted status and environment may be interpreted bidirectionally.

Nonobservational Assessments of the Home Environment

Variety of Experiences Checklist. Results of the planned comparisons in which gifted children were expected to have experienced a greater variety of experiences outside of the home during the preschool years was not borne out. Our earlier findings showed these variables to be correlated positively and significantly, albeit at low magnitudes, with cognitive development (A. W. Gottfried & A. E. Gottfried, 1984) during preschool period. However, there were no differences between the gifted and nongifted groups on this specific variable. Perhaps within a middle-class sample, fine-line differences are not found in the children's experiences outside of the home, but rather in their experiences within the home setting.

Home Environment Survey. The HES was analyzed for each of the factors at 5, 7, and 8 years. The factors, with the items loading on each, are listed in Table 6.1. We had specific hypotheses about the factors explicitly assessing the academically oriented materials in the home available to children and the involvement of parents in their children's academic and cultural activities; hence, these factors were analyzed with one-tailed *t* tests. Because we had no *a priori* expectation for the remaining factors, these were analyzed with two-tailed *t* tests.

At 5 years, there were three factors: Mother Provides Educational Stimulation, Educational Attitudes, and Provisions of Learning Materials. As one can readily see in Table 6.1, each of these factors contains items related to academically oriented activities. Therefore, we expected gifted children to score higher than nongifted children on all three factors. Our hypotheses were supported for two factors: Mother Provides Educational Stimulation ($t(83) = 3.24, p < .002$) and Provisions of Learning Materials ($t(83) = 1.95, p = .027$). Gifted children made more monthly trips to the library and had mothers who read to them more each day and spent more time with them on academic skills than did nongifted children. Gifted children were also provided with more learning materials such as activity books, electronic teaching aids, and computer experience. It is interesting to note the consistency of these findings with reading more to the child on the PHSI at 1.25 years and the academic stimulation and materials subscales of the HOME at 3.25 years. The third factor, Educational Attitudes, did not significantly differentiate the two groups. Examination of the items reveals that only one is directly related to academic attitudes: educational level child is expected to receive. Two of the items assess the actual amount of time the children and mothers watch TV each day, and the last is a measure of whether children have their own musical instruments. Clearly, these are a heterogeneous set of items and hence may account for nonsignificance in the analysis.

At 7 years, the three factors were Mother Provides Educational Stimulation, Educational Attitudes, and Mothers' Time Involvement with Child. The first two factors, as shown in Table 6.1, contain items similar to those bearing the same name at age 5 years, specifically, items relating to academic experiences. We made the same *a priori* predictions for these two factors, that is, we hypothesized that gifted children would score higher than nongifted children. We had no expectations for Mothers' Time Involvement with Child and therefore conducted a two-tailed test. Results of the planned comparisons analyses showed support for one of our hypotheses. Gifted children scored higher than nongifted children on Mother Provides Educational Stimulation (t(adjusted df = 37.6) = 2.33, p = .013). There was no significant difference between the groups for Educational Attitudes. These results are consistent with those from the 5-year analyses. In the school-entry years, gifted children receive more academically oriented materials and have mothers who are more involved with them in academic activities. But, the factor we labeled Educational Attitudes was apparently too heterogeneous in nature, and this possibly accounted for its nonsignificance. The third factor, Mothers' Time Involvement with Child, was unrelated to giftedness status. It therefore appears that the time, as measured in actual time, mothers spend with children does not differentiate the two groups of children. This becomes more apparent as we evaluate the 8-year data.

The items of the HES at the 8-year assessment are listed with their respective factors in Table 6.1. Consistent with prior hypotheses, we expected factors with an academic basis to significantly differentiate the two groups. These were Learning Opportunities and Reading Involvement with Children. We had no expectation for the remaining three factors: TV Time and Mothers' and Fathers' Time Involvement with Child. One-tailed t tests found support for both hypotheses. Learning opportunities were significantly higher for the gifted children compared to the nongifted children ($t(101) = 3.67$, $p < .001$). Gifted children had more access to real musical instruments, more of their own and family magazine/book/journal subscriptions, more private lessons, more experience with a computer at home, and higher educational aspirations by their parents. Ongoing reading to the child in the early years is consistently associated with gifted intelligence at 8 years. Reading Involvement with Child was also significant ($t(105) = 2.92$, $p = .002$). Gifted children were more likely to make more trips to the library each month, read by themselves more each day, and have their own dictionary. Again, as shown in the infancy measures and by other researchers (Colangelo & Dettmann, 1983; R. L. Cox, 1977; Terman, 1925–1929), activities involving reading continue to differentiate the gifted and nongifted groups. Results of the two-tailed t tests, for which we had no *a priori* hypotheses, were not significant. Thus, we found that academically oriented activities and experiences differentiated the gifted from the nongifted group, but not parental contact as measured by parental reports of actual time spent with children.

One can see that significant differences were consistently found for those factors reflecting academically oriented experiences and not for factors reflecting the amount of time parents spend with children per se. The amount of time family members watch TV was included in each of the HES questionnaires and consistently revealed nonsignificant differences between the groups. Our findings of differences in academically oriented materials and activities are in accord with those reported by Freeman (1979). We conclude that it is not necessarily the actual time parents devote to children, but the active involvement in academically and culturally oriented activities that differentiate the gifted from nongifted children. In a nutshell, it is the quality and not the quantity of involvement that is consequential.

While we were surprised that we found no differences for the factor labeled Educational Attitudes at ages 5 and 7 years, particularly in view that parents of gifted children are more highly educated, a closer look at the factor reveals a heterogeneous set of items. Only one—Educational Aspirations—directly assesses the educational/academic domain. Because of the developmental and psychological significance of this one item, we chose to analyze it separately at each age. This item was also the highest-loading item on the Educational Attitudes factor at ages 5 and 7 years and on the Learning Opportunities factor at age 8 years. Specifically, mothers were asked how much education they expected their child to receive by checking either high school degree, college degree, master's degree, or professional degree. The results of the chi-square analyses were significant at each age. The mothers of gifted children had higher educational aspirations for their child. At the 5-year assessment, 70% (14/20) of gifted children were expected to receive at least a master's degree as opposed to 31.7% (26/82) of nongifted children (χ^2 (3, N = 102) = 11.37, $p < .01$). The corresponding values for the 7- and 8-year assessments were 65.0% (13/20) and 32.6% (28/86) (χ^2 (3, N = 106) = 7.80, p = .05); and 70% (14/20) and 32.6% (27/83) (χ^2 (3, N = 103) = 12.76, p = .005). What is noteworthy in these analyses is that mothers of gifted children had higher educational aspirations for their children 3 years before we identified them as gifted. Further, not one mother of a gifted child checked only a high school degree, whereas 6% to 7% of the nongifted mothers did at each of the three assessments. Without knowing what aspirations mothers had for their children at birth or during early infancy, it is impossible to determine whether the intellectual status of the children influenced their expectations. Nevertheless, it is overwhelmingly evident that gifted children live in an environment that is supportive of educational achievements and intellectual advancement. Furthermore, mothers of gifted children were also more highly educated. Aspirations for their children may reflect their own educational attainment.

In summary, three major findings emerged from the aforementioned analyses of both the observational and nonobservational home assessments. First, it is evident that across the preschool and early elementary school years, gifted compared to nongifted children are provided with more opportunities and materials that foster intellectual and academic growth. Second, parents of gifted children are more involved in their children's academic activities. Third, reading activities differentiate gifted children from nongifted children starting in infancy and continuing into the early elementary years. This combination of provision of the materials and activities along with parental involvement is potent and a key dimension in enhancing children's intellectual development (Freeman, 1979; see also A. W. Gottfried, 1984b).

Child's Request for Activities. We hypothesized that intellectually advanced children would be more persistent in requesting stimulation outside of school and making demands on parents to provide additional activities. This was based on our finding suggesting that young children's differential cognitive development elicited differential levels of stimulation in the preschool years (A. W. Gottfried & A. E. Gottfried, 1984). Therefore, at the 8-year assessment, we asked parents to report on the lessons, sports, clubs, and hobbies that their children had requested. The total number of activities across the categories was analyzed. Results revealed that gifted children on the average requested more activities than nongifted children ($t(101) = 2.94, p = .002$). The mean number of activities requested by gifted children was 6.6 ($SD = 2.1$) as opposed to 5.0 ($SD = 2.3$) for nongifted children. Hence, we have support for our view that gifted children are actively seeking or placing greater demands on their parents for more environmental enrichment.

In order to determine which type of activities requested by children differentiated the giftedness status groups, a one-way MANOVA was conducted with the four types of activities as the dependent measures. The multivariate test was significant ($F(4, 98) = 5.88, p < .001$). The univariate tests showed group differences for lessons, clubs, and hobbies, but not for sports. Gifted children requested significantly more of these types of activities than did nongifted children. The data and univariate F values are presented in Table 6.3. Hence, we have presented evidence that gifted children actively seek out more environmental stimulation than do nongifted children. Moreover, the activities that gifted children requested are domain specific; that is, differences were not found across all extracurricular activities. It is interesting that

Table 6.3. Comparison of Means between Gifted and Nongifted Children: Activities Requested

Activity requested	Giftedness status		Univariate F
	Gifted	Nongifted	
Lessons	2.4(0.9)	1.6(1.1)	9.71**
Sports	1.1(1.1)	1.5(1.0)	2.15
Clubs	1.5(0.8)	0.9(0.7)	13.73***
Hobbies	1.6(1.1)	1.0(1.0)	5.53*

Note. Standard deviations in parentheses. $N = 103$.
*$p < .05$. **$p < .01$. ***$p < .001$.

nongifted children requested more sporting type of activities, although this difference did not reach statistical significance.

Family Relationship Variables

Family Environment Scale. This inventory was completed by mothers when the children were 3, 5, 7, and 8 years of age and by fathers at the 8-year assessment only. For mothers, we had directional hypotheses about four of the ten scales based on our earlier research (A. W. Gottfried & A. E. Gottfried, 1984) with preschool-aged children and that of Cornell (1984) with children between 6 and 11 years of age. These scales were Intellectual-Cultural Orientation, Cohesion, Expressiveness, and Conflict. When the FES was completed by mothers, we expected the families of gifted children to score higher than the families of nongifted children on the first three scales and lower on the last scale. Although we had no predictions about findings based on fathers' reports, we reasoned that their responses may be consistent with mothers. By contrast, Cornell found no significant differences for fathers as respondents in research with gifted children.

For the analyses of mothers' responses, we opted for repeated-measures ANOVA as opposed to the 16 t tests that would be required for planned comparisons. The ANOVA allowed a more powerful test while maintaining a constant Type I error rate. Thus, four 2×4 (Giftedness Status $\times$ Age: 3, 5, 7, and 8 years) repeated-measures ANOVAs were conducted, one for each of the four FES scales for which we had specific hypotheses. For mothers' reports on the Intellectual-Cultural Orientation scale, there was a significant main effect for Giftedness Status ($F(1, 99) = 11.41$, $p = .001$). The intellectually stimulating atmosphere was higher in the homes of gifted children ($M = 7.7$, $SD = 1.6$) than nongifted children ($M = 6.4$, $SD = 1.9$). The families of gifted children support a greater interest in political, social, intellectual, and cultural activities, and perhaps are more actively involved as well. Certainly, we know that gifted children have more academically oriented experiences. These experiences may also generalize to the political, social, and cultural domains.

There was less conflict reported in the homes of gifted children ($M = 2.2$, $SD = 1.7$) than nongifted children ($M = 2.9$, $SD = 1.9$). The repeated-measures ANOVA revealed a main effect of Giftedness Status ($F(1, 99) = 3.91$, $p = .05$). Similarly, there was more cohesion reported in the homes of gifted children ($M = 8.5$, $SD = 0.8$) as compared to nongifted children ($M = 7.9$, $SD = 1.5$). The repeated-measures ANOVA revealed a main effect of Giftedness Status ($F(1, 99) = 3.91$, $p = .05$). Thus, our findings are directly in line with those of Cornell (1984), who found significant differences on the same three scales. The gifted and nongifted groups differed in family Intellectual-Cultural Orientation, Conflict, and Cohesion. There was no difference in the Expressiveness domain.

Because fathers completed the FES at only one assessment period (age 8 years), *t* tests rather than repeated-measures ANOVAs were used to compare the groups. The analyses were conducted as planned comparisons because we expected to find results similar to those of mothers. Furthermore, we wanted to keep the analyses parallel with those of mothers. Significant differences were found for the Intellectual-Cultural Orientation scale only ($t(62) = 1.77$, $p < .05$). As with mothers, the intellectual-cultural atmosphere was greater in the homes of gifted children during early elementary school years. Collectively, the consistent results for mothers across the 5-year span and for fathers at 8 years on the Intellectual-Cultural Orientation scale are highly consistent with the more enriched environments that were noted on the observational and nonobservational measures of the home environment reported earlier. Not only do parents provide more materials and experiences, they also encourage an atmosphere that promotes intellectually stimulating discussions and involvement in cultural and political activities. Further, the results reveal that the stimulating intellectual atmosphere in the homes of gifted children is apparent from the preschool age through the early elementary school years.

The differences between the gifted and nongifted groups for the remaining three scales, Cohesion, Expressiveness, and Conflict, were not significant for fathers' report. Our findings—with the exception of the Intellectual-Cultural Orientation scale—are similar to those of Cornell (1984), who found no differences in any of the FES scales when fathers were respondents.

Family Inventory. This inventory was created in order to obtain a single global measure of family functioning. As described earlier, the factor analysis revealed one general factor and a smaller secondary factor. Both factors were analyzed here with specific predictions, based on our earlier work (Bathurst, 1988). Each parent completed this inventory at the 8-year assessment and the two scales were analyzed separately for mothers and fathers. We expected to find more positive family functioning and less family regulation in the group of gifted children. Results of the planned comparisons supported three of our four hypotheses. From mothers' reports, the family atmosphere was significantly more positive in the homes of gifted children than nongifted children ($t(101) = 1.89, p = .03$). The differences were not significant for fathers' report. For both parents, the families of gifted children when compared to nongifted children regulated family members' behavior less (mothers' reports: $t(101) = -1.78, p = .04$; fathers' reports: $t(64) = -1.90, p = .03$). These findings underscore the importance of parental involvement and suggest differences in the patterns of parental involvement in the homes of gifted and nongifted children. The families of gifted children enjoy doing things together, cooperate with each other, openly discuss feelings, and experience less tension than do families with nongifted children. They also tend to regulate family members and the home environment less. Thus, the families of gifted children are less rule oriented and have less well-defined roles as compared to families of nongifted children.

In summary, gifted children have homes with more cohesion among family members, a less conflictual atmosphere, and less control of family members in the form of rules and regulations. We have strong support for an atmosphere conducive to intellectual and cultural interests. These findings, coupled with results showing gifted children have more materials and experiences conducive to academic stimulation, allow us to paint a more colorful and complete picture of what the home environment experience is like for gifted children during their early years.

SUMMARY

1. The evidence is overwhelming that gifted children compared to nongifted children receive more enriched environments during the early

years (i.e., infancy, preschool, and early elementary). What is exciting about our results is that these differences are found years before children are identified as gifted.

2. While our findings directly support others who have studied gifted children after they are identified, we have provided substantial support for the notion of enriched environmental continuity from infancy to middle childhood for gifted children. The advantages provided to gifted children begin early in development and are noted consistently throughout the early elementary school years, perhaps even beyond.

3. Differences between the home and family environments of gifted and nongifted children were apparent in all three categories: distal environmental variables, proximal environmental variables, and family relationship variables. In every case, where differences were noted, they favored the gifted children.

4. Gifted children come from families with higher socioeconomic status and have parents who are more highly educated than nongifted children. These differences may account for the higher-quality home environments that are provided for gifted children. Gifted children had fathers a few years older than those of nongifted children. Family composition variables that did not distinguish the groups included fathers' occupational status (some differences emerged for mothers' occupational status), mothers' work status, mothers' intelligence, sex of the children, marital status, experience of divorce, age of mothers, and number of adults and children residing in the home.

5. Gifted children were predominantly firstborns, and often only borns.

6. Within the domain of the proximal home environmental variables, gifted children consistently had a more enriched cognitive environment than nongifted children. Parents were more involved, more responsive, and more nurturing in their children's academic endeavors and had higher educational aspirations for their children. These findings are consistent with our earlier findings during infancy and preschool (A. W. Gottfried & A. E. Gottfried, 1984) and with Freeman's (1979, 1991) results.

7. We also found evidence that children play an active role in eliciting environmental stimulation; children are not passive recipients of environmental and parental input. The gifted children placed more demands on parents for stimulating activities. Although it is impossible to determine from our data whether these children are more demanding from the early infancy period or whether they develop into more demanding children because parents provide more for them, one would

hypothesize that the process is one that is continuous, interactive, and effectual; that is, children affect their environment.

8. Within the family relationships domain, the families of gifted children endorse more culturally and intellectually stimulating activities by the time the children are 3 years old, and these differences remain through the early elementary years. These families have a greater degree of cohesion and less conflict. In addition, they impose fewer regulatory controls on family members.

In sum, children who become intellectually gifted grow up in a more advantageous home and family environment with regard to promoting cognitive growth. They experience cognitive enrichment, educational enhancement, and cohesive family relationships during their early years of development.

7

On Becoming Intellectually Gifted

We initiated the research in this book with the assumption that intellectual giftedness is a developmental process; that is, it does not just happen. Although the process of identifying which children are to be considered or designated as intellectually gifted occurs most often during the early elementary years (for both psychometric and educational reasons), it does not mean that this personal attribute is an all-of-a-sudden event. The foregoing findings strongly support the view that intellectual giftedness is a developmental phenomenon.

The intent of this chapter is not to summarize the results. Summaries of the specific findings for each domain investigated have been furnished at the conclusion of each content chapter (Chapters 3–6). The purpose here is to integrate the findings into a developmental perspective and put forth our own interpretation of how children become intellectually gifted. Our conceptualization on how children become intellectually gifted shall be known as the "Potentiality-Enrichment Theory." We view this as an initial stage of theory development and expect that future empirical work will help to elaborate the theory.

All theories of human behavior and development are based on probabilities, that is, the likelihood that certain behaviors or actions (or reactions) occur under specified conditions or that certain kinds of behaviors are likely to follow other types of behaviors. As noted in Chapter 3, one may develop a theory of how children become intellectually gifted but not of how an individual child emerges as intellectually gifted. The individual case profiles of intellectual quotients across time presented in Chapter 3 demonstrated that there were as many individual ontogenetic age patterns as there were gifted children. This strongly underscores the importance of acknowledging the variability or uniqueness in the course of intellectual performance over time, particularly during the early years. Explaining how an individual became gifted, accomplished, talented, or recognized in an area may rest on detailed biographical observations and accounts. Just as intellectually gifted children are statistically exceptional, individuals contained within the gifted population are also unique or exceptional in their own developmental way. We assert that each child who emerges as intellectually gifted does so at his or her own developmental tempo. For example, the concept of "late bloomers" would fit into our views on the individuality of becoming gifted. By the same token or principle, a highly gifted or exceptionally talented child may become an ordinary adult if continuity of environmental enrichment, support, or opportunity is diminished. Our theorizing focuses on behaviors and environmental experiences that are likely to exist in the early course of development in children who become intellectually gifted as a group.

POTENTIALITY-ENRICHMENT THEORY

Our Potentiality-Enrichment conceptualization of how children become intellectually gifted pertains to the interface of children's cognitive ability, their intrinsic motivation, and a cognitively stimulating home environment. Evidence for each of these aspects was obtained in this longitudinal study. The early evidence regarding a proneness to reach superior levels of cognitive performance was found during infancy on the Bayley, the preschool years on the McCarthy, and the early school years on academic achievement with the KABC achievement scale, WRAT-R, and Woodcock-Johnson. Group differences favoring children who became gifted compared to nongifted were obtained across all these measures and age periods, beginning at 1.5 years. More important from the theoretical perspective, the gifted in contrast to nongifted children were significantly more likely to attain superior intelligence scores at least once during the infancy and preschool periods. Individual children in the gifted group varied with respect to when these elevations occurred within each period. Moreover, they did not exhibit the same pattern of elevation on subtests of the McCarthy or Woodcock-Johnson. Therefore, there was a great deal of individuality in the expression of superior scores. Similarly, the case profiles across time corroborated the individuality of the spiked patterns. Our interpretation of these spikes is that they are indications of the ability of these children and their potential range of effect or signs of reach. Lastly, these results highlight the importance of employing a time-frame analysis in the assessment of superior cognitive ability. If a single point in time or age had been employed as is usually done in research and practice, we would have missed the identification of potential. Because of the highly variable developmental tempo in infants and young children, the use of a single time assessment is likely to fail to identify potentially gifted children. By contrast, with repeated assessments across time, the opportunity to express one's potential is given more latitude. These elevated scores may be early signs in the developmental course of intellectual giftedness and may serve as cues in its detection. Furthermore, superior cognitive competence may be revealed in everyday cognitive activities within the home environment, which in turn may catch the attention of a knowledgeable or astute parent.

Our findings regarding gifted children's advanced language during infancy and the preschool years are relevant here. Accelerated receptive and expressive language abilities may be indicators of potential intellectual/cognitive giftedness, not only for researchers, but for parents as well. Consequently, enhanced cognitive and language skills may elicit greater parental involvement and provision of cognitive stimulation and experiences.

There were, however, instances of spikes for children in the nongifted group as well. This raises the issue of why some children evidenced spikes in their early course of development but did not become gifted by age 8 years. There are several possible explanations: (1) they have not yet become gifted; that is, such children may be late bloomers; (2) the environmental advantages are not present; (3) parents failed to recognize the child's ability and consequently did not nurture the accelerated development; and (4) the child's own motivation is insufficient to encourage or elicit more advantageous environmental stimulation.

At the heart of superior intellect may be motivation for or pleasure inherent in acquiring knowledge, that is, intrinsic motivation. Our data indicate that cognitive mastery motivation and eventually academic intrinsic motivation are characteristics of the intellectually gifted from infancy and thereafter. During infancy and early childhood, the gifted children's test-taking behaviors showed that they became readily and enthusiastically engaged in the cognitive demands of these tests. They were rated as being significantly more goal directed; having greater absorption in tasks as indicated by longer attention spans; revealing more intense interest in and reactivity to the test materials; showing greater cooperation with the examiner; having a more positive emotional tone; and being less fearful in the testing situation. These data are also in accord with our other findings regarding children's testability. During the preschool years, children who become gifted were highly unlikely to be untestable compared to children who did not become gifted. As reported, the rate of untestable children among the nongifted was fourfold that of children who became gifted.

Gifted children also evidenced significantly greater academic intrinsic motivation, lower academic anxiety, and more positive perceptions of their academic competence at ages 7 and 8 years. In a follow-up study we conducted of the children at ages 9 and 10 years, the gifted continued to show superior academic intrinsic motivation as measured by the *Children's Academic Intrinsic Motivation Inventory* (A. E. Gottfried, 1986a). We also found continuity between early test-taking behaviors as measured in infancy and early childhood with academic intrinsic motivation scores during the school years (A. E. Gottfried & A. W. Gottfried, 1993). This means that such cognitive mastery motivation test-taking behaviors as indexed above are both precursors and predictors of future academic intrinsic motivation during the school years. Overall, the children who subsequently became gifted revealed superior motivation during infancy, preschool, and the school-age years. These data are also consistent with findings by A. E. Gottfried (1990) that academic intrinsic motivation is positively correlated with IQ. Children with higher IQs, and, in particular, gifted children, find more pleasure in learning and cognitive tasks, experience more intrinsic motivation, and are indeed more competent at such tasks and schooling. On the basis of these data, we hypothesize that children who are intellectually gifted are likely to be motivationally gifted, although we are not proposing a one-to-one correspondence between intelligence and motivation.

Our educational and achievement data are interpretable within a motivational as well as the cognitive framework. The gifted children had consistently higher academic achievement on both standardized tests and teacher and parent ratings, and their teachers rated the gifted children as significantly harder working, better behaved, and learning more in the classroom setting. Inasmuch as academic intrinsic motivation has also been shown to be positively correlated with academic achievement and a unique predictor of current and future achievement (A. E. Gottfried, 1985, 1990; A. E. Gottfried, Fleming, & A. W. Gottfried, 1994), gifted children's higher academic performance can be interpreted as containing a strong motivational component. Additionally, gifted children were highly unlikely to have their kindergarten entry delayed, and they were never retained in school. From a young age, children who become gifted are academically more ready for school entry (keep in mind our sample of children comprised young 5-year-olds at kindergarten entry), more successful in school, and evidence a greater orientation toward the cognitive challenges of school.

It has become increasingly common for schools to set earlier deadlines for kindergarten entry so that children who are accepted for the fall term must be 5 years old by June or September rather than by December. In some instances, there have been separate deadlines established for boys and girls, with boys having to be older than girls. The purpose of this practice is ostensibly to prevent "immature" children from entering kindergarten. We seriously question this policy, particularly for gifted children. Chronological age should not be used as an index for developmental status. Gifted children may suffer if they are denied entry into kindergarten on the basis of their chronological age. Gifted children who are forced to delay entry due to age alone may not be provided with adequate cognitive and/or academic stimulation. Denying them optimal environmental opportunity to develop their abilities may result in inadequate challenge and a reduction in their intrinsic motivation.

From our theorizing, we would propose that academically underachieving gifted children are less adequately motivated. The absence of sufficient environmental supports for intrinsic motivation, such as inadequately challenging cognitive tasks in the school and home environments, could undermine fruition of their intellectual potential (also see Monks et al., 1986; Rimm & Lowe, 1988; Tuttle et al., 1988; Whitmore, 1986). As theoretically proposed and empirically demonstrated, children's home environments, including the provision of adequate stimulation, mastery experiences, and parental encouragement of task endogeny, promote the development of mastery and academic intrinsic motivation (A. E. Gottfried, 1986b; A. E. Gottfried, Fleming, & A. W. Gottfried, 1994; A. E. Gottfried & A. W. Gottfried, 1991).

In our view, motivation is not simply a concomitant of intellectual giftedness. Rather, motivation is an essential component without which gifted children are unlikely to evidence their gift. The foundation for this statement rests on the integral nature or interface of intellect, motivation, and environment. These three aspects are inextricably intertwined in that each continuously promotes the others. For example, a child with a higher intellectual ability is likely to have greater mastery or intrinsic motivation that is further stimulated through active attempts to demand more stimulation of the environment. To the extent that the environment is accommodating to the child's efforts, higher stimulation, challenge, and mastery experiences are likely to be provided. This environmental provision in turn further fosters greater intellect and motivation.

Our research provided overwhelming evidence that gifted children are embedded in an intellectually and culturally advantageous home atmosphere. The intellectual ecology of the homes they grow up in is facilitative of cognitive advancement. This was indicated by the proximal, distal, and family relationship variables. Throughout the early years, they received a more cognitively enriched home environment. They were provided with significantly more environmental stimulation, parental involvement and responsiveness, and academically enhancing materials and experiences. These findings support our view that the parents of children who become gifted actively provide a more enriched cognitive and educational curriculum in their homes. Additionally, their families had higher intellectual and cultural orientations, higher family cohesiveness, and less regulation of family members. This latter finding regarding lower regulation of family members is in accord with theories regarding family processes that are conducive to the development of children's task endogeny and intrinsic motivation (A. E. Gottfried, Fleming, & A. W. Gottfried, 1994); that is, self-determination, a characteristic of intrinsic motivation, ought to be facilitated in homes with less external family regulation.

Parents of gifted children were more highly educated and they had higher educational aspirations for the children who became gifted. Mothers perceived gifted children as more highly developed intellectually compared to other young children of the same age. Gifted children were predominantly firstborns and quite often only borns, both of which place them in a particularly advantageous position to benefit from a greater degree of home environmental enrichment. Our research on home environment and early cognitive development has shown that firstborns compared to later borns receive a significantly greater level of proximal stimulation (A. W. Gottfried & A. E. Gottfried, 1984). While reflecting on the predominance of firstborns and only borns in the sample of gifted children, we considered how second and later borns become gifted when they are in a statistically less favored position. Our speculations led us to consider the possibility that a later-born, gifted child is even more superior in his or her intellect than a firstborn because he or she needs to counteract a less favorable family position. To follow up on this idea, we compared the 8-year IQ scores of the gifted firstborn and only-born ($N = 16$), second-born ($N = 3$), and later-born ($N = 1$)

children. The mean of the gifted second- and later-born children was higher than that of the gifted firstborns and only borns—140.25 versus 137.25, respectively. We then examined the IQ score of each child. Of the second borns, all of the IQ scores were above 140 (142, 143, and 145). The third-born child had an IQ score of 131. Of the firstborns and only borns, 6 of the 16 (37.5%) had IQ scores above 140 ranging from 141 to 145, whereas the IQ scores of the remaining 10 children were between 130 and 139. Hence, our hunch about the superiority of second and later borns was borne out. Admittedly, this finding is post hoc and speculative since it is based on only four second and later borns. However, we feel that it is a hypothesis worthy of further inquiry in larger samples. If it proves to be valid in other samples, the processes by which second and later borns become more highly gifted would need to be explored.

Not only were the gifted children furnished with more cognitively enriching environments, but they were also more active in eliciting developmentally enhancing experiences. Earlier findings from this longitudinal project suggested that young children differing in cognitive development elicit correspondingly different levels of home stimulation (A. W. Gottfried & A. E. Gottfried, 1984). Findings in the present research show that gifted children made significantly more requests of their parents for extracurricular activities. In a similar vein, Durkin (1966) found that children who were early readers were persistent in eliciting reading instruction from their parents. Hence, it is our conclusion that children who become intellectually gifted compared to nongifted are more environmentally engaged.

In addition to receiving and eliciting greater cognitive stimulation, we contend that intellectually gifted children benefit more—that is, in a more mentally sophisticated way—from environmental enrichment. First, with chronological age corrected, gifted children are (by definition) advanced in their mental age as presented in Chapter 3. Their patterns of intellectual abilities were not markedly different from the nongifted, but their level of development was advanced. Hence, this advancement provides an advantage for extracting and interpreting knowledge from their environmental interactions. Second, teachers' reports indicated that the children who became gifted learned more. Last, academic achievement was significantly higher in the gifted both as a group and as individuals; gifted children were more likely to evidence performance at superior levels.

Our findings are entirely consistent with the large body of data on the environments of gifted children and eminent adults. Our study is unique because this is the first empirical documentation of enriched environments, in infancy and early childhood, of children who ultimately become intellectually gifted. Our data also reveal considerable continuity in the elevation of environmental stimulation for gifted children during the early years. The fact that we are finding the same environmental profile during the early life of children who become gifted as obtained by other researchers and biographers for older children underscores the role of environments and the continuity or stability of enhanced home environmental stimulation in the course of development of the intellectually gifted. In our theorizing, the continuity or maintenance of environmental enrichment is a factor of utmost importance in the development of intellectual giftedness.

In summary, embedded in the Potentiality-Enrichment Theory of intellectual giftedness are the early behavioral and environmental aspects that emerge in the course of development of these children. First, children who become gifted were highly likely to exhibit superior intellectual performance levels (but not necessarily at the same age) during the early years. During infancy and the preschool years, they were advanced in receptive and expressive language abilities. Second, as early as infancy and into school, these children revealed greater intrinsic motivation. Early in development they were more engaged in tests or tasks placing cognitive demands on them. They were more adept in testing situations and highly unlikely to be untestable in testing conditions. Third, as early as infancy and thereafter they were embedded in a more enriched family atmosphere. By virtue of their parents' education and their birth order they are placed in an intellectually more advantageous position to receive cognitive environmental stimulation. They also elicit such stimulation and benefit more from it. Fourth, children who ultimately become gifted are highly unlikely to be delayed in their kindergarten entry or retained in a grade. Fifth, in the opening years of their education, these children demonstrate an overall higher level of academic achievement, superior levels of academic performance, greater academic intrinsic motivation, less anxiety about learning, and a more positive perception of academic competence. Sixth, gifted children are cognitively well rounded. Gifted IQ implies generalized high intelligence. Seventh, gifted children are socially competent and their intellectual giftedness emerges at no expense to their behavioral functioning, emotionality, or temperament.

IMPLICATIONS

We believe that the factors that have distinguished the gifted and nongifted groups can be used to provide applications for all potentially gifted children. These implications for practice are now discussed.

Identification Strategies and Motivational Assessment

Our data indicate that psychometric measures have a role in the assessment of giftedness from infancy throughout childhood. From infancy on, gifted children's performance on measures of cognitive ability and achievement was more likely to show at least one incidence of superior elevation compared to nongifted children. Hence, there were psychometric indicators of superior performance during infancy and early childhood that occurred prior to the child's attainment of an IQ of at least 130 at age 8 years. However, we would not advocate relying on a single elevation at one point in time during infancy or the preschool years as an index of gifted intellectual performance. A single elevated score during these early years may increase the probability that the child will become gifted from a statistical point of view; however, there is a matrix of factors operating in the pathway to becoming intellectually gifted, as presented throughout this book. Further, a child may not evidence a superior score at one particular time, and yet he or she could evidence a superior score at another point in time. Because children are unlikely to have histories of repeated intellectual assessments during infancy and the preschool years, histories of achievement test performance could be particularly helpful as they are often available from kindergarten onward. Occurrence of a superior score (at or above the second standard deviation) is associated with an increased likelihood that a child is or will become intellectually gifted. Children who attain even one elevated score on any achievement area could be selected for further assessment.

Individuality of the profiles of the gifted children's intellectual performance, as presented in Chapter 3, and in their achievement, as presented in Chapter 4, further supports the importance of examining performance over time. There simply is no one particular intellectual ability, achievement area, or time in development that could be used to identify all gifted children during the early years. Further, examining histories of achievement should not end when entry into the gifted programs begins. Rather, attempts to identify gifted children should be a continuous process to allow for inclusion of children who are not identified as gifted at one point, but who may become identified at a later point. Programs need to remain open to children who do become eligible, and not be restricted to those who happened to have been included early. For children who may become late bloomers, achievement histories and motivation may provide clues as to who they are.

Criteria for entry into gifted programs ought not to be restricted to IQ. Children with superior performance in a particular academic achievement area, such as math or writing, ought to have elementary school programs to accommodate their gifts. For example, there were some children in our nongifted group who did evidence superior academic achievement at the same level as the gifted. Children with superior academic achievement, without an accompanying gifted IQ score, are likely to be omitted from gifted programs. However, their exclusion may diminish their future achievement, academic intrinsic motivation, and ultimately cost society many potentially talented individuals.

We suggest that cognitive mastery and academic intrinsic motivation be included in the identification of gifted children. The inclusion of motivation as a criterion for identification of gifted children has been controversial. For example, on the one hand, Renzulli (1978) advocated the inclusion of task commitment as an identification criterion in order to detect gifted students who might otherwise be excluded by virtue of IQ scores lower than the limit selected. On the other hand, Gagne (1985) criticized the use of motivation for identification and proposed that motivation of gifted children should be a program goal rather than an identification index. Feldhusen and Hoover (1986) propose a view similar to that of Gagne.

Gagne's criticism of the use of motivation to identify gifted children seems based on a competence versus performance distinction. Gagne is concerned that students who are unmotivated, but evidence a gifted IQ, would be omitted from programs. Hence, Gagne's suggestion is for competence (i.e., presumed competence based on the IQ score) to be used preferentially in identification of gifted children. Following Gagne's argument, motivation is a performance variable, and as such, should not be used to identify giftedness.

Gagne also stated that motivation is just a catalyst for giftedness, and not essential to giftedness itself. It is our position that academic intrinsic motivation and early cognitive mastery motivation are integral to the process of giftedness, and not just catalysts. The definition of a catalyst is "one that precipitates a process or event, especially without being involved in or changed by the consequences" (Morris, 1978).

Hence, in Gagne's view, motivation is conceptualized as a separate element that serves to promote giftedness. The present research offers a position that contrasts with Gagne's interpretation. In the present research, intrinsic motivation was studied. This type of motivation is, by definition, enjoyment of the learning process, and an orientation toward mastery, persistence, and challenge (A. E. Gottfried, 1985). Theoretically, intrinsic motivation serves to advance and enhance intellectual development. For example, exposure to optimally discrepant stimuli plays a role in cognitive development and also the motivational process (Hunt, 1971). Our perspective is that intrinsic motivation is integral to intellectual development, not a catalyst or separate element. This view is supported by the empirical findings we presented as well as intrinsic motivation theories.

With regard to the gifted, motivation ought not be considered only a noncognitive personality trait (e.g., Heller & Hany, 1986; Perleth & Heller, 1994), a catalyst (Gagne, 1985), or limited to task commitment (Renzulli, 1986). While all of these diverse types of motivation may play a role in the attainment of intellectual excellence, intrinsic motivation is more inherently involved in intellectual development. As described above, intrinsic motivation is a cognitively based motive emerging from the interaction of the child with cognitive tasks that are of optimal challenge. It therefore promotes the process of reaching intellectual exceptionality. We agree with Renzulli that motivation ought to be used in the identification of gifted children. We take this position because giftedness can be nurtured more effectively if the motivational characteristics of children are identified. Our purpose in advocating that motivation be used in the identification process is to allow for the identification of a greater number of children. Hence, we view this as an inclusionary rather than an exclusionary method. Children who are highly intrinsically motivated could be included in gifted programs even if their actual IQ scores fall below the required cutoff. Since in our view gifted performance is not simply a product of IQ, but is integrally related to motivation, it is entirely appropriate to include academic intrinsic motivation in the identification process.

Behaviors such as goal orientation, persistence, and enthusiasm in and enjoyment of the learning process ought to be included in the assessment of giftedness of young children. Exceptionally strong or salient observed behaviors in these areas may be indicators of intellectual giftedness. For school-age children, strong motivation as evidenced by superior scores on the *Children's Academic Intrinsic Motivation Inventory* and the *Young Children's Academic Intrinsic Motivation Inventory* (A.

E. Gottfried, 1986a, 1990) could be used to supplement the process of identifying gifted children. These instruments would be especially useful for identifying particularly strong motivation in specific academic areas. For example, a child who is performing in the superior range on math achievement, and who likewise evidences strong math motivation, but who does not evidence superior IQ, should be considered as a candidate for gifted programs. Why should this child be denied access to a program suitable to his or her exceptional ability in one area in favor of a child with a gifted IQ who may not evidence the same level of performance and motivation?

Using motivation in the identification process may allow for earlier assessment, and hence provision of suitable stimulation. Intrinsic motivational assessment would not only aid in the identification of well-motivated children, but also those gifted children with lower motivation who could benefit from being placed in a gifted class that is more challenging to them.

In surveying the literature regarding motivation and giftedness, it became apparent that motivation is often used in a global sense without specifying the type of motivation being described. Some authors refer to motivation in the gifted as achievement motivation (Heller & Hany, 1986), task commitment (Renzulli, 1978), or do not specify the type of motivation at all but use the term nonspecifically (Gagne, 1985). This lack of consistency and specificity with regard to motivation is clearly inadequate. First, there are different types of motivation that vary with regard to their centrality versus externality to the cognitive process. The distinction between intrinsic and extrinsic motivation is a good example of this. External consequences are often used as incentives for cognitive performance, but the source of motivation is external to intellectual development rather than being integral to it as in the case of intrinsic motivation. As another example, achievement motivation emerges from an expectancy-value model (Petri, 1991) utilizing concepts involving multiplicative relationships between the motive to succeed and the probability and incentive values of success. These processes involve very different psychological variables than does intrinsic motivation. Hence, different types of human motivation may have different ramifications for the development of giftedness. Our main point here is not to catalog the types of motivation, but to challenge researchers to consider the implications of different types of motivation for gifted and nongifted children, and not to group all different types of motivation together under one common rubric.

Examining test score histories and motivation may aid in the assessment of children who are less likely to be identified as gifted. For example, in our study, firstborns were overwhelmingly more likely to be identified as gifted than later borns. Also, children of relatively lower SES were less likely to be gifted in our study, even though all children were middle class. Examining histories of test scores and motivationally relevant behaviors may provide a more comprehensive and extensive data base for the identification of potential giftedness in subpopulations of the gifted who are usually identified at a lower rate.

Environment and Parenting

Another implication of our research concerns the role of environment in the development of giftedness. Of course, it seems obvious that a maximally enriched home environment appropriate for each child be provided from early infancy onward. However, we advocate the early provision of educational enrichment programs. On the basis of our data, we do not believe that it is adequate to wait until the middle elementary school years for such programs. Children could be benefiting, cognitively and motivationally, from the provision of adequately stimulating and cognitively challenging environments earlier. Because giftedness does not just occur all of a sudden in middle childhood, nor does the supportive home environment occur all of a sudden in middle childhood but rather is enriched from infancy onward, neither should the school programs for gifted children be delayed until the middle or upper elementary school grades. In our opinion, this practice misses an important opportunity to develop a child's potential.

Our data have many implications for parenting of the gifted. There have been many treatments of this topic in the literature, and we do not seek to review these. Books are readily available to the public (e.g., Golant, 1991). Rather, the present data indicate some special aspects of parenting that deserve to be highlighted.

Gifted children's parents' perceptions of the advancement of their child's ability, relative to other children, emerged as early as infancy. These perceptions were consistent with the child's cognitive advancement (intellectual and verbal). In addition, parents of gifted children provided more stimulating and enriched environments from infancy through childhood. These two factors, parental perception and the provision of stimulating environments, can be very important to the development of exceptional intellectual ability. Parents who perceive that their children are more advanced than others may provide more environmental opportunities and experiences to foster cognitive development. These parents may have, or come to have, higher expectations for their child's ultimate development and academic achievement than parents with relatively lower perceptions of their child's development. Parents of such children may also have great pride in their child's advancement, which may enhance the child's cognitive and academic self-concept.

Bloom (1982) noted in his work with talented individuals that parents played an exceptionally important role in procuring the proper level of skill development for their children once they acknowledged the gift their children had. Bloom indicated that musical families selectively focused on music cues, and promoted those in the children, whereas athletic families focused on athletic cues. Bloom's point is that for many children, these cues may go unnoticed, albeit they may exist. In families bent toward a particular talent, the parent attends to the special behaviors consistent with that skill.

Bloom's work, as well as our own contained in this book, and that published earlier (A. W. Gottfried & A. E. Gottfried, 1984), suggests the importance of a bidirectional view of environmental stimulation. In the present study, gifted children not only had more cognitively stimulating homes, but also made more requests for extracurricular lessons and activities compared to nongifted children. Bloom's (1982) work implies that bidirectionality exists between the child's overt evidence of a special talent and the parents' acumen in detecting and responding to this talent.

We view the role of stimulation in intellectual development in general, and gifted intelligence in particular, as a continuous, bidirectional, active process between children and their parents. Additionally, a substantial body of evidence undeniably indicates that home environmental processes including cognitive and academic stimulation are significantly related to intelligence, cognitive development, and academic achievement (A. W. Gottfried & A. E. Gottfried, 1984; Kellaghan, Sloane, Alvarez, & Bloom, 1993). Less is known, however, about the nature of bidirectionality between children and parents. The manner in which gifted children may elicit higher levels of stimulation and the responsiveness of parents to children's behaviors and characteristics need further investigation.

We take exception to the concept of the hurried child with respect to early cognitive skill training, which Elkind (1981) conceives of as pushing children to satisfy parental needs. While he does acknowledge the importance of challenge, and the fact that some children do gravitate to learn academic skills on their own at an early age, he appears to have a static, rather than interactive, view of the role of environment. His treatment of the topic implies that children are being imposed upon by parental pressures. Although we acknowledge that some parents may indeed inappropriately push and pressure children, this does not appear to be the general case in the early development of children who attain gifted IQs. The opposite danger lies in the understimulation of potentially gifted children for fear of pushing them.

Aside from the role of environment, the present research supports several other implications for parenting gifted children. Parents need to be aware of the following. First, myths and stereotypes, such as maladjustment of the gifted, still abound, as presented in Chapter 1. Parents need accurate information that dispels these myths. Planning for their gifted child's future should not be influenced by inaccurate myths. Our scientific analysis of the gifted child within the family presents a positive picture of his or her development and family life. This is in accordance with other major literature, such as Terman's study. Second, parents need to be apprised of the uniqueness of each gifted child. There is no one pattern that characterizes gifted children as a whole. Developmental timing and areas of development that are accelerated differ from child to child. There is no one age at which giftedness occurs. Rather, extremely high performance can occur on cognitive and academic achievement tests at different times for different children. Gifted children do not necessarily excel across all areas. Third, testing of young children at one point in time can be misleading. As our analyses and recommendations point out, multiple-point testing, rather than single-point testing, is needed. Hence, if a child achieves a score in the gifted range at one point in time, that child may not necessarily test in the gifted range at a later time. Similarly, if a child is tested and does not attain a superior score, that does not necessarily mean that the child is not gifted or that he or she would not attain a gifted score at a later time. Early single-point testing can result in erroneous perceptions and expectations regarding either exceptionally high or average performance.

Our overall recommendation is for parents to follow their child's lead, and to be careful observers of their child's development. Parents should respond appropriately to their child's bids for stimulation based on the child's interest and responsiveness to different activities. Parents ought to provide experiences that enhance their child's development without inappropriately demanding achievement. Overall, their children's joy in the learning process is the ultimate goal without which, we believe, intellectual giftedness will not easily be evidenced. Hence, parents need to be aware of the concepts of intrinsic motivation and its inherent importance to the development of intellectual giftedness. If parents truly understand this, then appropriate stimulation and excellent development in all children, be they gifted or nongifted, can occur.

In conclusion, giftedness is not a chance event; it is not a coincidental phenomenon. There are early precursors, and possibly predictors, and definitely developmental and environmental aspects to its emergence. We assert that giftedness will blossom when children's cognitive ability, motivation, and enriched environments coexist and meld together to foster its growth.

References

Achenbach, T. M. (1991a). *Manual for the Child Behavior Checklist/4–18 and 1991 Profile.* Burlington: University of Vermont Department of Psychiatry.

Achenbach, T. M. (1991b). *Manual for the Teacher's Report Form and 1991 Profile.* Burlington: University of Vermont Department of Psychiatry.

Albert, R. S. (1980). Family position and the attainment of eminence: A study of special family positions and special family experiences. *Gifted Child Quarterly, 24,* 87–95.

Albert, R. S., & Runco, M. A. (1986). The achievement of eminence: A model based on a longitudinal study of exceptionally gifted boys and their families. In R. J. Sternberg & J. E. Davidson (Eds.), *Conceptions of giftedness* (pp. 332–357). New York: Cambridge University Press.

Austin, A. B., & Draper, D. C. (1981). Peer relationships of the academically gifted: A review. *Gifted Child Quarterly, 25,* 129–133.

Baldwin, B. T., & Stecher, L. I. (1923). *Mental growth curve of normal and superior children studied by means of consecutive intelligence examinations* (Vol. 2). Iowa City: University of Iowa.

Barbe, W. B. (1956). A study of the family background of the gifted. *Journal of Educational Psychology, 47,* 302–309.

Barbe, W. B. (1981). A study of the family background of the gifted. In W. B. Barbe & J. S. Renzulli (Eds.), *Psychology and education of the gifted* (3rd ed.). New York: Irvington Publishers.

Bates, E., O'Connell, B., & Shore, C. (1987). Language and communication in infancy. In J. D. Osofsky (Ed.), *Handbook of infant development* (2nd ed., pp. 149–203). New York: John Wiley & Sons.

Bates, J. E. (1980). The concept of difficult temperament. *Merrill-Palmer Quarterly, 26,* 299–319.

Bates, J. E., Freeland, C. A., & Lounsbury, M. L. (1979). Measurement of infant difficultness. *Child Development, 50,* 794–803.

Bathurst, K. (1988). The inventories of family functioning: A psychometric analysis. University of California at Los Angeles. *Dissertation Abstracts International, 49*(7), 2918B (University Microfilms No. DA 88–22158).

Bathurst, K., & Gottfried, A. W. (1987a). Untestable subjects in child development research: Developmental implications. *Child Development, 58,* 1135–1144.

Bathurst, K., & Gottfried, A. W. (1987b, April). *Confirmatory factor analysis of the Family Environment Scale using structural equation modeling.* Paper presented at annual convention of Western Psychological Association, Long Beach.

Bayley, N. (1969). *Bayley Scales of Infant Development.* New York: Psychological Corporation.

Bayley, N. (1970). Development of mental abilities. In P. H. Mussen (Ed.), *Manual of child psychology* (Vol. 1, pp. 1163–1209). New York: John Wiley & Sons.

Behar, L., & Stringfield, S. (1974). A behavior rating scale for the preschool child. *Developmental Psychology, 10,* 601–610.

Benbow, C. P., & Arjmand, O. (1990). Predictors of high academic achievement in mathematics and science by mathematically talented students: A longitudinal study. *Journal of Educational Psychology, 82,* 430–441.

Bloom, B. S. (1982). The role of gifts and markers in the development of talent. *Exceptional Children, 48,* 510–522.

Bornstein, M. H., & Sigman, M. D. (1986). Continuity in mental development from infancy. *Child Development, 57,* 251–274.

Bradley, R. H., Caldwell, B. M., Rock, S. L., Ramey, C. T., Barnard, K. E., Gray, C., Hammond, M. A., Mitchell, S., Gottfried, A. W., Siegel, L., & Johnson D. L. (1989). Home environment and cognitive development in the first three years of life: A collaborative study involving six sites and three ethnic groups in North America. *Developmental Psychology, 25,* 217–235.

Brody, E., & Brody, N. (1976). *Intelligence: Nature, determinants, and consequences.* New York: Academic Press.

Brody, L. E., & Benbow, C. P. (1986). Social and emotional adjustment of adolescents extremely talented in verbal or mathematical reasoning. *Journal of Youth and Adolescence, 15,* 1–18.

Brody, L. E., & Benbow, C. P. (1987). Accelerative strategies: How effective are they for the gifted? *Gifted Child Quarterly, 3,* 105–110.

Brody, N. (1992). *Intelligence* (2nd ed.). San Diego, CA: Academic Press.

Brown, K. W., & Gottfried, A. W. (1986). Cross-modal transfer of shape in early infancy: Is there reliable evidence? In L. P. Lipsitt & C. Rouce-Collier (Eds.), *Advances in infancy research* (Vol. 4, pp. 163–170). Norwood, NJ: Ablex.

Bryne, J. M., Backman, J. E., & Smith, I. M. (1986). Developmental assessment: The clinical use and validity of parental report. *Journal of Pediatric Psychology, 11,* 549–559.

Burns, G. L., Patterson, D. R., Nussbaum, B. R., & Parker, C. M. (1991). Disruptive behaviors in an outpatient pediatric population: Additional standardization data on the Eyberg Child Behavior Inventory. *Psychological Assessment, 3,* 202–207.

Buss, A. H., & Plomin, R. (1984). *Temperament: Early developing personality traits.* Hillsdale, NJ: Lawrence Erlbaum.

Cahan, S., & Gejam A. (1993). Constancy of IQ scores among gifted children. *Roeper Review, 15,* 140–143.

Caldwell, B. M., & Bradley, R. H. (1984). *Administration manual (revised edition) of the Home observation for measurement of the environment.* Little Rock: University of Arkansas.

Cameron, J., Livson, N., & Bayley, N. (1967). Infant vocalizations and their relationship to mature intelligence. *Science, 15,* 331–333.

Campbell, D. T., & Stanley, J. C. (1963). *Experimental and quasi-experimental designs for research.* Chicago: Rand McNally College Publishing.

Carter, K. R., & Ormrod, J. E. (1982). Acquisition of formal operations by intellectually gifted children. *Gifted Child Quarterly, 26,* 110–115.

Center for Talented Youth. (1993). *1993 CTY Talent Search: Seventh Grade.* Baltimore: Johns Hopkins University.

Chan, L. K. S. (1988). The perceived competence of intellectually talented students. *Gifted Child Quarterly, 32,* 310–314.

Chapin, F. S. (1955). *Experimental designs in sociological research.* New York: Harper.

Cherlin, A. J. (1992). *Marriage, divorce, remarriage.* Cambridge, MA: Howard University Press.

Ciha, T. E., Harris, R., Hoffman, C., & Potter, M. W. (1974). Parents as identifiers of giftedness, ignored but accurate. *Gifted Child Quarterly, 18,* 191–195.

Colangelo, N., & Brower, P. (1987). Labeling gifted youngsters: Long-term impact on families. *Gifted Child Quarterly, 31,* 75–78.

Colangelo, N., & Dettmann, D. F. (1983). A review of research on parents and families of gifted children. *Exceptional Children, 50,* 20–27.

Colligan, R. C. (1976). Prediction of kindergarten reading success from preschool report of parents. *Psychology in the Schools, 13,* 304–308.

Colligan, R. C. (1977). The Minnesota Child Development Inventory as an aid in the assessment of developmental disability. *Journal of Clinical Psychology, 33,* 162–163.

Corman, H. H., & Escalona, S. K. (1969). Stages of sensorimotor development: A replication study. *Merrill-Palmer Quarterly, 15,* 351–361.

Cornell, D. W. (1984). *Families of gifted children.* Ann Arbor, MI: UMI Research Press.

Cornell, D. G., & Grossberg, I. W. (1987). Family environment and personality adjustment in gifted program children. *Gifted Child Quarterly, 31,* 59–64.

Cox, C. M. (1926). *Genetic studies of genius: (Vol. 2) The early mental traits of 300 geniuses.* Stanford, CA: Stanford University Press.

Cox, R. L. (1977). Background characteristics of 456 gifted students. *Gifted Child Quarterly, 21,* 261–267.

Cronbach, L. J. (1991). Emerging views on methodology. In T. D. Wachs & R. Plomin (Eds.), *Conceptualization and measurement of organism-environment interaction* (pp. 87–104). Washington, DC: American Psychological Association.

Davis, H. G., & Connell, J. P. (1985). The effect of aptitude and achievement status on the self-system. *Gifted Child Quarterly,* **29**, 131–136.

Dean, R. S., & Steffen, J. E. (1984). Direct and indirect pediatric screening measures. *Journal of Pediatric Psychology, 9,* 65–75.

DeVoss, J. C. (1925). Specialization of the abilities of gifted children. In L. M. Terman (Ed.), *Genetic studies of genius: Vol. 1. Mental and physical traits of a thousand gifted children* (pp. 307–362). Stanford, CA: Stanford University Press.

Dixon, W. J. (Ed.) (1992). *BMDP statistical software manual* (Vol. 1, pp. 521–564). Los Angeles: University of California Press.

Durkin, D. (1966). *Children who read early: Two longitudinal studies.* New York: Teachers College Press.

Eccles, A. L., Bauman, E., & Rotenberg, K. (1989). Peer acceptance and self-esteem in gifted children. *Journal of Social Behavior and Personality, 4,* 401–409.

Eisert, D. C., Spector, S., Shankaran, S., Faigenbaum, D., & Szego, E. (1980). Mothers reports of their low birth weight infants' subsequent development on the Minnesota Child Development Inventory. *Journal of Pediatric Psychology, 5,* 353–364.

Elkind, D. (1981). *The hurried child.* Reading, MA: Addison-Wesley.

Ellis, H. (1904). *A study of British genius.* London: Hurst & Blackett, Ltd.

Eyberg, S. M. (1980). Eyberg Child Behavior Inventory. *Journal of Clinical Child Psychology, 9,* 29.

Fagan, J. F., III, & Detterman, D. K. (1992). The Fagan Test of Infant Intelligence: A technical summary. *Journal of Applied Developmental Psychology, 13,* 173–193.

Falbo, T., & Polit, D. F. (1986). Quantitative review of the only child literature: Research evidence and theory development. *Psychological Bulletin, 100,* 176–189.

Featherman, D. (1980). Retrospective longitudinal research: Methodological considerations. *Journal of Economics and Business, 32,* 152–169.

Feldhusen, J. F., & Heller, K. A. (1985). *Identifying and nurturing the gifted: An international perspective.* Toronto: Hans Huber Publishers.

Feldhusen, J. F., & Hoover, S. F. (1986). A conception of giftedness: Intelligence, self concept and motivation. *Roeper Review, 8,* 140–143.

Feldman, D. H. (1986). *Nature's gambit: Child prodigies and the development of human potential.* New York: Basic Books.

Freehill, M. F. (1961). *Gifted children: Their psychology and education.* New York: Macmillan.

Freeman, J. (1979). *Gifted children: Their identification and development in a social context.* Lancaster: MPT Press Limited.

Freeman, J. (1983). Emotional problems of the gifted child. *Journal of Child Psychology and Psychiatry, 24,* 481–485.

Freeman, J. (1988). Environment and high IQ—A consideration of fluid and crystallized intelligence. *Personality and Individual Differences, 4,* 307–313.

Freeman, J. (1991). *Gifted children growing up.* London: Cassell Educational Limited.

Fullard, W., McDevitt, S. C., & Carey, W. B. (1984). Assessing temperament in one- to three-year-old children. *Journal of Pediatric Psychology, 9,* 205–217.

Gagne, F. (1985). Giftedness and talent: Reexamining a reexamination of the definitions. *Gifted Child Quarterly, 29,* 103–112.

Gallucci, N. T. (1988). Emotional adjustment of gifted children. *Gifted Child Quarterly, 32,* 273–276.

Galton, F. (1869). *Hereditary genius.* London: Macmillan.

Games, P. A. (1990). Alternative analyses of repeated-measures designs by ANOVA and MANOVA. In A. von Eye (Ed.), *Statistical methods in longitudinal research* (Vol. 1, pp. 81–121). New York: Academic Press.

Garrity, L. I., & Servos, A. B. (1978). Comparison of measures of adaptive behaviors in preschool children. *Journal of Consulting and Clinical Psychology, 46,* 288–293.

George, W. C., Cohn, S. J., & Stanley, J. C. (Eds.). (1979). *Educating the gifted: Acceleration and enrichment*. Baltimore: Johns Hopkins University Press.

Gockenbach, L. B. (1989). A review of personality factors in parents of gifted children and their families: Implications for research. *Journal of Clinical Psychology, 45*, 210–213.

Goertzel, M. G., Goertzel, V., & Goertzel, T. G. (1978). *300 eminent personalities*. San Francisco: Jossey-Bass.

Golant, S. K. (1991). *The joys and challenges of raising a gifted child*. New York: Prentice-Hall.

Goldsmith, H. H., Buss, A. H., Plomin, R., Rothbart, M. K., Thomas, A., Chess, S., Hinde, R. A., & McCall, R. B. (1987). Roundtable: What is temperament? Four approaches. *Child Development, 58*, 505–529.

Gottfried, A. E. (1982). Relationships between academic intrinsic motivation and anxiety in children and young adolescents. *Journal of School Psychology, 20*, 205–215.

Gottfried, A. E. (1985). Academic intrinsic motivation in elementary and junior high school students. *Journal of Educational Psychology, 77*, 631–645.

Gottfried, A. E. (1986a). *Children's Academic Intrinsic Motivation Inventory*. Odessa, FL: Psychological Assessment Resources.

Gottfried, A. E. (1986b). Intrinsic motivational aspects of play experiences and play materials. In A. W. Gottfried & C. C. Brown (Eds.), *Play interactions: The contribution of play materials and parental involvement to children's development* (pp. 81–99). Lexington, MA: Lexington Books.

Gottfried, A. E. (1990). Academic intrinsic motivation in young elementary school children. *Journal of Educational Psychology*, **82**, 525–538.

Gottfried, A. E., & Gottfried, A. W. (Eds.) (1988). *Maternal employment and children's development: Longitudinal research*. New York: Plenum.

Gottfried, A. E., & Gottfried, A. W. (1991, November). *Home environment and children's academic intrinsic motivation: A longitudinal study*. Paper presented at the Lives through Time Conference on Longitudinal Research, sponsored by the American Psychological Association, Palm Springs, CA.

Gottfried, A. E., & Gottfried, A. W. (1993, March). *Motivation in intellectually gifted children: A longitudinal study from infancy through middle childhood*. Paper presented at the biennial meeting of the Society for Research in Child Development, New Orleans.

Gottfried, A. E., & Gottfried, A. W. (Eds.). (1994). *Redefining families: Implications for children's development*. New York: Plenum.

Gottfried, A. E., Gottfried, A. W., & Bathurst, K. (1988). Maternal employment, family environment, and children's development: Infancy through the school years. In A. E. Gottfried & A. W. Gottfried (Eds.), *Maternal employment and children's development: Longitudinal research* (pp. 11–58). New York: Plenum.

Gottfried A. E., Bathurst, K., & Gottfried, A. W. (1994). Role of maternal and dual-earner employment in children's development: A longitudinal study. In A. E. Gottfried & A. W. Gottfried (Eds.), *Redefining families: Implications for children's development* (pp. 55–97). New York: Plenum.

Gottfried, A. E., Fleming, J. S., Gottfried, A. W. (1994). Role of parental motivational practices in children's academic intrinsic motivation and achievement. *Journal of Educational Psychology, 86*, 104–113.

Gottfried, A. E., Gottfried, A. W., & Bathurst, K. (in press). Maternal and dual-earner employment status and parenting. In M. Bornstein (Ed.), *Handbook of parenting*. Hillsdale, NJ: Lawrence Erlbaum.

Gottfried, A. W. (1973). Intellectual consequences of perinatal anoxia. *Psychological Bulletin, 80*, 231–242.

Gottfried, A. W. (1984a). *Home environment and early cognitive development: Longitudinal research*. New York: Academic Press.

Gottfried, A. W. (1984b). Home environment and early cognitive development: Integration, meta-analyses, and conclusions. In A. W. Gottfried (Ed.), *Home environment and early cognitive development: Longitudinal research* (pp. 329–342). New York: Academic Press.

Gottfried, A. W. (1985). Measures of socioeconomic status in child development research: Data and recommendations. *Merrill-Palmer Quarterly, 31*, 85–92.

Gottfried, A. W., & Bathurst, K. (1983). Hand preference across time is related to intelligence in young girls, not boys. *Science, 221*, 1074–1076.

Gottfried, A. W., & Brody, N. (1975). Interrelationships between and correlates of psychometric and Piagetian scales of sensorimotor intelligence. *Developmental Psychology, 11*, 378–387.

Gottfried, A. W., & Gilman, G. (1983). Development of visual skills in infants and young children. *Journal of the American Optometric Association, 54*, 541–544.

Gottfried, A. W., & Gottfried, A. E. (1984). Home environment and cognitive development in young children of middle-socioeconomic-status families. In A. W. Gottfried (Ed.), *Home environment and early cognitive development: Longitudinal research* (pp. 57–115). New York: Academic Press.

Gottfried, A. W., & Gottfried, A. E. (1986). Home environment and children's development from infancy through the school entry years: Results of contemporary longitudinal investigations in North America. *Children's Environments Quarterly, 3*, 3–9.

Gottfried, A. W., & Rose, S. A. (1980). Tactile recognition memory in infants. *Child Development, 51*, 69–74.

Gottfried, A. W., Rose, S. A., & Bridger, W. H. (1977). Cross-modal transfer in human infants. *Child Development, 48*, 118–123.

Gottfried, A. W., Guerin, D. W., Spencer, J. E., & Meyer, C. (1983). Concurrent validity of the Minnesota Child Development Inventory in a nonclinical sample. *Journal of Consulting and Clinical Psychology, 51*, 643–644.

Gottfried, A. W., Guerin, D. W., Spencer, J. E., & Meyer, C. (1984). Validity of Minnesota Child Development Inventory in screening young children's developmental status. *Journal of Pediatric Psychology, 9*, 219–230.

Gottfried, A. W., Guerin, D. W., & Bathurst, K. (1989, April). *Infant predictors of IQ and achievement: A comparative analysis*. Paper presented at the biennial meeting of the Society for Research in Child Development, Kansas City, MO.

Gregory, R. J. (1992). *Psychological testing: History, principles, and applications*. Boston: Allyn and Bacon.

Gribbin, K., Schaie, K. W., & Parham, I. A. (1980). Complexity of life style and maintenance of intellectual abilities. *Journal of Social Issues, 36*, 47–61.

Gross, M. U. M. (1993). *Exceptionally gifted children*. London: Routledge.

Groth, N. J. (1975). Mothers of gifted. *Gifted Child Quarterly, 19*, 217–222.

Guerin, D., & Gottfried, A. W. (1987). Minnesota Child Development Inventories: Predictors of intelligence, achievement, and adaptability. *Journal of Pediatric Psychology, 12*, 595–609.

Guerin, D. W., & Gottfried, A. W. (in press-a). Developmental stability and change in parent reports of temperament: A ten-year longitudinal study from infancy through preadolescence. *Merrill-Palmer Quarterly.*

Guerin, D. W., & Gottfried, A. W. (in press-b). Infant difficultness: Convergent validity and temperamental consequences during childhood. *Infant Behavior and Development.*

Guerin, D. W., Gottfried, A. W., Oliver, P., & Thomas, C. W. (1994). Temperament and school functioning during early adolescence. *Journal of Early Adolescence, 14*, 200–225.

Guerin, D. W., Griffin, J. R., Gottfried, A. W., & Christenson, G. N. (1993). Dyslexic subtypes and severity levels: Are there gender differences? *Optometry and Vision Science, 70*, 348–351.

Hagen, E. (1980). *Identification of the gifted.* New York: Teachers College Press.

Hansen, R. A. (1977). Anxiety. In S. Ball (Ed.), *Motivation in education* (pp. 91–109). New York: Academic Press.

Hauser, R. M., & Featherman, D. L. (1977). *The process of stratification: Trends and analyses.* New York: Academic Press.

Hegvik, R. L., McDevitt, S. C., & Carey, W. B. (1982). The Middle Childhood Temperament Questionnaire. *Developmental and Behavioral Pediatrics, 3*, 197–200.

Heller, K. A. (1991). The nature and development of giftedness: A longitudinal study. *European Journal of High Ability, 2*, 174–188.

Heller, K. A., & Feldhusen, J. F. (Eds.). (1985). *Identifying and nurturing the gifted: An international perspective.* Toronto: Hans Huber Publishers.

Heller, K. A., & Hany, E. A. (1986). Identification, development and analysis of talented and gifted children in West Germany. In K. A. Heller & J. F. Feldhusen (Eds.), *Identifying and nurturing the gifted: An international perspective* (pp. 67–82). Toronto: Hans Huber Publishers.

Heller, K. A., Monks, F. J., & Passow, A. H. (Eds.). (1993). *International handbook of research and development of giftedness and talent.* Oxford: Pergamon.

Henderson, B. B., Gold, S. R., & McCord, M. T. (1982). Daydreaming and curiosity in gifted and average children and adolescents. *Developmental Psychology, 18*, 576–582.

Hernandez, D. J. (1988). Demographic trends and the living arrangements of children. In E. M. Hetherington & J. D. Arasteh (Eds.), *Impact of divorce, single parenting, and stepparenting on children* (p. 6). Hillsdale, NJ: Lawrence Erlbaum.

Hertzog, C., & Rovine, M. (1985). Repeated-measures analysis of variance in developmental research: Selected issues. *Child Development, 56*, 787–809.

Hoge, R. D. (1988). Issues in the definition and measurement of the giftedness construct. *Educational Researcher, 17*, 12–16.

Hoge, R. D., & Renzulli, J. S. (1993). Exploring the link between giftedness and self-concept. *Review of Educational Research, 63*, 449–465.

Hollingshead, A. B. (1975). *Four factor index of social status.* Unpublished manuscript, Yale University (Available from Department of Sociology).

Hollingworth, L. S. (1926). *Gifted children: Their nature and nurture.* New York: Macmillan.

Hollingworth, L. S. (1942). *Children above 180 IQ.* New York: World Book.

Hollingworth, L. S. (1976). The development of personality in highly intelligent children. In W. Dennis & M. W. Dennis (Eds.), *The intellectually gifted: An overview* (pp. 89–98). New York: Grune & Stratton. (Original work published 1942)

Hom, H. L. (1988, March). *Motivational orientation of the gifted student, threat of evaluation, and its impact on performance.* Paper presented at the biennial meeting of the Society for Research in Child Development, New Orleans.

Horowitz, F. D. (1987). A developmental view of giftedness. *Gifted Child Quarterly, 31,* 165–168.

Horowitz, F. D., & O'Brien, M. (Eds.). (1985). *The gifted and talented: Developmental perspectives.* Washington, DC: American Psychological Association.

Horowitz, F. D., & O'Brien, M. (1986). Gifted and talented children: State of knowledge and directions for research. *American Psychologist, 41,* 1147–1152.

Howe, M. J. A. (1990). *The origins of exceptional abilities.* Oxford: Blackwell.

Hresko, W. P., Reid, D. K., & Hammill, D. D. (1981). *The test of early language development.* Austin, TX: Pro-Ed.

Hubert, N. C., Wachs, T. D., Peters-Martin, P., & Gandour, M. J. (1982). The study of early temperament: Measurement and conceptual issues. *Child Development, 53,* 571–600.

Hughes, H. H., & Converse, H. D. (1962). Characteristics of the gifted: A case for a sequel to Terman's study. *Exceptional Children, 29,* 179–183.

Humphreys, L. G. (1985). A conceptualization of intellectual giftedness. In F. D. Horowitz & M. O'Brien (Eds.), *The gifted and talented: Developmental perspectives* (pp. 331–360). Washington, DC: American Psychological Association.

Humphreys, L. G. (1992). Commentary: What both critics and users of ability tests need to know. *Psychological Science, 3,* 271–274.

Hunt, J. McV. (1971). Intrinsic motivation and psychological development. In H. M. Schroder & P. Suedfeld (Eds.), *Personality theory and information processing* (pp. 131–177). New York: Ronald Press.

Huttenlocker, J. (1974). The origins of language comprehension. In R. L. Solso (Ed.), *Theories in cognitive psychology: The Loyola Symposium* (pp. 331–368). Hillsdale, NJ: Lawrence Erlbaum.

Ireton, H., & Thwing, E. (1972–1974). *Manual for the Minnesota Child Development Inventory.* Minneapolis: Behavioral Science Systems.

Ireton, H., & Thwing, E. (1979). *Manual for the Minnesota Preschool Inventory.* Minneapolis: Behavioral Science Systems.

Ireton, H., Thwing, E., & Currier, S. K. (1977). Minnesota Child Development Inventory: Identification of children with developmental disorders. *Journal of Pediatric Psychology, 2,* 18–22.

Jacobs, J. (1971). Effectiveness of teacher and parent identification of gifted children as a function of school level. *Psychology in the Schools, 8,* 140–142.

Janos, P. M., & Robinson, N. M. (1985). Psychosocial development in intellectually gifted children. In F. D. Horowitz & M. O'Brien (Eds.), *The gifted and talented* (pp. 149–195). Washington, DC: American Psychological Association.

Jastak, S., & Wilkinson, G. S. (1984). *Wide Range Achievement Test-Revised.* Wilmington, DE: Jastak Associates.

Karnes, M. B., & Johnson, L. J. (1986). Identification and assessment of gifted/talented handicapped and nonhandicapped children in early childhood. In R. J. Whitmore (Ed.), *Intellectual giftedness in young children: Recognition and development* (pp. 35–54). New York: Haworth Press.

Karnes, F. A., & Whorton, J. E. (1988). Attitudes of intellectually gifted youth toward school. *Roeper Review, 10,* 173–175.

Kaufman, A. S., & Kaufman, N. L. (1977). *Clinical evaluation of young children with the McCarthy scales.* New York: Grune & Stratton.

Kaufman, A. S., & Kaufman, N. L. (1983). *Kaufman Assessment Battery for Children: Administration and scoring manual.* Circle Pines, MN: American Guidance Service.

Keating, D. P. (1975). Precocious cognitive development of the level of formal operations. *Child Development, 46,* 276–280.

Keating, D. P. (1976). A Piagetian approach to intellectual precocity. In D. L. Keating (Ed.), *Intellectual talent: Research and development.* Baltimore, MD: Johns Hopkins University Press.

Kee, D. W., Gottfried, A. W., Bathurst, K., & Brown, K. (1987). Left-hemispheric language specialization: Consistency in hand preference and sex differences. *Child Development, 58,* 718–724.

Kee, D. W., Gottfried, A. W., & Bathurst, K. (1991). Consistency of hand preference: Predictions to intelligence and school achievement. *Brain and Cognition, 16,* 1–10.

Kellaghan, T., Sloane, K., Alvarez, B., & Bloom, B. S. (1993). *The home environment and school learning.* San Francisco: Jossey-Bass.

Kelly, K. R., & Jordan, L. K. (1990). Effects of academic achievement and gender on academic and social self-concept: A replication study. *Journal of Counseling and Development, 69,* 173–177.

Kincaid, D. (1969). A study of highly gifted elementary pupils. *Gifted Child Quarterly, 13,* 264–267.

Klausmeier, K., Mishra, S. P., & Maker, C. J. (1987). Identification of gifted learners: A national survey of assessment practices and training needs of school psychologists. *Gifted Child Quarterly, 31,* 135–137.

Krapp, A., Hidi, S., & Renninger, K. A. (1992). Interest, learning, and development. In K. A. Renninger, S. Hidi, & A. Krapp (Eds.), *The role of interest in learning and development* (pp. 3–25). Hillsdale, NJ: Lawrence Erlbaum.

Kulieke M. J., & Olszewski-Kubilius, P. (1989). The influence of family values and climate on the development of talent. In J. L. VanTassel-Baska & P. Olszewski-Kubilius (Eds.), *Patterns of influence on gifted learners: The home, the self, and the school.* New York: Teachers College Press.

Lehman, E. B., & Erdwins, C. J. (1981). The social and emotional adjustment of young, intellectually-gifted children. *Gifted Child Quarterly, 25,* 134–137.

Lesser, G. S., Fifer, G., & Clark, D. H. (1965). Mental abilities of children from different social-class and cultural groups. *Monographs of the Society for Research in Child Development* (Vol. 30, No. 2, Serial No. 102).

Li, A. K. F. (1988). Self-perception and motivational orientation in gifted children. *Roeper Review, 10,* 175–180.

Lombroso, C. (1891). *The man of genius.* London: Walter Scott.

Louis, B., & Lewis, M. (1992). Parental beliefs about giftedness in young children and their relation to actual ability level. *Gifted Child Quarterly, 36*, 27–31.

Ludwig, G., & Cullinan, D. (1984). Behavior problems of gifted and nongifted elementary school boys and girls. *Gifted Child Quarterly, 28*, 37–39.

Luftig, R. L., & Nichols, M. L. (1991). An assessment of the social status and perceived personality and school traits of gifted students by non-gifted peers. *Roeper Review, 13*, 148–153.

Luthar, S. S., Zigler, E., & Goldstein, D. (1992). Psychosocial adjustment among intellectually gifted adolescents: The role of cognitive-developmental and experiential factors. *Journal of Child Psychology and Psychiatry, 33*, 361–373.

MacMahon, B., & Pugh, T. F. (1970). *Epidemiology: Principles and methods*. Boston: Little, Brown.

Massoth, N. A. (1985). The McCarthy Scales of Children's Abilities as predictor of achievement: A five-year follow-up. *Psychology in the Schools, 22*, 10–13.

Massoth, N. A., & Levenson, R. L., Jr. (1982). The McCarthy Scales of children's abilities as a predictor of reading readiness and reading achievement. *Psychology in the Schools, 19*, 293–296.

Matheny, A. P. (1980). Bayley's Infant Behavior Record: Components and twin analysis. *Child Development, 51*, 1157–1167.

Matheny, A. P. (1989). Temperament and cognition: Relations between temperament and mental test scores. In G. A. Kohnstamm, J. E. Bates, & M. K. Rothbart (Eds.), *Temperament in childhood* (pp. 263–282). New York: John Wiley & Sons.

Maxwell, S. E., & Delaney, H. D. (1990). *Designing experiments and analyzing data*. Belmont, CA: Wadsworth.

McCall, R. B. (1977). Childhood IQs as predictors of adult educational and occupational status. *Science, 197*, 482–483.

McCall, R. B., & Carriger, M. S. (1993). A meta-analysis of infant habituation and recognition memory performance as predictors of later IQ. *Child Development, 64*, 57–79.

McCall, R. B., Hogarty, P. S., & Hurlburt, N. (1972). Transitions in infant sensorimotor development and the prediction of childhood I. Q. *American Psychologist, 27*, 328–348.

McCarthy, D. (1972). *Manual for the McCarthy scales of children's abilities*. New York: Psychological Corporation.

McDevitt, S. C., & Carey, W. B. (1978). The measurement of temperament in 3–7 year old children. *Journal of Child Psychology and Psychiatry, 19*, 245–253.

Meehl, P. E. (1971). High school yearbooks: A reply to Schwarz. *Journal of Abnormal Psychology, 77*, 143–148.

Miles, C. C. (1946). Gifted children. In L. Carmichael (Ed.), *Manual of child psychology* (pp. 886–953). New York: John Wiley & Sons.

Milgram, R. M., & Milgram, N. A. (1976). Personality characteristics of gifted Israeli children. *Journal of Genetic Psychology, 129*, 185–194.

Monks, F. J., van Boxtel, H. W., Roelofs, J. J. W., & Sanders, P. M. (1986). The identification of gifted children in secondary education and a description of their situation in Holland. In K. A. Heller & J. F. Feldhusen (Eds.), *Identifying and nurturing the gifted: An international perspective* (pp. 39–63). Toronto: Hans Huber Publishers.

Moore, T. (1967). Language and intelligence: A longitudinal study of the first eight years. *Human Development, 10,* 88–106.

Moos, R. H., & Moos, B. S. (1986). *Family Environment Scale manual* (2nd ed.). Palo Alto, CA: Consulting Psychologist Press.

Morris, W. (1978). *The American heritage dictionary of the English language.* Boston: Houghton Mifflin.

Nelson, K. (1973). Structure and strategy in learning to talk. *Monographs of the Society for Research in Child Development, 38* (1–2, Serial No. 149).

O'Brien, R. G., & Kaiser, M. K. (1985). MANOVA method for analyzing repeated measures designs: An extensive primer. *Psychological Bulletin, 97,* 316–333.

Olszewski, P., Kulieke, M., & Buescher, T. (1987). The influence of the family environment on the development of talent: A literature review. *Journal for the Education of the Gifted, 11,* 6–28.

Olszewski-Kubilius, P. M., Kulieke, M. J., & Krasney, N. (1988). Personality dimensions of gifted adolescents: A review of empirical literature. *Gifted Child Quarterly, 32,* 347–352.

Overall, J. E., & Woodward, A. (1977). Nonrandom assignment and the analysis of covariance. *Psychological Bulletin, 84,* 588–594.

Oviatt, S. L. (1980). The emerging ability to comprehend language: An experimental approach. *Child Development, 51,* 97–106.

Parkyn, G. W. (1953). *Children of high intelligence: A New Zealand study.* New Zealand: Whitcombe & Tombs.

Pendarvis, E. D., Howley, A. A., & Howley, C. B. (1990). *The abilities of gifted children.* Englewood Cliffs, NJ: Prentice-Hall.

Perleth, C., & Heller, K. A. (1994). The Munich longitudinal study of giftedness. In R. Subotnik & K. Arnold (Eds.), *Beyond Terman: Longitudinal studies in gifted education* (pp. 77–114). Norwood, NJ: Ablex.

Petri, H. L. (1991). *Motivation: Theory, research, and applications.* Belmont, CA: Wadsworth.

Piaget, J. (1954). *The construction of reality in the child.* New York: Basic Books.

Plomin, R., & DeFries, J. C. (1985). *Origins of individual differences in infancy.* New York: Academic Press.

Prior, M. (1992). Childhood temperament. *Journal of Child Psychology and Psychiatry, 33,* 249–279.

Radford, J. (1990). *Child prodigies and exceptional early achievers.* New York: Free Press.

Reis, S. M. (1989) Reflections on policy affecting the education of gifted and talented students: Past and future perspectives. *American Psychologist, 44,* 399–408.

Renzulli, J. S. (1978). What makes giftedness? Reexamining a definition. *Phi Delta Kappan, 60,* 180–184, 261.

Renzulli, J. S. (1986). The three-ring conception of giftedness: A developmental model for creative productivity. In R. J. Sternberg & J. E. Davidson (Eds.), *Conceptions of giftedness* (pp. 53–92). New York: Cambridge University Press.

Reschly, D. J., & Wilson, M. S. (1990). Cognitive processing vs. traditional intelligence: Diagnostic utility, intervention implications, and treatment validity. *School Psychology Review, 19,* 443–458.

Reynolds, C. R. (1985). Multitrait validation of the Revised Children's Manifest Anxiety Scale for children of high intelligence. *Psychological Reports, 56,* 402.

Reynolds, C. R., & Bradley, M. (1983). Emotional stability of intellectually superior children versus nongifted peers as estimated by chronic anxiety levels. *School Psychology Review, 12,* 190–194.

Rimm, S., & Lowe, B. (1988). Family environments of underachieving gifted students. *Gifted Child Quarterly, 32,* 353–359.

Robinson, A. (1985). The identification and labeling of gifted children: What does research tell us? In K. A. Heller & J. F. Feldhusen (Eds.), *Identifying and nurturing the gifted: An international perspective* (pp. 103–109). Toronto: Hans Huber Publishers.

Robinson, N. M. (1987). The early development of precocity. *Gifted Child Quarterly, 31,* 161–164.

Robinson, N. M., & Dale, P. S. (1992, February). *Precocity in language and its predictive significance.* Paper presented at Esther Katz Rosen Symposium on the Psychological Development of Gifted Children. Lawrence: University of Kansas.

Roe, K. V. (1978). Infants' mother-stranger discrimination at 3 months as a predictor of cognitive development at 3 and 5 years. *Developmental Psychology, 14,* 191–192.

Roe, K. V., McClure, A., & Roe, A. (1982). Vocal interaction at 3 months and cognitive skills at 12 years. *Developmental Psychology, 18,* 15–16.

Roedell, W. C. (1984). Vulnerabilities of highly gifted children. *Roeper Review, 6,* 127–130.

Roedell, W. C. (1989). Early development of gifted children. In J. L. Van Tassel-Baska & P. Olszewski-Kubilius (Eds.), *Patterns of influence on gifted learners: The home, the self, and the school.* New York: Teachers College Press.

Roedell, W. C., Jackson, N. E., & Robinson, H. B. (1980). *Gifted young children.* New York: Teachers College Press.

Rose, S. A., & Ruff, H. A. (1987). Cross-modal abilities in human infants. In J. D. Osofsky (Ed.), *Handbook of infant development* (2nd ed., pp. 318–362). New York: John Wiley & Sons.

Rose, S. A., Gottfried, A. W., Melloy-Carminar, P., & Bridger, W. H. (1982). Familiarity and novelty preferences in infant recognition memory: Implications for information processing. *Developmental Psychology, 18,* 704–713.

Rose, S. A., Gottfried, A. W., & Bridger, W. H. (1983). Infants' cross-modal transfer from solid objects to their graphic representations.

Saccuzzo, D. P., Johnson, N. E., & Russell, G. (1992). Verbal versus performance IQs for gifted African-American, Caucasian, Filipino, and Hispanic children. *Psychological Assessment, 4,* 239–244.

Saylor, C. F., & Brandt, B. (1986). The Minnesota Child Development Inventory: A valid maternal report form for screening development in infancy. *Journal of Developmental and Behavioral Pediatrics, 7,* 308–311.

Schneider, B. H. (1987). *The gifted child in peer group perspective.* New York: Springer-Verlag.

Schneider, B. H., Clegg., M. R., Byrne, B. M., Ledingham, J. E., & Crobmie, G. (1989). Social relations of gifted children as a function of age and school program. *Journal of Educational Psychology, 81,* 48–56.

Schofield, N. J., & Ashman, A. F. (1987). The cognitive processing of gifted, high, average, and low average ability students. *British Journal of Educational Psychology, 59,* 9–20.

Scholwinski, E., & Reynolds, C. R. (1985). Dimensions of anxiety among high IQ children. *Gifted Child Quarterly, 29*, 125–130.

Seaman, M. A., Levin, J. R., & Serlin, R. C. (1991). New developments in pairwise multiple comparisons: Some powerful and practicable procedures. *Psychological Bulletin, 110*, 577–586.

Shaywitz, S. E., Shaywitz, B. A., Fletcher, J. M., & Escobar, M. D. (1990). Prevalence of reading disability in boys and girls: Results of the Connecticut Longitudinal Study. *Journal of the American Medical Association, 264*, 998–1002.

Sheldon, P. M. (1954, February). The families of highly gifted children. *Marriage and Family Living*, 59–60, 67.

Shoemaker, D. W., Saylor, C. F., & Erickson, M. T. (1993). Concurrent validity of the Minnesota Child Development Inventory with high-risk infants. *Journal of Pediatric Psychology, 18*, 377–388.

Shure, M. B., & Spivak, G. (1974). *The PIPS test manual.* Unpublished manuscript, Hahnemann Medical College and Hospital, Philadelphia.

Silverman, L. K., & Kearney, K. (1988). Parents of the extraordinarily gifted. *Advanced Development, 1*, 1–10.

Solano, C. H. (1987). Stereotypes of social isolation and early burnout in the gifted: Do they still exist? *Journal of Youth and Adolescence, 16*, 527–539.

Sparrow, S. S., Balla, D. A., & Cicchetti, D. V. (1984). *Vineland Adaptive Behavior Scales Survey Form Manual (Interview edition).* Circle Pines, MN: American Guidance Service.

Sternberg, R. J., & Davidson, J. E. (Eds.). (1986). *Conceptions of giftedness.* Cambridge: Cambridge University Press.

Stevens, G., & Featherman, D. L. (1981). A revised socioeconomic index of occupational status. *Social Science Research, 10*, 364–395.

Storfer, M. D. (1990). *Intelligence and giftedness: The contributions of heredity and early environment.* San Francisco: Jossey-Bass.

Sturner, R. A., Funk, S. G., Thomas, P. D., & Green, J. A. (1982). An adaptation of the Minnesota Child Development Inventory for preschool developmental screening. *Journal of Pediatric Psychology, 7*, 295–306.

Subotnik, R., & Arnold, K. D. (1994). *Beyond Terman: Longitudinal studies in contemporary gifted education.* Norwood, NJ: Ablex.

Tabachnick, B. G., & Fidell, L. S. (1989). *Using multivariate statistics* (2nd ed.). New York: HarperCollins.

Tannenbaum, A. J. (1983). *Gifted children: Psychological and educational perspectives.* New York: Macmillan.

Terman, L. M. (1905). A study in precocity and prematuration. *American Journal of Psychology, 16*, 145–183.

Terman, L. M. (1925–1929). *Genetic studies of genius* (Vols. 1–4). Stanford, CA: Stanford University Press.

Terman, L. M., & Oden, M. H. (1947). *The gifted child grows up: Genetic studies of genius* (Vol. 4). Stanford, CA: Stanford University Press.

Terman, L. M., & Oden, M. H. (1959). *The gifted group at mid-life: Thirty-five years' follow-up of the superior child* (Vol. 5); *Genetic studies of genius.* Stanford, CA: Stanford University Press.

Thomas, A., Chess, S., & Birch, H. G. (1968). *Temperament and behavior disorders in children.* New York: New York University Press.

Tomlinson-Keasey, C. (1990). Developing our intellectual resources for the 21st century: Educating the gifted. *Journal of Educational Psychology, 82,* 399–403.

Tomlinson-Keasey, C., & Little, T. D. (1990). Predicting educational attainment, occupational achievement, intellectual skill, and personal adjustment among gifted men and women. *Journal of Educational Psychology, 82,* 442–455.

Toothaker, L. E. (1991). *Multiple comparisons for researchers.* Newbury Park, CA: Sage.

Tuttle, F. B., Jr., Becker, L. A., & Sousa, J. A. (1988). *Characteristics and identification of gifted and talented students* (3rd ed.). Washington, DC: National Education Association.

Ullman, D. G., & Kausch, D. F. (1979). Early identification of developmental strengths and weaknesses in preschool children. *Exceptional Children, 46,* 8–13.

Wachs, T. D. (1976). *Purdue Home Stimulation Inventories* (Sections I, II, and III). Unpublished manual, Purdue University.

Wachs, T. D. (1992). *The nature of nurture.* Newbury Park, CA: Sage.

Wachs, T. D., & Gruen, G. E. (1982). *Early experience and human development.* New York: Plenum.

Wechsler, D. (1974). *Manual for the Wechsler Intelligence Scale for Children.* San Antonio, TX: Psychological Corporation.

Wechsler, D. (1991). *WISC-III. Wechsler Intelligence Scale for Children—Third Edition.* San Antonio, TX: Psychological Corporation.

Whitmore, J. R. (1986). Predicting severe underachievement and developing achievement motivation. In J. R. Whitmore (Ed.), *Intellectual giftedness in young children: Recognition and development* (pp. 113–133). New York: Haworth Press.

Willerman, L., & Fiedler, M. F. (1974). Infant performance and intellectual precocity. *Child Development, 45,* 483–486.

Witty, P. (1940). A genetic study of fifty gifted children. In G. M. Whipple (Ed.), *Intelligence: Its nature and nurture.* 39th Yearbook of the National Society for the Study of Education. Chicago: University of Chicago Press.

Witty, P. (Ed.). (1951). *The gifted child.* Boston: D. C. Heath.

Woodcock, R. W., & Johnson, M. B. (1977). *Woodcock-Johnson Psycho-Educational Battery.* Allen, TX: DLM Teaching Resources.

Yadusky-Holahan, M., & Holahan, W. (1983). The effect of academic stress upon the anxiety and depression levels of gifted high school students. *Gifted Child Quarterly, 27,* 42–46.

Yoder, A. H. (1894). The study of the boyhood of great men. *Pedagogical Seminary, 3,* 134–156.

Index

Breinigsville, PA USA
25 September 2010
246071BV00002B/5/A

9 780306 484438